# The Making of the European Union

# The Making of the European Union

## Foundations, Institutions and Future Trends

Sten Berglund

*Professor of Political Science, University of Örebro, Sweden and Humboldt University, Berlin, Germany*

Joakim Ekman

*Doctor of Political Science, University of Örebro, Sweden*

Henri Vogt

*Research Fellow, Centre for European Studies, University of Helsinki, Finland*

Frank H. Aarebrot

*Professor of Comparative Politics, University of Bergen, Norway*

**Edward Elgar**
Cheltenham, UK • Northampton, MA, USA

© Sten Berglund, Joakim Ekman, Henri Vogt and Frank H. Aarebrot 2006

All rights reserved. No part of this publication may be reproduced, stored in a retrieval system or transmitted in any form or by any means, electronic, mechanical or photocopying, recording, or otherwise without the prior permission of the publisher.

Published by
Edward Elgar Publishing Limited
Glensanda House
Montpellier Parade
Cheltenham
Glos GL50 1UA
UK

Edward Elgar Publishing, Inc.
136 West Street
Suite 202
Northampton
Massachusetts 01060
USA

A catalogue record for this book
is available from the British Library

**Library of Congress Cataloguing in Publication Data**
The making of the European Union : foundations, institutions and future trends / edited by Sten Berglund ... [et al.]
    p. cm.
Includes bibliographical references and index.
    1. European Union–History. 2. European Union. I. Berglund, Sten, 1947-

JN30.M285 2006
341.242'2–dc22
                                                              2005056795

ISBN-13: 978 1 84542 025 3
ISBN-10: 1 84542 025 X

Printed and bound in Great Britain by MPG Books Ltd, Bodmin, Cornwall

# Contents

| | | |
|---|---|---|
| *List of Figures* | | vii |
| *List of Tables* | | ix |
| *Notes on the Authors* | | xi |
| *Preface* | | xiii |
| 1 | Introduction | 1 |
| 2 | The Origins of the European Union | 9 |
| 3 | Patterns of Inclusion and Exclusion in Europe | 27 |
| 4 | Support for the European Union | 59 |
| 5 | Support for Deeper Political Integration: The External Dimension | 111 |
| 6 | The Challenge of Euroscepticism and Nationalism | 139 |
| 7 | *Politikverdrossenheit*, Globalisation and Individualism | 163 |
| 8 | Conclusions: The Future of the European Union | 195 |
| *Appendix: Chronology of European Integration* | | 203 |
| *Index* | | 231 |

# Figures

| | | |
|---|---|---|
| 2.1 | Two parallel historical processes of European integration | 15 |
| 2.2 | Early currency unions, 1865–1927 | 20 |
| 2.3 | Membership in the International Postal Union, 1875–2001 | 21 |
| 2.4 | Implementing the metric system, 1795–1910 | 22 |
| 3.1 | The structure of the chapter | 28 |
| 4.1 | Objects and levels of political support | 61 |
| 4.2 | In favour of future enlargements of the EU | 67 |
| 4.3 | A positive image of the European Union | 69 |
| 4.4 | EU membership: a good thing? | 70 |
| 4.5 | EU membership: a bad thing, 1991–2004 | 71 |
| 4.6 | Positive evaluation of EU membership | 73 |
| 4.7 | Trust in the European Commission | 75 |
| 4.8 | Trust in the European Parliament | 76 |
| 4.9 | Multivariate logistic regression model of EU benefit item | 93 |
| 4.10 | Net effects of a multivariate logistic regression model of EU benefit item | 94 |
| 4.11 | Geographical distribution of net probability effect (young age) | 95 |
| 4.12 | Geographical distribution of net probability effect (urban location) | 96 |
| 4.13 | Geographical distribution of net probability effect (positive assessment of household financial situation) | 97 |
| 4.14 | Geographical distribution of net probability effect (satisfaction with democracy) | 99 |
| 4.15 | Share of respondents who say their country has benefited or will benefit from EU membership by the impact of all the independent variables in the simplified model | 101 |
| 5.1 | The image of the role played by the US in the world among EU citizens | 126 |
| 6.1 | Resistance to a multicultural society | 156 |
| 6.2 | Limits to a multicultural society | 157 |
| 7.1 | Contextualising the future of the EU | 165 |

7.2  Two parallel current and future determinants
     of European integration					191

# Tables

| | | |
|---|---|---|
| 2.1 | Stein Rokkan's conceptual map of Europe | 10 |
| 2.2 | The early banks, 1400–1860 | 20 |
| 2.3 | Patterns of innovation | 23 |
| 3.1 | Some analytical dimensions of citizenship | 30 |
| 3.2 | Some features of citizenship laws in Europe | 36 |
| 3.3 | Number of non-nationals and acquisition of citizenship in Europe | 38 |
| 3.4 | Religions in Europe | 41 |
| 3.5 | Some indicators of religious freedom in Europe | 43 |
| 3.6 | The year of attaining universal suffrage for men and women | 46 |
| 3.7 | Women in European parliaments and the WEF 2005 ranking | 48 |
| 3.8 | Death penalty in Europe | 51 |
| 3.9 | Possible consequences of inclusion and exclusion | 55 |
| 4.1 | Indicators of public support for the EU | 62 |
| 4.2 | National identity and European bias | 64 |
| 4.3 | Attachment to Europe | 65 |
| 4.4 | Support for the EU among the EU15 | 79 |
| 4.5 | Support for the EU among the ten enlargement countries | 79 |
| 4.6 | Support for the EU by wave of enlargement: 10 per cent cut-off | 80 |
| 4.7 | Support for the EU by wave of enlargement: 15 per cent cut-off | 81 |
| 4.8 | Support for the EU by wave of enlargement: 20 per cent cut-off | 81 |
| 4.9 | Support for the EU by region: 10 per cent cut-off | 82 |
| 4.10 | Support for the EU by region: 15 per cent cut-off | 82 |
| 4.11 | Support for the EU by region: 20 per cent cut-off | 83 |
| 4.12 | Support for the EU in new and old states: 20 per cent cut-off | 84 |
| 4.13 | Percentage of respondents who think their respective countries benefit from the EU | 86 |
| 4.14 | Countries sorted by percentages satisfied with democracy and the development of household financial situation | 88 |

| | | |
|---|---|---|
| 4.15 | Percentage of respondents who think their country benefits from the EU (respondents grouped in terms of their democratic and financial satisfaction and/or dissatisfaction) | 90 |
| 5.1 | Opinions on a common foreign policy | 115 |
| 5.2 | Attitudes towards the EU as an international actor by support for EU membership in EU15 | 117 |
| 5.3 | Share of respondents per country 'against' a common defence and security policy | 118 |
| 5.4 | Support for a common European voice in world politics | 120 |
| 5.5 | Countries perceived as a threat to peace in the world | 123 |
| 5.6 | Perceived influence on the globalisation process | 125 |
| 5.7 | Opposition to enlargement in EU15 | 129 |
| 5.8 | Support for a larger and more powerful Union | 131 |
| 6.1 | A typology of nationalism in the EU | 141 |
| 6.2 | Euroscepticism on the conceptual map of Europe | 144 |
| 6.3 | Euroscepticism by accession waves and proximity to city-belt Europe | 145 |
| 6.4 | Types and indicators of party-based Euroscepticism | 148 |
| 6.5 | Party-based Euroscepticism | 150 |
| 6.6 | Eurosceptical parties: electoral and parliamentary support | 152 |
| 6.7 | Party-based Euroscepticism, public opinion and xenophobia (a summary) | 160 |
| 7.1 | Turnouts in the elections to the European Parliament | 167 |
| 7.2 | Comparison between turnouts in the national parliament (NP) and the European Parliament (EP) elections | 169 |
| 7.3 | Interest in politics in a number of European countries | 170 |
| 7.4 | Trust in societal institutions and personal future expectations in EU15 and trust in societal institutions in the new member states | 172 |
| 7.5 | Attitudes to globalisation and support for EU membership in EU15 and attitudes to globalisation in the new member states | 174 |
| 7.6 | Attitudes to globalisation in the old EU member states | 177 |
| 7.7 | Who can control globalisation? Data on EU15 and new member states | 178 |
| 7.8 | Indicators of social trust | 182 |
| 7.9 | Social trust and interest in politics | 183 |
| 7.10 | The meanings of the European Union in EU15, the new member states, Bulgaria and Romania | 184 |
| 7.11 | The meanings of the European Union in EU15 | 186 |
| 8.1 | Findings and conclusions conducive to three alternative scenarios | 198 |

# Notes on the Authors

Frank H. Aarebrot (b. 1947) is professor of comparative politics at the University of Bergen, Norway. He is the author and co-author of numerous articles and chapters within the field of comparative politics, among others: 'Analysis and Explanation of Variation in Territorial Structure', in Stein Rokkan et al., *Centre–Periphery Structures in Europe* (Campus Verlag 1987). He has published *The Political History of Eastern Europe in the 20th Century* (with Sten Berglund, Edward Elgar 1997), *The Handbook of Political Change in Eastern Europe* (co-edited and co-authored with Sten Berglund and Tomas Hellén, Edward Elgar 1998), *Politics and Citizenship on the Eastern Baltic Seaboard* (co-edited and co-authored with Terje Knutsen, Nordic Academic Press 2000), *Challenges to Democracy: Eastern Europe Ten Years after the Collapse of Communism* (co-authored with Sten Berglund, Henri Vogt and Georgi Karasimeonov, Edward Elgar 2001), and *The Handbook of Political Change in Eastern Europe, Second Edition* (co-edited and co-authored with Sten Berglund and Joakim Ekman, Edward Elgar 2004).

Sten Berglund (b. 1947) is professor of political science at the University of Örebro, Sweden and Humboldt University, Berlin, Germany. His previous publications include *The New Democracies in Eastern Europe: Party Systems and Political Cleavages* (co-edited and co-authored with Jan Åke Dellenbrant, Edward Elgar 1991 and 1994), *The Political History of Eastern Europe in the 20th Century* (with Frank Aarebrot, Edward Elgar 1997), *The Handbook of Political Change in Eastern Europe* (co-edited and co-authored with Tomas Hellén and Frank Aarebrot, Edward Elgar 1998), *Challenges to Democracy: Eastern Europe Ten Years after the Collapse of Communism* (co-authored with Frank Aarebrot, Henri Vogt and Georgi Karasimeonov, Edward Elgar 2001), *Baltic Democracy at the Crossroads: An Elite Perspective* (co-edited with Kjetil Duvold, Norwegian Academic Press 2003), and *The Handbook of Political Change in Eastern Europe, Second Edition* (co-edited and co-authored with Joakim Ekman and Frank

H. Aarebrot, Edward Elgar 2004).

Joakim Ekman (b. 1970) holds a Ph.D. in political science from the University of Örebro, Sweden. His current research interests comprise European politics, democratization and political socialization, and his works include *National Identity in Divided and Unified Germany* (doctoral thesis, 2001) and *The Handbook of Political Change in Eastern Europe, Second Edition* (co-edited and co-authored with Sten Berglund and Frank H. Aarebrot, Edward Elgar 2004). His works have also appeared in the *European Journal of Political Research* and *Journal of Communist Studies and Transition Politics*.

Henri Vogt (b. 1967) is Research Fellow at the Department of Political Science, University of Helsinki, Finland. He holds a M.Soc.Sc. from the University of Helsinki and a D.Phil. in politics from the University of Oxford. His books include *Between Utopia and Disillusionment: A Narrative of the Political Transformation in Eastern Europe* (Berghahn Books 2005), *Challenges to Democracy: Eastern Europe Ten Years after the Collapse of Communism* (co-authored with Sten Berglund, Frank Aarebrot and Georgi Karasimeonov, Edward Elgar 2001), and *A Responsible Europe? Ethical Foundations of EU External Affairs* (co-edited with Hartmut Mayer, Palgrave 2006). In 2005–2008, he is the President of the Nordic International Studies Association. His current research on the impact of European regional organisations on Eastern European democratisation is funded by the Academy of Finland (project number 108239).

# Preface

This book project was initiated under the auspices of the research project *Conditions of European Democracy* (1999–2004), financed by the Tercentenary Fund of the Bank of Sweden. It is also the last contribution by the project leaders to a series of books, published by Edward Elgar: *The Political History of Eastern Europe in the 20th Century* (1997); *The Handbook of Political Change in Eastern Europe* (1998); *Challenges to Democracy: Eastern Europe Ten Years after the Collapse of Communism* (2001); and *The Handbook of Political Change in Eastern Europe, Second Edition* (2004). The present volume applies an all-European perspective that sets it apart from the previous books with their focus on post-communist Central and Eastern Europe. In the final analysis, however, the present volume on the *Making of the European Union* is essentially a continuation of our efforts to understand, from a comparative perspective, the political landscape of Europe after the end of communism.

The authors wish to express their gratitude to the Tercentenary Fund for its generous support over the years. They also wish to thank their respective academic institutions, the Political Science Section of Örebro University, the *Nordeuropa-Institut* of the Humboldt University, Berlin, the Political Science Department of the University of Helsinki, and the Department of Comparative Politics of the University of Bergen. Finally, we wish to thank Otto Leirbukt and Ossi Piironen for their research assistance. Otto Leirbukt assisted Frank Aarebrot in his data analyses; Ossi Piironen assisted Henri Vogt in his inventory of indicators.

This is a co-authored volume, for which we all bear responsibility. A certain division of labour was nevertheless necessary. Henri Vogt and Sten Berglund drafted the introductory chapter; Chapter 2 was drafted by Frank Aarebrot; Chapters 3 and 7 by Henri Vogt; Chapter 4 by Sten Berglund, Joakim Ekman and Frank Aarebrot, Chapter 5 by Joakim Ekman, Chapter 6 by Sten Berglund and Joakim Ekman, and the Conclusions by Sten Berglund.

*Sten Berglund*   *Joakim Ekman*   *Henri Vogt*   *Frank H. Aarebrot*

# 1. Introduction

At the time of finishing work on this book, in July 2005, the process of European integration had drifted into a serious crisis, perhaps into the most serious one since the Danes voted against the Treaty of the European Union in the summer of 1992. The French and Dutch citizens blatantly rejected the Treaty establishing a Constitution for Europe in their referendums on 29 May and 1 June 2005, respectively, thus freezing the constitutional process for at least a year. Only two weeks later, the heads of EU states could not agree upon the financial framework for the Union for the years 2007–13. National interests seemed to prevail over the breathtaking rhetoric of European unity.

We do not yet know what the concrete effects of these setbacks (setbacks from Brussels' point of view) will be, but it seems to us obvious that the foundations, justification, and future aims of the integration process will have to be rethought, redefined, and even reconstructed. Above all, the linkages between people and the elites must become more meaningful, the notions of democracy and true European plurality brought to the core of all integration activities instead of the current calls for efficiency and tedious standardisation. We hope that this volume can provide a number of thought-provoking ideas for this renewal exercise.

**Starting Points**

An avalanche of more or less academic books has been produced on the old continent's economic and political integration over the last decades. And it does not take clairvoyance to predict that within the next few months we will see yet a new wave of EU books, inspired by the above-mentioned difficulties and propagating – in our view prematurely – 'The End of the European Union'. We believe, however, that this book is distinct from most of these volumes for at least four reasons or, to be more precise, their combined impact.

First, we are not so much interested in the actual functioning of the Union, its daily policies, increasing global influence or internal controversies, but seek to map out what we call the *outer limits* or overall conditions of the integration process. We try to describe and analyse the historical, mental, intellectual, and attitudinal denominators of integration; denominators that have shaped the process so far and will shape it in the future. The focus is on the foundations, including earlier historical efforts of European-level political cooperation; public views, both in relation to the deepening and widening of the EU; and future scenarios of integration.

Second, and closely related to the first point, we apply a citizen's or bottom-up perspective on the integration process. The European Union – and its organizational forerunners – was initially part of an elite-driven project for peace and prosperity in Western Europe. The elite (and technocratic) perspective thus goes a long way towards accounting for the many twists and turns in the history of European integration after the Second World War. But it is perhaps precisely this elite-tied nature of the European integration project that has now accumulated into a fatal problem, a problem that EU studies have helped construct and reconstruct: the views and attitudes of average Europeans have not been sufficiently listened to. The difficulties that the constitutional process has encountered can well be interpreted from this perspective; to many a member of Euro-elites it appears virtually impossible to understand that it is fully legitimate to vote 'no' in a referendum.

Hence, it seems that the EU enjoys more support amongst political elites than it does at the grass-root level. But no political entity can flourish in the long run if it is not backed up by ordinary people, by the masses – or at least no democratic entity can do that. Popular support is thus crucial for the success of the European Union, regardless of how and in what direction it develops. But support is a multi-faceted term. It can mean very many different things, it contains many dimensions, and it can become manifested in many ways. People may, for example, support 'Europe', the idea of ever closer cooperation between the European countries, but still vote against the Draft Constitution, because they feel that the Euro-politicians do not do enough to fight the forces of globalisation and the loss of companies and jobs to countries with cheaper labour. Mapping and analysing these different dimensions of support for the EU and its institutions in member and candidate countries is a matter of major significance, not only for the European Commission but also for the scientific community at large.

Two issues are particularly important if we apply a citizen's perspective, namely how people perceive their own country – and the identity that it stands for – and the sense of balance to be struck between further enlargement and deepening of the European Union. When we talk about people's attitudes towards the EU, it is evident that we also talk about their relationship with their respective nation-states. Whether federalists or functionalists, the founding fathers of what is now known as the European Union expected increasing economic and political cooperation to result in the withering away not only of the nation-state but also of nationalist sentiments. The focus and the loyalties of the citizens would gradually shift from the national to the overarching European level. It has become more and more evident that this has not happened. On the contrary, national identities may have become even more important than they were, say, thirty years ago. Also, as we discuss more thoroughly in Chapter 3, there are still a great number of mechanisms in place that protect national cultures and polities, mechanisms of exclusion that make integration in many respects problematic. All in all, the crucial question of integration is not the extent to which national identities will be replaced by a European identity, but the extent to which these national cultures are able to incorporate 'Europe' into themselves (Wæver 2002, 25).

In recent years, it has been evident that enlargement has dominated the EU agenda to the detriment of deepening with the notable exception of the monetary union. The breakdown of Soviet-style socialism in Eastern Europe in 1989–90, and subsequently in the Soviet Union, changed the political map of Europe profoundly. In a bold move designed to bridge the gap between East and West, the EU responded by opening its doors to the new democracies of Eastern Europe. In May 2004, the Baltic countries of Estonia, Latvia and Lithuania, Poland, Hungary, the Czech Republic, Slovakia and Slovenia joined Malta and Cyprus as full members of the Union. In 2007, Bulgaria and Romania are scheduled to follow suit. These represent system changes of the same magnitude as other historical turning points such as the collapse of the Austro-Hungarian Empire in the wake of the First World War, the building of Cold War structures in the aftermath of the Second World War and more recently the peaceful breakdown of the Soviet-style regimes in Central and Eastern Europe.

But enlargement may have exceeded its limits. Many already now feel that it has proceeded too fast, without a precise and shared understanding of where the borders of Europe actually lie. There are those who would like to see a Europe with a distinct, small, and maybe Christian core – French President Jacques Chirac is possibly the best known envoy of this view – and those who advance the idea of open borders, of continuing enlargement. For Zygmunt Bauman (2003, 7), among others, Europe is defined in terms of a 'European culture' that knows no borders. 'Europe', he says, 'is allergic to borders'. However that may be, it has become ever more evident that we need to create a Europe with several speeds, a Europe that can flexibly decide upon the modes of cooperation for each issue area separately. The findings of this book also implicitly support this idea of flexibility: the mental fences across Europe are already so low – the continent has indeed become more and more homogenous – that it opens up possibilities for a variety of cooperative arrangements across the continent.

The third distinctive point of this book is that we apply a broad comparative perspective, where European nation-states constitute the primary units of analysis. In other words, we search, time and again, for the relationship of individual European countries to the continent's integration project. In order to answer we make use of a number of analytical dimensions or cleavages (cf. Lipset and Rokkan 1967; Berglund and Aarebrot 1997; Berglund et al. 2001; Berglund et al. 2004). There are the 'regional' distinctions between north and south, east and west, and between Balkan, Mediterranean, Central European and Scandinavian countries. There are also the religious division lines, above all that between Catholicism and Protestantism. We also refer to such categories as core and periphery, big and small member states and the original six member states versus the newcomers. Closely related to this we also try to combine macro-sociological, historical analysis with survey-based analysis of the support that the EU enjoys among the European citizenries.

The most important of these distinctions is undoubtedly that between 'East' and 'West'. In fact, the original idea of this book was to explore the remains of the iron curtain, to ask to what extent we can still differentiate between the former communist countries and the established member states. We quickly realised that this would have been too narrow a perspective: there are of course differences between the East and West, but more often than not other cleavages provide explanations that seem to be more to the point.

This leads us to the fourth and final point, a point that could also be understood as a specification of the first one. We try to incorporate what we call a systemic perspective into the analysis. Put differently, we treat the European Union as a political entity very much comparable to the state. The European Union has many, but not all, the attributes of a state. The key government institutions are there. The monetary union is there, and so are several of the standard symbols of statehood: the flag, the national anthem and permanent diplomatic representation outside the European Union. The European Commission is not just any European government; it represents the top level of a complex system of internationalised governance, also including other key government institutions like the European Parliament and the Council of Ministers plus a set of more or less loosely defined issue- or policy-specific institutions and organisations, possibly from all three levels of the union: local/regional, national and supranational or federal. The national level is presumably more transparent than the EU level, but certainly not without informal networks somewhat removed from political science textbook accounts of political representation and accountability in Western democracies.

The systemic perspective paves the way for three different research strategies (Easton 1965a; 1965b). We may focus on the elite level, the formal and informal actors behind the decisions made in the name of the European Union. This is what we would have to do, if we want to identify the different governance networks within the EU. Interesting as this might be, this is not our choice. Another option would be to make system output the primary object of our investigation. Output refers to the decisions or, for that matter, the 'non-decisions' that come out of the political system. This is the obvious choice for those with an interest in policy and policy outcomes. We rejected this option as well in favour of the ultimate source of political legitimacy in any political system, that is, the people, the voters or the European citizens. In terms of David Easton's simple model of political life (Easton 1965b), their opinions and attitudes compose a central element of systemic input.

The European Commission has monitored public opinion in member countries and applicant countries for more than three decades. The former communist countries of Eastern Europe have also been included in large cross-national EU-related surveys over the past 10–15 years. The Commission has an interest in attitudes towards the EU as such, its institutions and general direction. Several of the items included in the questionnaires are thus of immediate relevance for assessing the nature of input into the European political system. This is the systemic approach we have opted for. Chapter 4 on levels and layers of support for the European Union is explicitly cast within this framework, but the framework plays an important role throughout the volume.

**Structure of the Book**

As indicated by the title, the volume breaks down into three parts or sections. There is a section revolving around the foundations of the EU, a section focusing on public support for Union institutions and policies, and finally a section on obstacles or hurdles on the bumpy road of European integration.

The first section breaks down into two chapters dealing with what could be called 'integration propensity'. Chapter 2 provides an overview of the earlier integration processes on the European continent. It shows that the current wave of integration is by no means unique, but concrete efforts of integration have existed on the continent for a long time already. For example, the introduction of the metric system in 1875 or the establishment of the International Postal Union a year later can be understood from this perspective. The chapter also discusses the most important dynamism of the process of European integration, its basic source of energy, namely how Europe has developed through economic bottom-up cooperation, on the one hand, and political top-down integration, on the other hand. The other chapter of the first section, Chapter 3, poses the question of the inclusive or exclusive nature of European nation-states. The idea is that the patterns of inclusion/exclusion of the nation-states determine, at least to some extent, their willingness to integrate under the umbrella of 'Europe'. In order to understand these patterns, the chapter analyses, for example, the citizenship laws and religious heterogeneity of European countries.

The second section focuses on support for the EU and its institutions within the expanding Union. It is partly a question of mapping, partly a question of analysis. We describe countries and, for that matter, citizens in terms of attachment to the European Union, and we also set out to account for or explain the variations in support for the European Union. Such issues as trust in EU institutions, image of the Union, people's national vs. European identity are explored in Chapter 4. We also ask whether people only support the performance of the system, or whether they actually pledge allegiance to the very principles of integration. The results convincingly show that a lot still needs to be done for a 'true' European-level political community to emerge. Chapter 5, in turn, analyses Europeans' attitudes to deepening integration in the field of foreign and security policy. The idea is that because these policies have traditionally belonged to the very core functions of the nation-state, it is particularly interesting to see whether Europeans are willing to transform authority in these fields to the all-European level. The news seems good from the perspective of future integration: the majority of them are. It is obvious, however, that these views have been heavily conditioned by the US foreign policies in the first half of the 2000s, the war against terrorism and on Iraq. To what extent this specific support for Europe as an alternative to the US will turn into general support for integration thus proves the crucial question in the chapter.

The third section on obstacles against European integration is also divided into two chapters. Chapter 6 explores the impact of what seems to be the two major stumbling blocks of the ongoing process of Europeanisation – the resurgence of nationalism in defence of the nation-state in at least parts of Europe and the growing political indifference, sometimes bordering on outright hostility, throughout the European Union. Chapter 7 continues along the same path, but turns it into a boulevard. It asks to what extent people's increasing individualism, on the one hand, and the process of globalisation, on the other hand, limit or even damage the possibilities of European integration. Europeans may have grown so individualistic and hedonistic that they no longer are willing to attach themselves to the conduct of common affairs, to politics, including the European Union. And they may feel that the European Union simply strengthens the forces of globalisation that, like an invisible hand, moves their jobs to cheaper countries. The concluding chapter, then (Chapter 8), presents a number of scenarios for the future of integration, scenarios that also seek to take into account the views of ordinary Europeans.

The main empirical sources of the book are the surveys gathered by the European Commission and other institutions and organizations. The *Eurobarometers* and *Candidate Countries Eurobarometers* are the most important of these. In addition, we also use statistical, electoral and historical data. Thus, although we do seek to present and utilise a number of theoretical and conceptual frameworks, the emphasis is clearly on empirical analysis – in spite of the fact that we occasionally face the most common difficulty of empirical research: there is no suitable data available, at least not yet.

*

The European Union is historically unique. It is a large-scale attempt at social, economic and political integration by democratic countries, cooperating towards this end out of their free will. We are still far removed from the democratic, federal European super-state envisaged by some of the founding fathers and favoured by some of Europe's contemporary leaders. But the achievements are nevertheless impressive and, as opposed to previous integration projects, from Charlemagne to Hitler, they have been achieved by consent and without coercion.

The EU would not be conceivable without democracy. Only democracies qualify for membership, the founding treaties are based on democratic values, and EU government institutions are expected to be responsive as well as responsible. The EU is often said to be plagued by a 'democratic deficit', and – in the opinion of the authors of this volume – it will remain plagued by such a deficit until the United States of Europe has become a reality, that is, a federal European state with federal as well as state legislatures and executives. Small countries are understandably reluctant to accept such constitutional arrangements and the current pragmatic form of European governance with its emphasis on indirect representation is likely to prevail for yet some time. This makes it difficult to build popular support for common EU institutions, but it somehow does not seem to be equally difficult throughout the union. Some EU citizens are more supportive of the EU than other, and comparative analyses of the variations over time and space should provide clues about the causal chain.

# REFERENCES

Bauman, Zygmunt (2003), *Europe: An Unfinished Adventure*, Cambridge, Polity Press.
Berglund, Sten and Frank H. Aarebrot (1997), *The Political History of Eastern Europe: The Struggle between Democracy and Dictatorship*, Cheltenham, UK and Lyme, USA, Edward Elgar.
Berglund, Sten, Frank H. Aarebrot, Henri Vogt and Georgi Karasimeonov (2001), *Challenges to Democracy: Eastern Europe Ten Years after the Collapse of Communism,* Cheltenham, UK and Northampton, MA, USA, Edward Elgar.

Berglund, Sten, Joakim Ekman and Frank H. Aarebrot, eds (2004), *The Handbook of Political Change in Eastern Europe, Second Edition*, Cheltenham, UK and Northampton, MA, USA, Edward Elgar.
Easton, David (1965a), *A Framework for Political Analysis*, New York, Prentice-Hall.
Easton, David (1965b), *A Systems Analysis of Political Life*, New York, London and Sydney, John Wiley & Sons.
Lipset, Seymour Martin and Stein Rokkan (1967), 'Cleavage Structures, Party Systems and Voters Alignments: An Introduction', in Seymour Martin Lipset and Stein Rokkan, eds, *Party Systems and Voter Alignments: Cross-National Perspective*, New York, Free Press.
Wæver, Ole (2002) 'Identity, Communities and Foreign Policy: Discourse Analysis as Foreign Policy Theory', in Lene Hansen and Ole Wæver, eds, *European Integration and National Identity: The Challenge of the Nordic States*, London and New York, Routledge.

# 2. The Origins of the European Union

Observers of the inner workings in Brussels often emphasise that European integration had better be understood as ongoing processes rather than in terms of political structures. This is the point of departure of this chapter. Are the integration processes limited to the life span of the European Union or do they reach beyond the calamities of the end of the Second World War and the forced solidarity of the Cold War?

The states that constitute the Union today are descendants of the Westphalian system, currently challenged by supranational authorities such as the United Nations Security Council, the North Atlantic Treaty Organization and, last but not least, the European Union. These are not the only challenges. Prior to the establishment of the Westphalian system of modern states, medieval Europe comprised a very large number of internationally recognised principalities. During the last century and notably in the aftermath of the two great world wars several of these principalities – but by no means all of them – had been given a second chance in the form of modern statehood, almost always at the expense of the losing states. Today, many of the former winners are faced with claims for regional autonomy or even separatist claims from ancient principalities within their borders. It is far from certain that this process has come to an end.

Nevertheless, in today's Europe the challenged states remain dominant in terms of institutional strength. Lipset and Rokkan's seminal conceptual map of Europe (Flora et al. 1999; Lipset and Rokkan 1967; Rokkan 1975) updated by Berglund and Aarebrot (1997) summarises the pattern of state formation in the period after the Peace of Westphalia in 1648 and up to now (Table 2.1). A fundamental distinction is made between old former empire states, somewhat younger and weaker empire states and more recent and relatively small periphery states devolved from the empire states of the Westphalian system during the last 150 years (Tilly 2000). Another distinction is that between states with unchallenged political authority and states where religious authority is in a position to challenge political rulers through supra-national *ecclesia*. Four classes of countries follow a rough north–south gradient. First, in the Protestant countries with a state-church, the clergy was incorporated into the bureaucratic apparatus of the state where Protestant ministers became central agents for the nation-building strategies. Secondly, a class containing countries secularised in the wake of the French and Russian revolutions and mixed countries with large Catholic minorities and National Orthodox churches with a long tradition of subservience to the state. In these cases, the churches were in no position to challenge the state-building elites, and were not central to the nation-building strategies. Thirdly, a class of Catholic counter-reformation countries and non-secularised Orthodox countries – notably Greek Orthodox – where supranational ecclesiastical authority made for divided loyalty between State and Church among the clergy, curtailing the priests' potential as instruments for state- and nation-building. The fourth class contains the Muslim countries where the Holy Scripture of the Koran prescribes a universal community of all believers, thereby making state-building a highly problematic enterprise on religious grounds. In these countries, state- and nation-building has more often than not occurred in direct confrontation with religious beliefs among major segments of the populations.

*Table 2.1: Stein Rokkan's conceptual map of Europe (revised and updated)*

| Religious heritage | Late, devolved states from western seaward empires | Early states formed in western seaward empires | City-belt Europe | States based on former core nations of Central European empire states | Late, devolved states from Central European empires | Late, devolved states from eastern empires | Eastern empires |
|---|---|---|---|---|---|---|---|
| Protestant countries | Iceland Norway *(Scotland) (Wales)* | *Denmark England* | | Sweden | Finland | Estonia Latvia | |
| Mixed countries, substantially secularised countries or National Orthodox countries | *(Ulster)* | *France* | Netherlands Switzerland | Germany | Czech Rep. | Belarus Ukraine | Russia |
| Counter-reformation countries and non-secularised Orthodox countries | Eire Malta Cyprus | Spain Portugal | Belgium Luxemburg Italy | Austria Hungary | Poland Slovakia Slovenia Croatia | Lithuania Romania Bulgaria Serbia and Monte-negro FYROM Greece | |
| Muslim countries | | | | | Bosnia | Albania (Kazoo) | Turkey |

*Source:* Revised from Berglund and Aarebrot (1997).

The original six member of the EEC from 1957 are placed at the very centre of the conceptual map (Table 2.1). The founding members comprised four of the five city-belt states as well as the two secularised and/or mixed empire states; France to the west of the city belt and Germany to the east.

All six contain substantial Catholic populations: three are counter-reformation and three are secularised and/or mixed. To some extent, an inspection of the map lends credence to the notion of the EEC as a peace project. The two historically warring empire states are separated by the city belt as a buffer of sorts. With the exception of the Swiss lands there is a striking continuity from the structuring of the Carolingian heritage at the Compromise of Verdun in 843 into a German, French and a Lotharingian Realm.

When the EEC was extended into the EC in 1973, the two western, Protestant empire states of Denmark and Great Britain were included along with one state devolved from Britain, Eire. Two states devolved from the former Danish Empire State, Norway and Iceland, have chosen to remain outside the EU, as did the Danish Home Rule Territories of Greenland and the Faeroe Islands. In terms of the terminology of the conceptual map, countries comprising the territories of the former Protestant empire states with their strong tradition of state- and nation-building were brought in. Indeed, it is tempting to point out that these two former empire states and their devolved states and territories have proven at times in the aftermath of the extension to be quite hesitant and sometimes troublesome Europeans.

The breakdown of right wing authoritarian regimes was the direct occasion for the second wave of enlargement. The demise of the military regime in Greece and the collapse of fascism in Portugal and Spain paved the way for their EC membership in 1981 and 1986, respectively (Linz and Stepan 1996). In terms of the conceptual map, this meant that the two last remaining western empire states, both counter-reformation, were brought in. Greece became the first Orthodox country to join, historically devolved from an eastern empire. By 1990, the EC comprised all western empire states, four of five city-belt states, but only two devolved periphery states and only one Central European empire state. All the three new members shared a tradition of dualism between state-building and a supranational ecclesia.

The two most recent waves of enlargements are also derived from the collapse of non-democratic regimes: the demise of the Soviet Union and communism as a state ideology from 1989 onwards (Berglund et al. 2004). These events enabled formerly neutral countries to apply for membership, and Sweden, Finland and Austria all joined the EU in 1995. Non-neutral Norway seized the opportunity to make a second attempt at membership; the European Commission welcomed the application but the Norwegian voters turned it down. This third wave of extensions brought in two more Central European empire states – one Protestant, the other counter-reformation – and one Protestant devolved periphery state.[1]

The fourth enlargement wave followed in 2004 and comprised two distinct groups of applicant countries: eight former communist countries and the two Mediterranean islands of Malta and Cyprus, historically devolved from the British Empire. One of the countries, Hungary, became the last Central European empire state to join the EU. Six of the countries are historically devolved from Central European empires and the last three are the Baltic states, historically devolved from an eastern empire: Russia. All the three first classes of religious heritage (Table 2.1) are represented among the newest members.

In the conceptual map, the current member states of the EU are marked in italics. It is noteworthy that all states formed on the remains of western seaward empires and Central European empires have become members. None of the states formed on the basis of the cores of the former eastern empires are members. No Muslim country has yet been accepted as a member. There are non-members among all types of younger, devolved states. This 'exceptionalism' can most easily be found if we inspect the conceptual map diagonally, from Protestant states devolved from western empire states in the upper left-hand corner, to Muslim eastern empires in the bottom right-hand corner (Table 2.1). There is, however, a major distinction between two groups of non-members as we read down the diagonal. The Nordic non-members – Iceland and Norway – as well as the resisters in the city belt – Switzerland and Liechtenstein[2] – have chosen to remain outside the EU themselves. Contrary to this, the Balkan countries as well as Turkey are eager to join, but are not yet fully accepted by the EU.[3] This diagonal also reflects another implication of Rokkan's theory of state- and nation-building. When moving from west to east, we see that state-building has been hampered by a late start. Central and Eastern Europe was dominated not by states, but by empires up until the First World War, whereas in Western Europe state-building roughly began with the Peace of Westphalia in 1648. As we move from north to south, we see that nation-building encounters difficulties with increasing potential for resistance by supranational religious authorities and their clergy. The northern countries could enlist their Protestant ministers as nation-building agents. The countries of the south-eastern corner would be expected to be the less institutionally developed nation-states and should therefore not be able to offer the same level of resistance to the EU institutions as their north-western counterparts.

If we add the 'Eurosceptic' member states (see Chapter 4) to the European countries that have deliberately opted out of the union (Iceland, Norway and Switzerland), we get a group of at least six countries, including Britain, Denmark and Sweden. Is this merely a coincidence, or is there a structural explanation? It is tempting to put forward a hypothesis of institutional *relativism*. The EU institutions face two completely contrary criticisms from governments and citizens in the member states. Some argue that the EU institutions are too strong and that they impose their rules and regulations on member states, while others argue that the EU institutions are too lax, thus paving the way for the forces of the free market at the expense of the democratic institutions of the member states. Both arguments are put forward in most member states since they are to some extent related to left wing and right wing ideologies. However, the left wing assertion that the EU institutions are too lax is particularly prevalent in the countries of the north-west. This might be a function of relative perception of the EU institutions based on a historical experience of strong institutions created by long and highly successful state- and nation-building processes. Contrary to this, governments and citizens in countries with weaker national institutions might consider the EU institutions as awesome.

## Two Historical Explanations of Integration

The use of the conceptual map to understand European integration invites us to apply a longer time perspective. It would be our argument that it is possible to envisage the institutional integration of Europe as well as its constituent states by means of two modes of understanding: a unilinear mode and a mode of two parallel, sometimes competing, sometimes complementary, processes.

The unilinear model of understanding departs from the notion that there is a 'normal' European condition of competing and warring states and principalities throughout the last millennium. This 'normal' condition has on few occasions been interspersed by serious attempts to conquer the entire European continent and subjugate it to one ruler.[4] When these attempted conquests failed, they left behind a heritage that influenced the continent when it reverted to its 'normal' condition of competing states. Generally speaking, the unilinear history of European integration can be summarised in terms of a few turning-points, intimately associated with the unsuccessful architects of a new world order.

Charlemagne (747–814) was first in line. His attempts to re-establish the West Roman Empire led to the incorporation of most of Central European Christendom, but the integrity of the realm did not survive his succession and the disintegration of the empire was formalised by the Compromise of Verdun in 843. Even so, the Carolingian Empire left behind the idea of a Holy Roman Empire, the supremacy of Catholic Universalism, and a set of norms associated with civilised behaviour or *courtoisie*. This medieval system ended with another attempt at unification: the Habsburg claim to a European empire by Charles V (1500–1558) and Philip II (1527–98). When their hopes went down with the Spanish Armada, the Westphalian system of modern states emerged, and with it a permanent division between a Protestant and Catholic Europe. The armies of the French Revolution and Napoleon (1792–1804, 1804–15) were next to challenge the European state system. After Waterloo, old Europe was restored in terms of statehood, but the French ideas of citizenship and democracy remained and gradually transformed the West European states into mass democracies during the 19th century. This European order disintegrated during the First World War. After the war there was a short-lived attempt at restoring a democratic order, which Hitler set out to quench and replace by a European regime totally dominated by Nazi Germany. The German military campaigns in Western and Eastern Europe were initially very successful, but the German *Wehrmacht* was eventually pushed back by an anti-Hitler coalition, also including the United States. On the ruins of the Third Reich, the idea of stronger European cooperation emerged, but European sovereignty was curtailed by the two external victors, the United States and the Soviet Union. Thus, in this unilinear understanding of European history, the EU institutions can be considered part of the normalisation process after the last aborted conquest.

Does this understanding fully justify the existence of the EU? The organisation is obviously much more than a mere regulatory mechanism to ensure the strength of and cooperation between democratic states. Indeed, the original Treaty of Rome has as its main objective the integration of the European economies through a customs union. After its inception, some of the major advances of the EU include regional economic development and lately a common currency, both measures that go beyond what one might reasonably be expected of an organisation designed just to prevent another conquest.

We would argue that an alternative mode of understanding European integration is better suited to fully grasp the role of the EU in a historical perspective. This mode entails a notion of two *parallel* processes. First, the notion of conquest must be assumed to be a more general phenomenon than the four all-European attempts referred to above. Indeed, the notion of empire states in a conceptual map presupposes that all these states at one point or another have set out to and sometimes succeeded in conquering their neighbours. Conquest and subsequent incorporation of new lands constitute the central elements in Rokkan's concept of state-building and have taken place more or less continuously throughout European history. Second, cooperation between cities, principalities and states to mutual economic benefit has also been going on more or less continuously throughout European history, more often than not originating in the city belt. These dual processes of military–political incorporation and political–economic integration have sometimes reinforced one another and sometimes worked against one another. In a sense there are two parallel processes – one from the top and down, the other from the bottom and up as illustrated in Figure 2.1.

The state-building histories of France and Switzerland may highlight the logic of the model. The French case comes close to the ideal type of the classical state-building model. Ever since the Merovingians asserted their kingship on the Frankish tribes of the former Roman province of Gaul, an internationally recognised principality has existed defining a French territory. Subsequent French dynasties had consistently tried, albeit with varying success, to expand the French empire state. The centralisation of power in France was further enhanced through the introduction of royal despotism, economic mercantilism and linguistic standardisation under the auspices of Richelieu (1585–1642) and Colbert (1619–83). When Republican France emerged during the Revolution of 1789 and again after 1871, the foundation for rapid democratisation and nation-building had already been laid. Moreover, as Eugène Weber (1976) rightly points out, the economic integration of Southern France was completed by the end of the 19th century. The result was the pronounced predominance by Paris as a conquest centre over provincial cities and countryside.

*Figure 2.1: Two parallel historical processes of European integration*

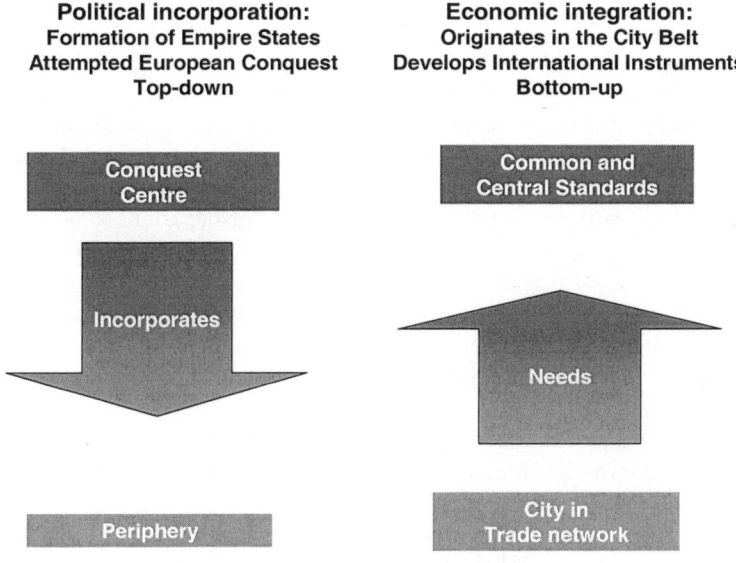

In contrast, Switzerland began in what is today a rural region – in the three *Ur-Kantonen* of Schwyz, Unterwalden and Ur. The representatives of these three cantons formed an alliance in 1294 in the form of an 'Oath Commonwealth' (*Eidsgenossenschaft*). Their strategic location around the *Vierwaldstädtersee* enabled them to control and tax the Trans-Alpine trading route, and the purpose of their union was to exploit this advantage and defend themselves against external enemies. The Swiss territorial entity grew as more cantons joined the Commonwealth, but remained a loose confederation until the French occupation (1798–1803). The loose character of the confederation is best illustrated by the fact that the treaty included no provisions for common citizenship and that the cantons had the right to feud when foreign enemies did not threaten. Moreover, as Switzerland grew by association, it came to include Protestant as well as Catholic cantons; German, French, Italian and Rhaeto-Romanic speakers. The unifying cultural symbols were limited to their common history, stories like the legend of Wilhelm Tell, and other myths. When Switzerland regained her independence in 1815, the Swiss decided to keep the federal capital of Bern and the bureaucratic institutions installed by the French occupying powers, thus transforming themselves from a confederation to a federation. A civil war, the so-called *Sonderbundkrieg* (1847–48), over the right of the Catholic cantons to secede, testifies to the resilience of the confederal structures. As a result Switzerland today has a relatively insignificant city as its capital and is dominated by the strong German and French speaking communities around Zurich and Geneva (Fossedal 2002).

The French case illustrates the top-down model of classical state-building, whereas the Swiss case is closer to a model where common economic interests gradually promote development into statehood, from the bottom up. But most countries cannot be read as easily with the help of the two modes of explanation. The unification of Germany from Prussia to the *Hohenzollern Reich* is a case in point. Modern German state-building can be understood both ways given the same points of departure – the formal and final dissolution of the Holy Roman Empire of the German Nation in 1806 and the national romantic revolutions of 1848 were based on the notion of popular rule for all peoples using the German tongue. The latter idea suited neither the Austrian Emperor, eager to retain his multi-ethnic possessions, nor the Prussian King, equally keen on expanding his Protestant realm into a great power.

Austria and Prussia clashed at the Frankfurt Parliament in 1848–51, where Otto von Bismarck was active as a young Prussian diplomat. Prussia promoted the idea of a 'small' Germany, excluding Austria, while Austria called for a greater Germany, in effect re-establishing the Holy German Empire under the Habsburg throne. In the end, after the demise of the national romantic revolution, neither Austria, nor Prussia, accepted the definition of Germany offered by the Frankfurt parliament. From this point on, until the unification of Germany in 1870, German state-building can be interpreted in two ways.

Bismarck promoted himself as the Iron Chancellor. This implied that Germany had been unified according to the state-building model. Successive wars against Denmark, Austria and France forced the remaining German states to accept Prussian leadership within a new empire. But the process can also be interpreted from a bottom-up perspective. The introduction of a railway system beginning in the 1850s made it possible for industrial entrepreneurs and the Prussian state to link the stone coals deposits of Silesia to the iron ore of the *Erzgebirge* and produce steel in the Ruhr area of Prussian Westphalia. This new infrastructure changed the situation on the ground, making German economic interests less dependent on the flow of the Rhine and the Elbe. But it also created a problem. On their way between Westphalia and the rest of Prussia the trains had to pass through a number of minor German states. Customs between these states had to be eliminated, if steel production were to be competitive. The North German Customs Union (*Nord-Deutscher Zollverein*) was a natural consequence. The new German empire was essentially a west–east oriented territory, thus conforming to the new economic realities. What is then the correct model, state-building by the Iron Chancellor or new economic interests forging a new territorial entity? The answer is: both are. Germany is a product of the two modes reinforcing one another.

At the European level, the dual mode model of integration implies continuous aspiration on the part of empire states to conquer and expand and similar aspirations originating mainly in the city belt to coordinate, standardise and facilitate commerce. Within the framework of the unilinear model, the EU is portrayed as a product of an aborted attempt by Germany to conquer and subjugate the European continent. In the dual mode model, however, the EU is cast as nothing but the last in a long series of integration projects as old and ubiquitous as the conquest strategies of empire states.

*

Territorial consolidation based on common economic interests also requires institutions. The conquest centres have their military headquarters and chancelleries; the trading cities have their banks and stock exchanges. All these institutions are essential for the functioning of a modern state.

An obvious institutional adaptation to the twin processes illustrated in Figure 2.1 would seem to be *federalisation* or *devolution*. Immediately, we would expect the states that have emerged according to the economic integration model from the bottom up to have a more federal or devolved structure than the empire states created from the top down. Whereas this is true even today for Switzerland and France respectively, it is by no means the case if we take a general view of contemporary Europe. The city-belt states comprise relatively unitary states like the Netherlands, Luxembourg and Italy.[5] States based on former historical empires include federal Germany and Austria as well as devolution processes in the UK and Spain. However, the very expectation of a rational constitutional process at the inception of European states might be fallacious. 'Founding fathers' actively discussing federal versus unitary structure at the birth of a nation is more typical of settler-states beyond Europe, such as the USA, Canada and Australia. The interaction between the two processes of integration across European history renders not one but several points in time when political elites have revised the institutional framework for geographical power in Europe. Thus, the territorial structure of the city-belt states at the beginnings of modern European statehood provides a better fit with the expected pattern. The United Dutch Provinces were almost as confederate as Switzerland in 1648. Germany, and particularly the territories surrounding the Rhine, consisted of a very large number of independent and semi-independent territorial entities where the Holy Roman Empire of the German Nation had been reduced to a *de jure* formality. Italy did not exist at all, but comprised a set of states that were internationally recognised as independent entities at the time of the Peace of Westphalia. Contrary to this, Prussia, Austria, France, Spain and Portugal were empires and kingdoms centrally ruled under varying degrees of despotism or enlightened despotism. The present UK consisted of a unitary England ruled by king and parliament with Scotland, Wales and Ireland as subject nations. The Europe of 1648 gives a better fit to our model than Europe today.

To understand this modern discrepancy we have to consider the interaction between the top-down and the bottom-up models. The Netherlands, Rhineland and Switzerland were occupied by the armies of the French Revolution, which brought with them not only the idea of popular democracy, but also the centralised French style of government. Thus, the new kingdom of the Netherlands became a unitary state during the French occupation and the Swiss confederation became a federation under the influence of the French occupiers. When Belgium and Luxembourg split from the Kingdom of the Netherlands under the Treaty of London of 1837, they retained the Dutch unitary structure. The empire states came under increased pressure from various regional identities during the 19th and 20th centuries, after 1848 in particular. Unified Germany had a federal structure at its inception in 1871. This structure was retained during the Weimar Republic and in the constitution of the present day Federal Republic. In fact, Germany was only ruled as a unitary state *de facto* during Nazi rule. In Spain, the periods of democratic rule have all been marked by demands from Catalonia and the Basque countries for regional autonomy. The Austrian empire had to transform itself into a dual monarchy after its defeat to Prussia in 1867, and a federal constitution was enshrined in the Austrian republic as it emerged after the Second World War. In Britain, the Irish independence movement was a *leitmotif* of British politics during the Victorian era, only abetted by the treaty of Irish independence of 1926. In the post-war period, the pressure for devolution has increased particularly since the 1970s, only to be formalised during the Blair government. Periods of centralised governance imposed by occupying armies have interacted with pressure for devolution rooted in national ideas.

## Historical Patterns of Integration

It is impossible to understand the present territorial and institutional structures of European countries, if we do not take into consideration the interaction between the top-down and the bottom-up processes in a perspective beyond national histories. A bird's-eye view of the EU institutions suggests that they have stronger similarities with the historical structures of the city belt than with the political machinery of empire states. Generally speaking, there are at least four kinds of institutions for economic integration:

- Financial institutions such as stock exchanges and banks, notably currency banks and national banks.
- Institutions and standards for monetisation, in particular standards for national coins and currencies.
- Infrastructural institutions such as mail systems, telecommunications and regulatory agencies for transport networks.
- Institutions supervising and maintaining national standards of measurement and weight. Lately also agencies supervising industrial standards as well as various types of consumer protection.

All modern states have developed such institutions, albeit of varying longevity and scope. Given the predominance of this kind of institutions in Brussels, the EU tends to challenge the authority of equivalent national institutions. Thus the new European Central Bank (ECB) has replaced the national currency banks in some member countries and threatens existing currency banks in others. Twelve of the member countries have replaced their national currency with the euro. The structural funds and other European infrastructure programmes interfere with traditional authority structures in the member states. A constant stream of EU directives forces national governments to modify existing standards and regulations almost on a daily basis.

But these clashes between European institutions for economic integration and similar institutions on the national level were not unknown prior to the European Union. Admittedly, the EU as an organisation represents a superstructure for these institutions, whereas in the past international economic institutions were generally legitimised through separate treaties. Nevertheless, international institutions challenging states and princes have ancient roots. Sovereign territorial authorities have always had the option of readily abiding by supranational norms, delaying their acceptance or rejecting them. We can therefore identify a pattern of diffusion with respect to the continental penetration of European institutions for economic cooperation.

*Table 2.2: The early banks, 1400–1860*

| Year | Name | Year | Name |
|---|---|---|---|
| 1401 | Bank of Barcelona, Spain | 1621 | Bank of Nuremberg, Germany |
| 1407 | Bank of St. George, Genoa, Italy | 1635 | Bank of Rotterdam, Netherlands |
| 1487 | Fuggers Bank, Augsburg, Germany | 1656 | Bank of Sweden |
| 1566 | Royal Exchange, London | 1694 | Bank of England |
| 1585 | Bank of Genoa, Italy | 1695 | Bank of Scotland |
| 1587 | Bank of Venice, Italy | 1762 | Barings Bank, England |
| 1609 | Bank of Amsterdam, Netherlands | 1768 | Russia establishes two public banks |
| 1609 | Public Bank of Barcelona, Spain | 1770 | Clearing House, London |
| 1616 | Bank of Middelburg, Netherlands | 1778 | Savingsbank in Hamburg, Germany |
| 1619 | Bank of Hamburg, Germany | 1800 | Bank of France |
| 1619 | Hamburg Girobank, Germany | 1860 | Crédit Agricole, France |
| 1621 | Bank of Delft, Netherlands | 1860 | Russian State Bank |

*Source*: Davies and Davies (1999).

The invention of the letter of credit was one of the most fundamental innovations for economic modernisation. It enabled merchants in one commercial city to transfer money to another city in another country without running the risks associated with the transporting of precious metals. Banking institutions were a prerequisite for letters of credit to work, as was recognition of these very banks as trustworthy and legitimate by governments and markets alike.

*Figure 2.2: Early currency unions, 1865–1927*

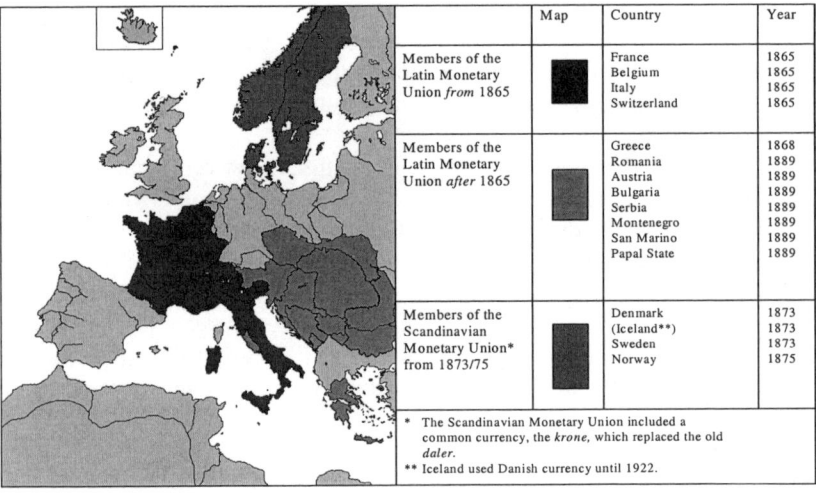

*Source*: Davies and Davies (1999).

Table 2.2 indicates the diffusion of banking institutions from 1400 to 1860. The early banks originated in Catalonia and Northern Italy and had spread across the Alps by 1500. When the Westphalian system was established in 1648, a banking system was already in place in the city belt, including London. Generally speaking, empire states like Sweden, France and Russia were latecomers in this process, as were periphery states with the notable exception of Scotland.

As a general rule, national currencies have been exactly that, the prerogative of states. Nevertheless, it would be wrong to believe that an international currency such as the euro is an innovation of our times. The 19th century saw two international monetary unions in Europe: the Latin Monetary Union from 1865 onwards and the Scandinavian Monetary Union from 1873. The latter even had a common currency, the crown. Both these unions collapsed as a result of the First World War and the monetary crisis in its wake. The innovators were the states that joined the Latin Monetary Union at its inception: France, Belgium, Italy and Switzerland – three city-belt states and one empire state as brought out by Figure 2.2.

*Figure 2.3: Membership in the International Postal Union, 1875–2001*

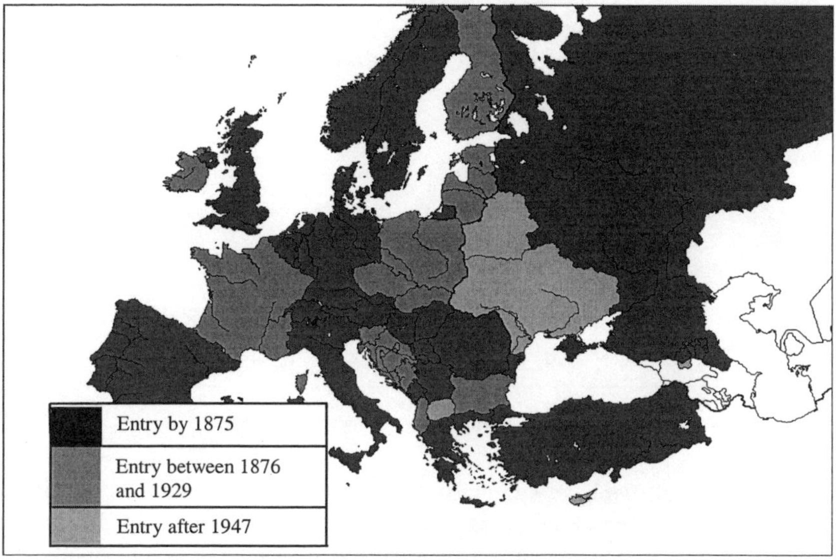

Entry by 1875
Entry between 1876 and 1929
Entry after 1947

Source: International Postal Union (http://www.upu.int/members/en/members.html).

The International Postal Union was a major project for infrastructural development. It made one language, French, mandatory for all postal services and it furnished legitimacy to an important innovation: the postal stamp. Many European countries had ratified the treaty at its inception in

1876, including all the city-belt countries. The laggards were Austria–Hungary and some of the newly independent countries in the Balkans (Figure 2.3).

Creating national standards for weight and length was another top priority among modernising absolutist rulers in the 18th century. With the French Revolution came the idea of an international standard for length and weight: the metre. This norm was legitimised by the International Metric Convention of 1875, which established the International Metric Commission in Paris: the keepers of the Standard Metre. Initially, the metre was enforced on the Netherlands and Spain by the armies of the French Revolution. The Metric Convention included Central Europe and Scandinavia, Denmark joined later, Russia, and notably Britain, were latecomers. Thus, by 1875 all city-belt states and continental empire states had gone metric (see Figure 2.4).

*Figure 2.4: Implementing the metric system, 1795–1910*

| Map | Country | Year |
|---|---|---|
| Implemented metric system before 1871 | France | 1795 |
| | Belgium | 1816 |
| | Netherlands | 1820 |
| | Spain | 1859 |
| Implemented metric system between 1871 and 1876 | Italy | 1871 |
| | Germany | 1872 |
| | Portugal | 1872 |
| | Norway | 1875 |
| | Switzerland | 1875 |
| | Austria | 1876 |
| | Hungary | 1876 |
| | Sweden | 1878 |
| Implemented metric system after 1876 | Serbia and Montenegro | 1883 |
| | Romania | 1884 |
| | Finland | 1887 |
| | Denmark | 1907 |
| | Iceland | 1910 |
| Limited use of the metric system | Greece | 1836 |

*Source:* IBPM's Homepage (http://www.bipm.fr/en/convention/member_states/)

In Table 2.3, we have summarised the patterns of innovations discussed above. For all four cases of early international institutional challenges to nation-states we observe that a majority of city-belt states are among the innovators. Moreover, several empire states are also among the founders of these institutions, at least one western but sometimes even eastern empire states. Periphery states are seldom among the innovators. This has a natural explanation, since they have – more often than not – emerged as sovereign states only recently.[6] This should not be interpreted to indicate that small peripheral states are less interested in international cooperation than others. It is rather the other way around.

*Table 2.3: Patterns of innovation*

| Pre-EU penetration strategy | Institutional example | Innovation criterion | City-belt states | Western empire states | Eastern empire states | Periphery states |
|---|---|---|---|---|---|---|
| Institutions | Banks | Before 1650 | North Italy Western Germany Netherlands | Spain UK | | |
| Monetisation | Currency Unions | 1865 | Italy Switzerland Belgium | France | | |
| Infrastructure | The Postal Union | Before 1875 | Benelux Switzerland Italy | Spain Portugal UK Denmark | Sweden Austria–Hungary Russia Turkey | Norway Greece |
| Standards | The Metre | Before 1878 | Benelux Switzerland Italy | Spain Portugal France | Germany Austria–Hungary Sweden | Norway |

When we inspect the expansion of the European Union, the traditional innovation pattern seems to repeat itself (Table 2.3). Four of the six core members are city-states. Switzerland is in fact the only notable exception to this rule. The two former empire states were already part of the Carolingian empire and have been innovators in several of the early integration processes. The first wave of expansion included Britain and her client states Denmark and Ireland; the second wave included former South European dictatorships – Portugal, Spain and Greece. The collapse of the Soviet Union made it possible for Sweden, Finland and Austria to reconsider their traditional policies of neutrality. Together they constitute the third wave of enlargement. The fourth and current wave includes most of the countries established in Central and Eastern Europe after the First World War and the former British Mediterranean strongholds of Malta and Cyprus.

Today, it may be easier to define the EU by listing the countries that are not members. The latter breaks down into two types: countries with a strong financial sector heavily dependent on the absence of international supervision such as Switzerland, Liechtenstein and the British Channel Islands. The other category includes countries heavily dependent on export of raw material such as Norway's oil, gas and fish and fishery-dependent Iceland, and the Danish dependencies of the Faeroe Islands and Greenland. Many voters in raw material-exporting countries perceive the interests of raw material exporters to clash with regulations intended to protect consumers and support processing industries in more industrialised EU member states.

The following chapters will focus on the expectations Europeans have towards EU institutions. Here we pose the question if historical experience can have an impact on these expectations. Europeans have witnessed integration as state-building from the top down as well as economic cooperation based on enlightened self-interest to form cooperative institutions from the bottom up. They have had the experiences of the French as well as those of the Swiss.

Admittedly, the state-building mode may have been more prevalent throughout European history than economically based integration. Hence, institutions of power tend to be more prominent in the minds of contemporary Europeans than institutions for economic cooperation. Not only Europeans, for that matter: Henry Kissinger, former US Secretary of State, was known to complain that there was no European foreign minister to call. Since the Maastricht Treaty the EU has tried to meet some of these state-building expectations by instituting elements of a common European foreign policy and lately even by appointing an EU foreign minister to answer calls from American Secretaries of State. The plans for a common European defence force belong in the same category. But when push comes to shove, the core of the EU institutions remains: the apparatus for economic integration. There is therefore a possible contradiction between popular attention to the instruments of state-building and the reality of what EU institutions actually do. This goes towards accounting for a certain degree of disenchantment on the part of the voters as evidenced by the low turnout in European elections. History shows that integrating a territory from the bottom up through the cooperation of enlightened interests is a slow and incremental process. Conquest, on the other hand, may be dramatic and heroic.

One of the aims of this book is to explore if, and to what extent, Europeans appreciate the slow and cumbersome road of accepting continental governance through economic integration. But the distinction between economic and political integration is admittedly fluid and all the following chapters actually revolve around measures of state- and nation-building initiated by Brussels.

But first we will have to examine the national legal frameworks, particularly in terms of citizenship, within which the European integration process is bound to operate. The idea of a European citizenship has to compete with its traditional national counterparts throughout Europe, just like the burghers of the old city in the network had to strive to become Dutch or Swiss citizens. On both these levels, the national and European, the crucial question is whether citizenship is defined in inclusive or exclusive terms.

## NOTES

1. Finland has been classified as devolved from a Central European empire state: Sweden. This is not unproblematic. Finland was politically an integral part of Sweden until it was ceded to Russia in 1809. It gained a great deal of autonomy from Tsarist Russia, established a parliamentary system in 1906 and was finally granted full independence by Lenin in 1917. Finnish nationalism has historically been torn between opposition to the Swedish heritage of cultural and political domination and resistance to Russian rule. Our classification is based on the far longer period of Swedish domination (Jussila et al. 1998).
2. We have chosen not to include any of the European mini-states in the map.
3. Bulgaria and Romania are scheduled to join the EU in 2007 (Karasimeonov 2004; Crowther 2004). Croatia has applied, but negotiations were put on hold by the EU (in March, 2005) and made contingent upon Croatia's cooperation with the international War Crimes Tribunal in the Hague. Finally, on 3 October 2005, Croatia was accepted again, and the country is expected to join the EU as a full member in 2009. Also, in October 2005, following intense debates among the EU25 states, the Council decided to open accession talks with Turkey.
4. It is noteworthy that another civilization on the Eurasian continent, China, has based its cosmology on an opposite notion of normality. In Chinese culture, the normal state of the world is 'One China', ruled as an empire under the Mandate of Heaven. The aberration is periods in Chinese history when the civilization has been divided into several polities under one culture, notably the so-called period of the 'Warring States' (475–221 BC).
5. Belgium has been a unitary state for most of its existence as a modern state and has been federalised only in the last decades.
6. Norway and Greece are classified as innovators in the summary table. It may be noted that they have exerted national pride internally, but not externally. Notably their early concern with international standards was mainly a way of making their international presence noticed.

## REFERENCES

Berglund, Sten and Frank H. Aarebrot (1997), *The Political History of Eastern Europe: The Struggle between Democracy and Dictatorship*, Cheltenham, UK and Lyme, USA, Edward Elgar.

Berglund, Sten, Joakim Ekman and Frank H. Aarebrot, eds (2004), *The Handbook of Political Change in Eastern Europe, Second Edition*, Cheltenham, UK and Northampton, MA, USA, Edward Elgar.

Crowther, William (2004), 'Romania', in Sten Berglund, Joakim Ekman and Frank H. Aarebrot, eds, *The Handbook of Political Change in Eastern Europe, Second Edition*, Cheltenham, UK and Northampton, MA, USA, Edward Elgar.

Davies, Glyn and Roy Davies (1999), *A History of Money – from Ancient Times to the Present Day*, Cardiff, University of Wales Press.

Flora, Peter, Derek Urwin, Stein Kuhnle and Stein Rokkan (1999), *State-Formation, Nation-Building, and Mass Politics in Europe: The Theory of Stein Rokkan, Based on his Collected Works*, Oxford, Oxford University Press.

Fossedal, Gregory A. (2002), *Direct Democracy in Switzerland*, Washington, DC, Transaction Publishers.

International Postal Union (2005), web page (http://www.upu.int/members/en/members.html).

Jussila, Osmo, Seppo Hentilä and Jukka Nevakivi (1998), *Finlands politiska historia*, Espoo, Schildts.

Karasimeonov, Georgi (2004), 'Bulgaria', in Sten Berglund, Joakim Ekman and Frank H. Aarebrot, eds, *The Handbook of Political Change in Eastern Europe, Second Edition*, Cheltenham, UK and Northampton, MA, USA, Edward Elgar.

Linz, Juan and Alfred Stepan (1996), *Problems of Democratic Transition and Consolidation: Southern Europe, South America and Post-Communist Europe*, Baltimore and London, Johns

Hopkins University Press.
Lipset, Seymour Martin and Stein Rokkan, eds (1967), *Party Systems and Voter Alignments: Cross-National Perspectives, International Yearbook of Political Behavior*, New York, Free Press.
Rokkan, Stein (1975), 'Dimensions of State Formation and Nation-Building: A Possible Paradigm for Research on Variations within Europe', in Charles Tilly, ed., *The Formation of National States in Europe*, Princeton, Princeton University Press, pp. 562–600.
Tilly, Charles (2000), *Coercion, Capital and European States: AD 990–1992*, Oxford, Blackwell.
Weber, Eugène (1976), *Peasants into Frenchmen: The Modernization of Rural France, 1870–1914*, Stanford, Stanford University Press.

# 3. Patterns of Inclusion and Exclusion in Europe

An underlying hypothesis informed the preceding chapter: historical institutional arrangements across the European continent influence – constrain and make possible – the current integration process and people's attitudes to it; to what extent will no doubt remain unanswered. In the following we switch our perspective from the level of institutional arrangements towards the level of individuals and their collectives, but in one sense the analysis continues along the same path: we will deal with another underlying aspect of what could be called 'integration propensity'.[1]

The point of departure is that as we try to make sense of the current public views on integration, we need to be au fait with the relationship between people and the nation-state, in particular how they have been made or not made *citizens*, given freedoms and rights or protected from random social threats. In other words, people's affections, loyalties, and identities in relation to the polity that has traditionally governed them play a significant part as they now need to relate themselves with that novel political entity, the European Union. For instance, if people had reason to trust their national political system, we should expect them to trust the European polity as well, especially if national political leaders espouse it. But an alternative pattern of reasoning may be just as plausible: one explanation for the apparent distrust in the European Union in the Nordic countries (see Chapter 4 for a more detailed analysis) is that the citizens of these countries have feared that the EU does not and will not treat them as well as their nation-states have.[2]

For our analysis we have singled out only one feature of the national political entities, namely that of their *inclusiveness* versus *exclusiveness*. The idea is thus to explore to what extent European nation-states have been willing to make citizenship inclusive, to incorporate different political and cultural elements into them, and whether we can find specific patterns of inclusion–exclusion in different parts of Europe. Most importantly, we ask in what ways and to what extent the patterns (or norms or habits or laws) of inclusion/exclusion have changed in recent years, and how these changes possibly affect European integration. For these questions to be meaningful in light of the aims of this book, we also make a strong assumption: the more inclusive the European nation-states are the better chances integration has in the long run; integration necessarily means toleration towards increasingly different norms, habits and looks (see Figure 3.1). This assumption is by no means as unproblematic as it may seem at first sight, however, but leads us straight to what is possibly the most essential dilemma of integration: Europe must be inclusive for that is what the so-called European values seem to imply, but it must also be exclusive so that these very values remain a meaningful category and avoid 'dilution' (see e.g. Cederman 2001, 3). But whatever the case, we believe that inclusion must dominate over exclusion, both internally and with relation to the outside world, if integration is to flourish.

*Figure 3.1: The structure of the chapter*

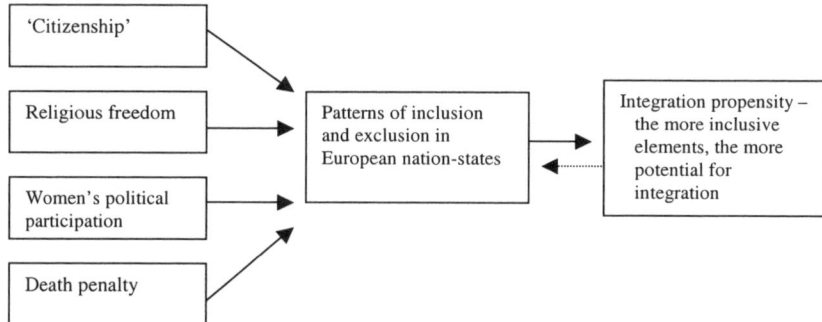

To illustrate the patterns of inclusion/exclusion, we scrutinise four indicators: 'citizenship' (including, for instance, immigration and acquisition of citizenship); religious freedom; women's political participation; and the use of death penalty. The two first of these are more significant; the two latter merely reinforce the overall arguments. To a degree the choice of these indicators was arbitrary – it might have been possible to find better ones – but what is important is that they do make it possible to draw a number of important conclusions. It is also noteworthy that the indicators primarily deal with *political* inclusion/exclusion, or political citizenship, even though the question is of multidimensional phenomena, social, economic and cultural (cf. T.H. Marshall's classical distinction between three different types of citizenship). Once again, concentrating solely on this dimension suffices from the perspective of our basic arguments. The analysis focuses on the current situation, although a more historically oriented presentation would also have been appropriate in this context, but that would have required a volume of its own. The analysis is primarily based on statistical evidence and on close reading of national legislations.

Finally, it is obvious that our starting point could easily be turned around: in today's Europe, national citizenships not only condition European 'citizenship', but the latter determines the former. This is usually referred to with the notion of Europeanisation, though 'Westernisation' might be a more accurate term; the continent is in many respects becoming more and more similar, even homogeneous. We have consciously tried to have a different angle in this chapter, but Europeanisation is clearly an important element of our analysis, too (one arrow in the figure above therefore points backwards). It has become increasingly difficult to analyse national and regional levels separately (cf. Kauppi 2005).

Before turning to the four indicators, let us start the chapter with a brief conceptual overview of the meanings of 'inclusion' and 'exclusion' in terms of citizenship.

**Citizenship, Inclusion, Exclusion**

Citizenship has always been a matter of, to use the words of Tzvetan Todorov (2000, 28), *les deux grands principes – autonomie de la collectivité, autonomie de l'individu*; the origins of these two principles can indeed be traced to antiquity, to the Greek city-states and the philosophy of the Stoics. The terms used for them have varied a great deal since, and they also seem to be a source of endless controversy. For example, one of the prevailing current debates in the field of International Relations, the debate between cosmopolitanism and communitarianism, is essentially based on the seemingly irreconcilable conflict between the individual and community (see e.g. Heater 2004; Meehan 1993; Cochran 2000).

The modern or liberal understanding of citizenship, as it emerged during 18th century Enlightenment, took its foundations from individualistic principles and made these applicable to each and everyone; it was based on universal human rights, universal suffrage. The foundations of citizenship were thus imposed, somewhat paradoxically, from outside the community itself (cf. Balibar 2001, 245).[3] This individualistic and inclusive understanding of citizenship was soon challenged, however. Nationalism, in the political form in which it emerged in the late 18th and early 19th centuries, was clearly a backlash against the universalism of Enlightenment. Citizenship was reserved for members of a national community; it became an ethnic and linguistic and thus exclusive category.

In recent European history, we can easily detect different variations of this distinction between ethnic-nationality-based and individual-based notions of citizenship – although most existing political communities are mixtures of both. Table 3.1 provides a list of the most frequently cited variations. What are often called German and French notions of citizenship – Germany as a *Kulturnation* and France as *état-nation* – is possibly the most widely known variation. The German tradition has emphasised the (ethnic) cultural community; one descent, one culture, one language (*jus sanguinis*). The distinction between the state and the nation has been virtually non-existent. This may be about to change, however. In the new citizenship law from 1999, there is now only a very weak reference to 'former Germans', and even this does not necessarily mean ethnic Germans.[4] In contrast, the tradition that emerged in France in the aftermath of the Great Revolution has been based on political responsibilities and rights that anyone who lives within the borders of France can in principle possess. Citizenship is thus defined in spatial or territorial terms (*jus soli*), and the sphere of politics also opens up for foreigners (Parisot 1998, 84–7 and 160–63).

*Table 3.1: Some analytical dimensions of citizenship*

| Collective | Individual |
|---|---|
| Greek city-states | Stoics |
| Republican | Liberal |
| Intergovernmental | Federal |
| German | French |
| *jus sanguinis* | *jus soli* |
| 'East' | 'West' |
| Particular | Universal |
| Nationalism | Technocracy |
| Communitarianism | Cosmopolitanism |

A closely related distinction is that between what has often been described as the West European – as opposed to the East European – way of understanding nation and national identity. The differences between the West and East European approaches to history are in fact often described as major. West European scholars in particular have tended to see nationalism in Eastern Europe as much more violent, non-civic and inherently more *mythos*-based than nationalism in Eastern Europe. An extreme example of this might be the role that dead bodies played in the crises of the former Yugoslavia. Some Serbs, as they fled from their lands in Croatia in the early 1990s, dug up the bones of their ancestors and took the bones with them to their new places of residence. Such an understanding of history is obviously very exclusive: people are not free agents but their fate is determined by the fate of their ancestors, a very exclusive group of people indeed (Verdery 1999; Pocock 1997).

Even if we decided to agree with the thesis of different perceptions of history, we need to bear in mind that these differences may be a reflection of even deeper social and politico-emotional structures. For example, societies have differing historical threat perceptions, and different senses of security, that determine the nature of the relations between the individual and the community. East European societies were parts of great empires until the early 20th century, many of them severely repressed. As ideas of independence emerged in them in the 19th century, it was essential to make history a mechanism of anti-repression and resistance – even to 'blur' it when necessary – and thus make it inherently exclusive. In the former communist countries, the legacy of communism has also played a part: until 1989, 'objective' historiography was not allowed, which left many essential historical questions untouched, without an answer – which may have strengthened the sense of community in these countries. After the demise of communism, the peoples of Eastern Europe embarked upon a process of *Vergangenheitsbewältigung* of their own; history was restored as an open and objective discipline. The political use of history will thus also assume new forms. In what ways these forms will contribute to mechanisms of exclusion and inclusion is a highly relevant question for the future of the entire region.

\*

As the discussion above indicates, in the context of citizenship the categories of inclusion and exclusion are by no means clear-cut. We may be inclined to assume that the community-based understanding of citizenship is exclusive and the individual-based inclusive, but reality usually turns out to be much more complex, both from a philosophical perspective and in concrete policy terms. The social and politico-legal patterns of inclusion often vary significantly. In legal terms, Germany has obviously been a fairly exclusive country – Turks living there for decades have not been granted citizenship. But in terms of social acceptance and cohesion, the situation has been clearly different; otherwise it would be impossible to explain the continuous stream of Turks to the country over the past few decades. Using a notion of social citizenship would certainly be justified.

A more interesting example is, as many scholars close to the communitarian strain of thought have remarked, the fact that adherence to 'universal values' – in the EU context, 'European values' – always excludes those not willing to support these values. This is the ultimate form of exclusion, a form often confronting today's non-Christian communities in Europe. France's decision to ban the use of headscarves (and other religious symbols) in state schools in 2004 serves as a good case in point here: the decision was based on the 'universal' principle of secular education, and it may have had good and inclusive intentions, but in practice it may lead to an increased sense of exclusion among those desiring to carry these very symbols.

Another inherent problem in the individual-based conception of citizenship is that it may lead to a highly technocratic political system. That system, while emphasising the individual's capacities, comes to rely on bureaucratic and scientific expertise and not on the mechanisms of democracy – and consequently becomes exclusive for its citizens. Indeed, technocracy, at least in its Faustian form, is easily the dark side of individualism. When we talk about indifference to politics in Chapter 7, this is in fact a highly relevant argument. On the other hand, strong, initially exclusive communities may value democracy highly,[5] and therefore bring into being various functional mechanisms of organising ethnic, religious and political differences within them; the capacity to organise, harness, and cultivate these differences is one of the most elementary features of a functioning democracy (Saukkonen 2003). The eventual result may then be an inherently inclusive community. But, of course, strong feelings of community can also lead to negative, exclusive nationalism, and ultimately to xenophobia.

The classical EU debate between the so-called federalists and intergovernmentalists can also be problematised in terms of inclusion and exclusion. We can argue that intergovernmentalists, as they emphasise the importance of national governments, have a more exclusive mindset than federalists, but there are alternative interpretations as well. Intergovernmentalism may mean that nations remain meaningful democratic entities, entities that can create inclusive social mechanisms. Federalism, in turn, necessarily involves the centralisation of power, which may lead to less plurality and therefore a greater democratic deficit – which is a mechanism of exclusion. Moreover, particularly in Eastern Europe there are a great number of people who embrace a federalist Union, because it seems to provide security guarantees for their states, guarantees against Russia. Also in this respect, strong federalism may actually be a more exclusive and 'nationalist' category than intergovernmentalism, often thought to spring from nationalist – and therefore exclusive – sentiments.

This leads us to the final remarks of this section. If we think about the development of European (Union) citizenship (or its pre-forms) through the distinction of community/individual, it is evident that it has been closer to the individualistic pattern – in spite of the term 'community'. Particularly during the early decades of European integration, European 'citizenship' was nothing more than a matter of freedom of movement and freedom of residence; there was hardly any idea of an overarching common Europeanness; the modest hope was that European nations would learn to live in peace with each other. The technocratic dimension was also clearly visible: in the ideas of the founding fathers of European integration, what is now known as the EU was to become an expert institution capable of resisting the random, watered compromises of daily politics (Monnet 1997, 513).

However, in the 1970s and 1980s community-influenced aspects of European citizenship gradually started to gain more relevance. In 1972, the Belgian and Italian prime ministers explicitly talked about the 'European citizen' (this is the earliest reference we have found), by proposing that 'we could as of now decide to establish a European Citizenship which would be in addition to the citizenship which the inhabitants of our countries possess' (quoted in O'Leary 1996, 18). In 1984, an ad hoc committee, the so-called Adonnino Committee, put forward proposals concerning culture, youth exchange, health, social security, free movement of people, town twinning and symbols of EC identity (Panebianco 2004, 19). Owing to this report, a number of measures were taken in the latter half of the 1980s to increase the sense of community in Europe. A European flag and anthem were introduced and student exchange programmes launched. In the 1990s, then, various identity-political programmes came to have a central role in the development of the European Union.[6] The current European constitutional process can also be understood from the community perspective: in many people's view, it should function very much in the same way as *Verfassungspatriotismus* in Germany has over the past 50 years; a sense of community emerges through adherence and allegiance to a constitution. But whatever 'community-measures' have been and will be taken, the individual-based conception still seems to prevail. The main consequence of this has been that integration has remained a project of and for the elites. Integration has also meant exclusion; the French and Dutch 'no' to the Union's Draft Constitution in May–June 2005 can easily be interpreted as a demonstration against this.

\*

In the following analysis of the nature of citizenship in Europe, both communitarian and individualistic elements are present. Two of the four indicators that we concentrate on, 'citizenship' and the position of religion in society are primarily related to collective notions of nationhood. The granting of citizenship to 'foreigners' and religious freedom seem to challenge the traditional homogeneity of European nation-states. The two other indicators, women's political rights and capital punishment, are more individualistically oriented. They illustrate how individuals have been given rights or protection.

Of particular importance is that the four factors tell us something about the forms of exclusion and inclusion in Europe. Three of the indicators, migration/citizenship, religious freedom, and women's political rights are explicitly matters of inclusion: they show how easy or difficult it is to formally become a member of society; how well differences in terms of religion are tolerated; how and to what extent women, a group accounting for half the population or more, have been granted political rights. But even the fourth indicator, death penalty, has something to say about inclusion/exclusion: it shows to what measures the state is willing to resort in order to protect its integrity, internal coherence; punishments are usually mechanisms of exclusion.

These indicators are obviously very crude and formal, that is, they do not tell much about the mechanisms of inclusion/exclusion on the individual or micro-level. Moreover, the legal aspects of our analysis are complicated; the statistical standards vary a great deal in Europe,[7] and the thrust of the study calls for a high level of abstraction. We are therefore well advised not to rule out the possibility of errors and misinterpretations and to present our findings as tentative rather than final and definitive.

**Citizenship**

The first of our indicators, 'citizenship', is in fact a combination of several issues. Firstly, we will take a brief look at the legal framework for granting citizenship, including dual citizenship and naturalisation requirements. Secondly, we will explore the flows of immigrants into Europe and the number of non-nationals throughout the European continent. And thirdly, and this is in a sense a combination of the other two issues, we will review how many people have in reality been granted citizenship in various corners of Europe. The logic is simple: exclusiveness and inclusiveness can be analysed both in legal terms, and in terms of the actual flows of people.

Table 3.2 compresses some basic features of citizenship laws in Europe. The first important observation is that in most member states, old as well as new, citizenship laws have been renewed or amended recently, often several times; this process of change will hardly come to a halt any time soon. There are at least two obvious reasons for this. First, and as will be shown below, the number of people aspiring to change their nationality has steadily been growing over the past decades, particularly in Western Europe. Second, human rights-related pressure put on European countries by the regional organisations like the Council of Europe, OSCE and the EU, has forced many countries to revise their citizenship laws so as to better match the *Zeitgeist* of open borders, of increasing mobility of people, goods and capital; Eastern European laws have been under particularly close scrutiny after the end of communism. Indeed, citizenship laws consitute a very good example of Europeanization.

However, although the laws have become more and more similar to one another, we can still find a great number of differences in them, including the kind of differences that reflect society's willingness to incorporate and integrate 'foreign' elements. Moreover, the general trend seems to be towards more inclusive laws and legal practices, but this is by no means always the case. We will return to this shortly.

As was noted earlier, two principles – *jus soli* and *jus sanguinis* – have traditionally determined the nature of citizenship laws, but in today's Europe this distinction has become almost irrelevant – a fact that is not often realised. *All* countries grant citizenship to children whose parents, or at least mother, are citizens of that country. There are, however, still a few countries left in the case of which we can speak of a fairly strong *jus sanguinis* principle, that is, citizenship is primarily an ethnic and linguistic category and its origins can go back several generations. In our sample Latvia and Estonia represent such countries, primarily as a legacy of Soviet rule. Section 2 of the Citizenship Law of Latvia, for example, automatically grants citizenship to 'persons who were Latvian citizens on 17 June 1940 and their descendants who have registered in accordance with the procedures set out in law'. However, and as analysed in detail by Elena Jurado (2002), compared with the situation right after these countries regained their independence in 1991, their citizenship laws and practices are now much closer to what may be called 'European standards'.

It is more interesting to determine to what extent the principle of *jus soli* is used. As Table 3.2 shows, most European countries do *not* recognise *jus soli*, if we do not take into account the typical clause 'natural persons under 15 years of age found on the territory of the country shall be citizens except when it is proved that they gained citizenship of another state by birth'. Although some countries have recently included elements of *jus soli*, notably Germany in 1999, it thus seems that European countries have not been willing to become inclusive in this respect.

However, in the Mediterranean countries and the British Isles at least some elements of the *jus soli* principle apply. This may possibly be explained by history and culture: most of these countries have been culturally important, even self-conscious, and they have over centuries attracted great numbers of immigrants; in this context *jus soli* has been practical and it has not been experienced as threatening the country's homogeneity. Ireland cannot be described in these terms, although it is the only European country with a genuine *jus soli* principle. The country's citizenship law, Article 6, simply declares that: 'Every person born in Ireland is an Irish citizen from birth.'

Dual citizenship is an issue that has been very much on the agenda in Europe in recent years. The general trend seems to be towards ever wider acceptance of dual citizenship. For example, Sweden and Finland have adopted new citizenship laws that for the first time accept 'full' dual citizenship, that is, upon naturalisation and when a person is granted the citizenship of another state. More than half of the EU countries, however, still do not recognise dual citizenship, or at least have strict restrictions about the conditions under which dual citizenship is possible.

*Table 3.2: Some features of citizenship laws in Europe*

|  | Current citizenship laws (amendments or other relevant legislation in brackets) | jus soli ('yes' in brackets = clear jus soli elements) | Dual citizenship allowed... ...upon acceptance of another citizenship | Dual citizenship allowed... ...upon naturalisation | Naturalisation requires language skills |
|---|---|---|---|---|---|
| Austria | 1985 (1993) | No | No[1] | No[1] | Yes |
| Bulgaria | 1968 (latest 1989) | No | Yes | No | Yes |
| Croatia | 1991 (1992; 1993) | No | No | No | Yes |
| Czech Rep. | 1993 (latest 1996) | No | No[1] | No | Yes |
| Denmark | 1951 (2002) | No | No | No | Yes |
| Estonia | 1995 (1995; 1998) | No | No | No | Yes |
| Latvia | 1998 | No | Yes | No | Yes |
| Lithuania | 2002 (2003) | No | No | No | Yes |
| Luxembourg | 1968 (1986) | No | No | No | Yes |
| Malta | 1964 (latest 2000) | No | Yes | Yes | Yes |
| Poland | 1962 (several times) | No | No | No | No |
| Slovenia | 1991 (latest 2002) | No | Yes | No | Yes |
| Netherlands | 2000 (2003) | (Yes) | No[1] | No | Yes |
| Spain | 1989 (latest 2002) | (Yes) | Yes | No[2] | Yes |
| Belgium | 2000 | (Yes) | No | Yes | No |
| Cyprus | 1967 (1983) | No | No | Yes[3] | No |
| Finland | 2003 | No | Yes | Yes | Yes[1] |
| France | (2003) | (Yes) | No | Yes | Yes |
| Germany | 1999 | (Yes) | No | No[1] | Yes |
| Greece | 1975 (Const.; 2003) | Yes | No | Yes[3] | Yes |
| Hungary | 1993 | No | No | Yes[3] | Yes[1] |
| Ireland | 1956/1986 (1994) | Yes | Yes | Yes | No |
| Italy | 1992 | No | Yes | Yes | No |
| Portugal | 1981 (1994) | (Yes) | Yes | Yes | Yes |
| Romania | 1991 | No | Yes | Yes | Yes |
| Slovakia | 1993 | No | Yes | No | Yes |
| Sweden | 2001 | No | Yes | Yes | No |
| Turkey | 1964 (2004) | No | Yes | Yes | Yes |
| UK | 1981 (2002) | (Yes) | Yes | (Yes) | (Yes) |

*Notes*: Most countries that are here not classified as *jus soli* usually confer citizenship to children whose parents are not known (or who are stateless) but who are found/born in their territory. (1) A number of exceptions; (2) Treaties on dual citizenship with Ibero-American countries, Andorra, the Philippines, Portugal and Equatorial Guinea; (3) Not specifically mentioned in the law.

*Sources*: In addition to the citizenship laws of each country, the Council of Europe web page (see http://www.coe.int/T/E/Legal_Affairs/; Eurostat (2000) *Documentation of Eurostat's database on international migration: Acquisition of Citizenship*; Eurostat Working Papers (3/2000/E/n°3); United States Office of Personnel Management/Investigations Service (2001) *Citizenship Laws of the World*, IS-1.

Possibly the most interesting point here is the extent to which naturalisation – acquisition of citizenship – requires some sort of command of the majority or state language. As Table 3.2 shows, most European countries still expect the person who wishes to become a citizen to have sufficient relevant language skills; in addition, most states also expect the applicants to adhere to 'the country's way of life'. In the analyses of this chapter, this is possibly the strongest example of how European nation-states seek to protect their homogeneity, be exclusive, and not in fact strive for creating a unified European citizenry.

The specificity of the language requirements varies a great deal. The Estonian citizenship law (Article 8), for example, gives a detailed list of requirements, including listening and reading comprehension, speech and writing. The Croatian citizenship law, in turn, demands that the applicant is 'proficient in the Croatian language and Latin script'. In Denmark, the regulations concerning citizenship have become stricter in recent years, and also the required language skills are now more demanding than before. The new Swedish citizenship law, in contrast, appears to be the most liberal in this respect. No knowledge of Swedish culture is required; it suffices if the applicant 'has led and can be expected to lead a respectable life'.

This is the legal context, but what about reality? Before turning to the numbers of people who have gained citizenship through naturalisation, we need to make a few comments regarding the first four columns of Table 3.3. First, birth rates have been on a very low level in all of Eastern Europe, and a great number of people have left for Western Europe in search of a better standard of living. This has resulted in a significant decrease in the number of inhabitants in most of these countries. Only Poland and Slovakia have growing populations, but even their growth rates are very modest. Turkey's rapidly increasing population represents a very different kind of 'problem'. Many would perceive it as a threat, if Turkey were to become a member of the EU.

Secondly, it is easy to find a geographical pattern when looking at the number of people who have been registered as residents but do not have citizenship rights (non-nationals; here also 'foreigners')[8]: the numbers are clearly lower in the new (2004) than in the old EU member states, and especially in North-Western Europe. None of the ten countries where foreigners account for more than 4 per cent of the population are new member states, and of the original six founders of the EU, only Italy has less than 4 per cent foreign residents.

Noteworthy also is the dramatically increasing electoral support of right-wing populist parties in many of the West European countries at the very centre of the migration flows: *Vlaams Belang* (previously *Vlaams Blok*) in Belgium, *le Front National* in France, and the FPÖ in Austria being the primary examples (see Chapter 6). In Eastern Europe, by contrast, migration will not become a significant social and political problem in the foreseeable future, and the emergence of parties founded on anti-immigration seems unlikely. Estonia and Latvia are special cases here: they have a significant non-national population composed mainly of the Russians that moved or were moved to these countries during communism.

Table 3.3: Number of non-nationals and acquisition of citizenship in Europe

|  | Population 1995 | Population 2000 | Per cent of non-nationals 1995 | Per cent of non-nationals 2000 | Acquisition of citizenship 2000 | Acquisitions of citizenship per number of non-nationals 2000 (per cent) |
|---|---|---|---|---|---|---|
| Austria | 7 943 000 | 8 002 000 | 8.5 | 9.5 | 24 300 | 3.2 |
| Belgium[3] | 10 130 000 | 10 239 000 | 9.1 | 8.8 | 62 100 | 6.9 |
| Cyprus | 646 000 | 691 000 | 5.7 | 8.4 | 300 | 0.5 |
| Czech Rep. | 10 333 000 | 10 278 000 | 1.0 | 2.2 | 7 300 | 3.2 |
| Denmark | 5 216 000 | 5 330 000 | 3.8 | 4.9 | 18 800 | 7.3 |
| Estonia | *1 448 100* | 1 372 000 | n.a. | 20.0 | 3 400 | 1.2 |
| Finland | 5 099 000 | 5 172 000 | 1.2 | 1.7 | 3 000 | 3.4 |
| France[1] | 56 577 000 | 58 749 000 | 6.4 | 5.6 | 150 000 | 4.6 |
| Germany | 81 539 000 | 82 164 000 | 8.6 | 8.9 | 186700 | 2.5 |
| Greece[5] | 10 454 000 | 10 559 600 | 1.5 | 1.7 | *807* | 0.1 |
| Hungary | 10 337 000 | 10 221 000 | 1.3 | 1.5 | 5 400 | 3.5 |
| Ireland | 3 597 000 | 3 777 000 | 2.7 | 3.4 | 1 100 | 0.9 |
| Italy[3] | 57 268 000 | 57 680 000 | 1.2 | 2.2 | 11 600 | 0.9 |
| Latvia[4] | *2 529 500* | 2 377 000 | n.a. | 25.5 | 13 500 | 2.2 |
| Lithuania[4] | *3 643 000* | *3 512 100* | n.a. | 0.9 | 500 | 1.6 |
| Luxembourg | 407 000 | 435 000 | 32.7 | 36.6 | 700 | 0.4 |
| Malta | 376 000 | 389 000 | 1.9 | 2.3 | n.a. | n.a |
| Poland | *38 580 600* | *38 653 600* | n.a. | 0.1 | *1 070* | 2.5 |
| Portugal | 10 013 000 | 10 198 000 | 1.6 | 1.9 | 1 100 | 0.6 |
| Slovakia[2] | *5 364 000* | *5 401 000* | 0.4 | 0.5 | 2 886 | 10.2 |
| Slovenia | 1 990 000 | 1 988 000 | 2.4 | 2.2 | 2 100 | 4.9 |
| Spain | 39 196 000 | 39 733 000 | 1.2 | 2.3 | 16 700 | 1.8 |
| Sweden | 8 816 000 | 8 861 000 | 6.1 | 5.5 | 43 500 | 8.9 |
| Netherlands | 15 424 000 | 15 864 000 | 4.9 | 4.1 | 50 000 | 7.7 |
| UK[2] | *58 025 000* | 58 886 000 | 3.4 | 4.0 | *82 200* | 3.5 |
| Bulgaria[4] | *8 427 400* | *8 190 900* | n.a. | 0.3 | n.a. | n.a. |
| Croatia | *4 670 200* | *4 567 500* | n.a. | n.a. | n.a. | n.a. |
| Romania[4] | *22 712 400* | *22 455 500* | 0.0 | 0.0 | 200 | 15.4 |
| Turkey[2] | *61 737 000* | *67 420 000* | 0.4 | n.a. | n.a. | n.a. |

*Notes*: (1) Census results from 1990 and 1998. Acquisition of citizenship data for year 2000: OECD, Quarterly Labour Force Statistics 2004, No. 4; (2) Population data: OECD, Quarterly Labour Force Statistics 2004, No. 4; (3) Acquisition of citizenship data for year 2000: OECD, Quarterly Labour Force Statistics 2004, No. 4; (4) Citizenship data: Council of Europe (2002) *Recent demographic developments in Europe 2002*. Citizenship data concerning Latvia: www.csb.lv (Central Statistical Bureau of Latvia) [Latvian citizens 1.77 mil; Latvian non-citizens 504 000; Foreign nationals 103 000].

*Data in italics*: Eurostat, population statistics 2004. Exceptions in the acquisition of citizenship data: Greece (year 1998, source: Eurostat yearbook 2004), Poland and Slovakia (year 2001, Eurostat yearbook 2004); Turkey (1995 data concerning non-nationals from year 1991). Clarke et al. (1998) provide an overview of the naturalisation figures in Europe in the 1980s and early 1990s.

Though the number of non-nationals is generally increasing, there are also countries where the figures have at least occasionally been in decline. This was the case in Belgium, France, Sweden, Slovenia (with significantly fewer non-nationals) and the Netherlands in the latter half of the 1990s. We only present comparable data from one year (2000), but the table suggests that the primary reason for this was simply that significant numbers of people were granted citizenship (shaded cells in Table 3.3). This can naturally be interpreted as a sign of a fairly inclusive citizenship policy. In Germany and Austria the granting of citizenship seems less common in spite of the high numbers of foreigners, although in absolute numbers Germany does get a significant group of naturalised citizens yearly. (Slovakia and Romania are insignificant here because of the very low number of non-nationals.)

What general conclusions can we draw on the basis of the data presented in Tables 3.2 and 3.3? The overall picture indicates increasing levels of mobility, and as the legal frameworks have been liberalised, also gradually improving standards of inclusion. When it comes to the actual flows of people, the countries of Western and Northern Europe have been and will most likely continue to be much more attractive than those of Eastern Europe; the high standards of living have drawn people from the rest of the continent and elsewhere – and the labour markets have needed cheap labour. In legal terms, however, it is impossible to find any similar geographical patterns: there are significant differences in legislation, but they are related to geography and the cultural traditions of a specific region to only a limited degree. Differences pertain to individual countries, and they cannot be explained by any common denominators.

Finally, a word of caution is in order. In some countries, the liberal policies promoted by European regional organisations have already been reversed, and other countries are under strong pressure to tighten their immigration policies as well. Denmark and the Netherlands are the primary cases in point here.[9] As a result of the increased popularity of populist right-wing parties, and with the change of government coalition in the early 2000s, Denmark and the Netherlands embarked on a distinctly restrictive course. In 2003, for example, they only made 6 500 and 25 000 naturalisation decisions, respectively, which was considerably less than in 2000 or late 1990s (see Table 3.3; *Statistics Denmark*; *Statistics Netherlands*).

It is probably even more significant that on the European level, too, and more specifically in the so-called Hague Programme, some hints of stricter immigration policies are visible, partly owing to the post-9/11 effect. Although the EU seeks to develop 'an area of freedom, security and justice', it also increases its role 'in securing police, customs and judicial cooperation'. If the need to tighten border controls is acknowledged at the European level, individual member states will hardly go against this stream. Whether this will lead to problems in the creation of a European citizenry remains to be seen, but at least it will not contribute positively to its inclusiveness.

## Freedom of Religion

Religion plays an increasingly important role in the debates on social coherence in current Europe. In this, on-the-surface secularised continent, religion, once again, seems to divide people more intensely than anything else; skin colour and sexual orientation are insignificant in comparison. Migration of non-Christians, particularly Muslims, to Europe and the right of the communities formed by them to practise their own customs now challenge – or are believed to challenge – those values that European Christianity has traditionally embraced. As a result, politics easily enters the realm of morals.

As Table 3.4 shows, when measured in percentages, 14 out of the 27 states in our sample have sizeable Muslim minorities. These can be of a truly substantial size, and can also form local majorities. Those of France and Germany total some 4 million people (in France many estimate that the number is much higher, up to 8 million), and also in Britain the number of Muslims is over one million, although Muslims are not among the three biggest religious communities in the country. The growth of these religious minorities has been rapid, sometimes very rapid. In France, for example, the crude estimation is that the number of Muslims has increased by approximately one million every ten years over the past 30 years. The reason is not only migration: birth rates are somewhat higher among the Muslims than in other parts of society. We must remember, however, that as in the case of Christians, a significant part of the Muslims are 'secularised', although the estimations of this vary a great deal.

Religious minorities currently entice a great deal of public attention, but this may in fact give a false picture of Europe's religious composition. There are still a significant number of countries with Christian (usually Catholic) majorities accounting for more than 90 per cent of the population – although Turkey's 97 per cent Muslim majority is clearly the highest figure of religious homogeneity in Europe. Even in the Nordic states, usually regarded as overwhelmingly secular, well over 80 per cent still belong to the Lutheran Evangelical Church. It is obvious that given these high figures, the underlying cultural, behavioural and social patterns of society are still clearly determined by the dominant religion, and that there are certainly a number of mechanisms in place to protect these dominant religions. This does not mean, of course, that religion would play a particularly significant role in people's daily lives; the question is of 'deeper' mechanisms of social reproduction. Italy and Spain can have some of the lowest birth rates in Europe, in spite of the papal ban on contraception – and still be profoundly Catholic.

Finally, it is noteworthy that some of the most secular countries, at least nominally, can be found among the former communist countries (Estonia, Latvia, and the Czech Republic). In this respect, too, the era of communism did have a major lasting impact. In Poland, the logic has been very different, though. The Catholic Church functioned as an alternative polis for ordinary Poles during the decades of communism. The communist system thereby indirectly supported the continuous strong position of religion in the country.

*Table 3.4: Religions in Europe*

|  | Largest religious community | Percentage of population 2001 | Second largest religious community | Percentage of population 2001 | Third largest religious community | Percentage of population 2001 |
|---|---|---|---|---|---|---|
| Austria | Catholics | 75.1 | Protestants | 5.3 | Muslims | 2.1 |
| Belgium | Catholics | 80.9 | Muslims | 2.4 | Protestants | 1.0 |
| Bulgaria | Orthodox | 71.6 | Muslims | 11.8 | Protestants | 1.4 |
| Croatia | Catholics | 88.4 | Orthodox | 5.7 | Muslims | 2.3 |
| Czech Rep. | Catholics | 39.0 | Protestants[2] | 4.0 | Orthodox | 0.2 |
| Denmark | Lutherans | 85.8 | Muslims | 2.2 | Catholics | 0.6 |
| Estonia | Orthodox | 20.3 | Lutherans | 13.7 | Jewish | 0.2 |
| Finland | Lutherans | 85.0 | Orthodox | 1.1 | Jehovah W. | 0.3 |
| France | Catholics | 65.5 | Muslims | 7.1 | Protestants | 1.2 |
| Germany | Lutherans | 35.6 | Catholics | 33.5 | Muslims | 4.4 |
| Greece | Orthodox | 92.1 | Muslims | 3.3 | Protestants | 0.6 |
| Hungary | Catholics | 60.1 | Protestants | 24.2 | Jewish | 0.8 |
| Ireland | Catholics | 91.6 | Anglicans | 2.2 | Presbyter. | 0.3 |
| Italy | Catholics | 79.9 | Muslims | 1.2 | Protestants | 0.1 |
| Latvia | Catholics | 14.8 | Lutherans | 14.6 | Orthodox | 7.7 |
| Lithuania | Catholics | 72.1 | Orthodox | 2.4 | Protestants | 1.3 |
| Luxembourg | Catholics | 90.9 | Protestants | 1.1 | Jewish | 0.1 |
| Malta | Catholics | 94.5 | Others | 5.5 |  |  |
| Netherlands | Catholics | 31.0 | Protestants[1] | 21.0 | Muslims | 4.5 |
| Poland | Catholics | 90.7 | Orthodox | 1.4 | Protestants | 0.7 |
| Portugal | Catholics | 92.2 | Protestants | 1.5 | Other chris. | 1.1 |
| Romania | Orthodox | 86.8 | Catholics | 5.1 | Protestants | 3.6 |
| Slovakia | Catholics | 60.4 | Evangelicals | 6.3 | Orthodox | 4.1 |
| Slovenia | Catholics | 82.9 | Orthodox | 2.4 | Muslims | 1.5 |
| Spain | Catholics | 92.0 | Muslims | 0.5 | Protestants | 0.3 |
| Sweden | Lutherans | 86.5 | Muslims | 2.8 | Catholics | 1.8 |
| Turkey | Muslims | 97.2 | Christians | 0.6 |  |  |
| UK[3] | Anglicans | 43.6 | Catholics | 9.3 | Protestants | 8.4 |
| EU-15 | Catholics | 49.8 | Protestants | 14.9 | Anglicans | 6.9 |
| EU-25 | Catholics | 53.4 | Protestants | 13.3 | Anglicans | 5.8 |
| Europe total (2003) | Catholics | 38.2 | Orthodox | 21.9 | Protestants | 10.2 |

*Notes*: It was not possible to make distinctions between different Muslim groups. (1) Dutch Reformed Church and Calvinists; (2) Evangelicals and Hussites; (3) In the UK, Muslims are the fourth largest religious community (2 per cent of the population).

*Source*: Statistics Finland (http://www.tilastokeskus.fi/tup/maanum/taulukot.html).

Table 3.5 gives a somewhat more nuanced picture of the mechanisms through which dominant religions are protected in Europe, and thus of the demand of religious homogeneity in Europe. The first significant observation is that *all* European countries guarantee freedom of religion in their constitution. However, a great number of countries still have what can be called state religion, that is, churches that have in one way or another a privileged position in society. The formulas establishing this position are sometimes ambiguous, to the point of making classification a delicate exercise. The new Bulgarian Constitution, for example, does not talk about a state religion, but states that 'Eastern Orthodox Christianity is considered the *traditional* religion in the Republic of Bulgaria' (Article 13; emphasis added).

Especially in Catholic countries, constitutions include references to God and, although not explicitly stated, this God is undoubtedly the Christian God. Poland, for example, does not officially have a state church, but the preamble of the country's constitution makes a distinction between those citizens 'who believe in God as the source of truth, justice, good and beauty' and 'those not sharing such faith'. The Irish constitution (Article 44), in turn, declares: 'The State acknowledges that the homage of public worship is due to Almighty God. It shall hold His Name in reverence, and shall respect and honour religion.' In Spain, God is not mentioned in the Constitution but the Catholic Church is (Article 16): 'There shall be no State religion. The public authorities shall take the religious beliefs of Spanish society into account and shall in consequence maintain appropriate co-operation with the Catholic Church and the other confessions.'

Catholicism is by no means the only explanatory factor in this respect, though; the timing of the constitution also proves significant. Denmark, normally viewed as a very secular and liberal-minded country but with a Constitution from 1953, still officially has a state religion. It is even decreed that 'The King shall be a member of the Evangelical Lutheran Church' (Article 6). Finland, by contrast, has a new constitution, from the year 2000, which no longer stipulates that the traditional national churches, the dominant Evangelical Lutheran Church and the small Orthodox Church, have privileged positions. Even so, these two churches are still regarded as having a state church position.

France (along with Turkey) is still the prime example of an explicitly secular state. The second article of the *Constitution de la Cinquième Republique* states that 'France is an indivisible, secular (*laïcité*), democratic and social Republic'. As we have already discussed in the context of the recent headscarf ban, there is always an inherent risk, however, that this secularism turns into an exclusive ideology.

What is perhaps an even better indicator of the position of the Church is the way in which religious education has been included in the primary and secondary school curricula. It is, however, immensely difficult to get a full picture of the situation in this respect; the pieces of information given in Table 3.5 need to be regarded as crude approximations. Many countries, for example France and the Netherlands, have several parallel educational systems, some of which are founded on religious beliefs. Even in the Nordic countries, where private schools are very few, and private religious schools even fewer, there are for instance Waldorf schools where ethical education plays a significant role. What can be stated, though, is that most European countries require that their offspring participate in some sort of religious or ethical education in primary or secondary schools. In most cases, teaching is still based, in one way or the other, on Christian values. France, the Czech Republic, and Turkey are the countries in which religious education in public schools is most clearly restricted or forbidden.

*Table 3.5: Some indicators of religious freedom in Europe*

|  | Constitutional freedom of religion | State religion | Religious teaching in schools | Additional information |
|---|---|---|---|---|
| Austria | Yes | No | Yes (12 official religious societies) |  |
| Belgium | Yes | No | Yes (6 official religious societies) |  |
| Cyprus | Yes | No | Yes, mandatory (Greek orthodox) | Turkish Cyprus is a 'secular republic' |
| Czech Republic | Yes | No | No |  |
| Denmark | Yes | Yes | Yes, attendance optional (Lutheran) | The Lutheran state Church has the right to tax their members |
| Estonia | Yes | No | Yes, attendance optional (ecumenical) |  |
| Finland | Yes | Yes (Luth & Orth) | Yes, mandatory (personal faith) | The two state churches collect church tax in connection with their members' income tax. |
| France | Yes | No | No | Strictly secularized state |
| Germany | Yes | No | Yes, optional (Christian) | The ten 'public law corporations' have the right to levy taxes |
| Greece | Yes | In theory, no; in practice, yes (Orth.) | Yes, mandatory for the Orthodox | Govt. finances the Orthodox Church and recognizes the church's canon law |
| Hungary | Yes | No | Yes, optional after school religious instruction | Four 'historical religions' enjoy some privileges |
| Ireland | Yes | No (but see the text) | Yes, attendance optional |  |
| Italy | Yes | No (but see add. info) | Yes, optional | The Catholic church enjoys a number of privileges. |
| Latvia | Yes | No | Yes, voluntary (mostly 'traditional' religions) |  |

## Table 3.5: (continued)

| | | | | |
|---|---|---|---|---|
| Lithuania | Yes | No | Yes, on the consent of the parents (only 'traditional' religions) | The nine 'traditional' religions receive regular state subsidies; enjoy tax exemptions etc. |
| Luxembourg | Yes | No | Yes (Catholic, Protestant or an ethics course) | |
| Malta | Yes | Yes | Yes; instruction mandatory (Catholic), attendance voluntary | |
| Netherlands | Yes | No | No in state schools; many of them give religious/ethical teaching | |
| Poland | Yes | No (but see the text) | Yes, usually Catholic | Roman Catholic church has some privileges (close ties with the state) |
| Portugal | Yes | No | Yes, optional attendance | Roman Catholic church has some special privileges (e.g. 'church tax') |
| Slovakia | Yes | No | Yes, mandatory attendance (religion or ethics) | |
| Slovenia | Yes | No | Possible, but not common | |
| Spain | Yes | No (but see extra) | Yes, attendance optional | Catholic Church enjoys substantive privileges: e.g. govt. funding, voluntary 'church tax' |
| Sweden | Yes | No | Yes, but not confessional | Separation of Church and State in 2000 |
| UK | Yes | Yes (Church of England/ Scotland) | Yes, mandatory (Christian, but not nondenominational) | |
| Bulgaria | Yes | Yes (traditional religion) | Yes, optional (Christian and Muslim) | Formation of political parties along religious lines is prohibited |
| Croatia | Yes | No (but see extra) | Yes, but attendance optional | Catholic Church in a privileged position (state funding, etc.) |
| Romania | Yes | No (but see extra) | Yes, optional (mostly Orthodox) | Constitution: 'Religious wedding may be celebrated only after civil marriage' |
| Turkey | Yes | No | No | 'Secular state', but restrictions for freedom of religion often reported |

All in all, the trend in many parts of Europe seems to be towards increased tolerance and inclusion in relation to different religions. Confessional religious teaching is less and less common in public schools, and members of minority religions are increasingly provided with religious education in their own religion. Had we analysed such religion-related moral issues as abortion or euthanasia, the trend would have been even more pronounced. The bottom line, however, is that the development is much slower than normally admitted; and the need to protect the traditional values strong.

The developments of Finnish religious teaching may serve as a good illustration of this. The Finnish Law on Basic Education was amended in 2003, by removing all references to *confessional* religious teaching. The new wording reads: 'religious teaching needs to be provided in the own religion of the majority of each class'. The change thus appeared significant in principle but it has remained cosmetic in reality. Moreover, the alternative available for those who do not belong to the state churches since the 1970s, the subject called 'ethics', is still chosen by a small minority of some 3 per cent, although in parts of the capital Helsinki – a more secularised and culturally heterogeneous city than the rest of the country – the figure is close to 30 per cent (information provided by the Finnish Ministry of Education).

The overall impression is thus clear: Europe is less religiously free than is usually believed. Christian churches have in many different ways secured their position in society. These reproductive mechanisms are often more or less subtle, but they are nevertheless there. The school system is by no means the only example. Many state churches have the right to tax their members; a very significant proportion of all public holidays are Christian; many countries, including Austria, the Netherlands, and the UK, still have blasphemy laws although they are hardly ever used.

At the same time, however, it is obvious that the countries of Europe are more and more seeking to take into consideration people's different religious and moral convictions, at least formally. The changes are, however, taking place slowly, and they are often vehemently resisted. Above all, there is no general solution as to how to include the new Muslim communities into the traditionally Christian societies, of how to include but still protect the traditional values. The so-called compartmentalisation in the Netherlands, functional in 1918–67, might provide a useful analogy here. Different religious and political communities organised a significant part of their social life within their own sphere of influence, within 'pillars'. The system guaranteed the different communities a sense of autonomy, which gave them a sense of national identification and eventually promoted political integration (Lijphart 1969). Through initially exclusive segregation, the overall system became inclusive.

**Women's Political Participation**

We now turn to the more 'individualistic' indicators, and first take a look at the way in which women have been given political rights in Europe. Again we are dealing with a hugely complicated issue, and can only scratch the surface of it here. But the importance of women's rights is hard to deny: hardly any other issue testifies as convincingly to the development of European societies towards higher levels of what could be called *internal inclusion*.

The geographical pattern was reasonably evident when we discussed migration in Europe, whereas in the case of religious freedom it was more difficult to draw geographical division lines, apart perhaps from the fact that some East European countries have become highly secularised. In the case of women's political participation, again, it is relatively easy to make distinctions along a North–South (or Protestant–Catholic) axis. As Table 3.6 shows, in Southern Europe, universal women's suffrage was introduced much later than in Northern Europe. In the former area, this happened after the Second World War, but in the latter already during the first two decades of the 20th century, in most cases after the First World War.

*Table 3.6: The year of attaining universal suffrage for men and women*

|  | Introduction of universal female suffrage | The difference between male and female voting rights (years) |
|---|---|---|
| Finland | 1906 | 0 |
| Denmark | 1915 | 0 |
| Austria | 1918 | 11 |
| Estonia | 1918 | 0 |
| Germany | 1918 | 47 |
| Hungary | 1918 | 0 |
| Latvia | 1918 | 0 |
| Poland | 1918 | 0 |
| Luxembourg | 1919 | 1 |
| Netherlands | 1919 | 2 |
| Czech Republic[1] | 1920 | 0 |
| Slovakia[1] | 1920 | 0 |
| Lithuania | 1920 | 0 |
| Sweden | 1921 | 10 |
| Ireland | 1928 | 10 |
| United Kingdom | 1928 | 10 |
| Turkey[2] | 1930 | 7 |
| Portugal | 1931 | 20 |
| Spain | 1931 | 24 |
| France | 1944 | 96 |
| Bulgaria | 1944 | 65 |
| Italy | 1945 | 33 |
| Slovenia[3] | 1945 | 25 |
| Croatia[3] | 1945 | 25 |
| Romania | 1946 | 27 |
| Malta | 1947 | 26 |
| Belgium | 1948 | 29 |
| Greece | 1952 | 75 |
| Cyprus | 1960 | 0 |

*Notes*: (1) Elections to the Czechoslovak National Assembly; (2) Local elections; the first democratic parliamentary elections were held in 1950 in Turkey. The secular Turkish republic was founded by Kemal Atatürk in 1923, and '7 years' refers to that date; (3) Parts of the Kingdom of Serbs, Croats and Slovenes until 1929, when the country changed its name to Yugoslavia.

*Sources*: Women in Parliaments 1945–1995; Worldwide Statistical Survey. Inter-parliamentary Union (1995); Wide (2004) 'Kvinnors politiska representation i Västeuropa 1950–2000: Vad förklarar variationen i tid och rum?' Unpublished manuscript.

## Patterns of Inclusion and Exclusion in Europe 47

Another significant observation is that many of the countries that introduced male and female suffrage simultaneously – apart from Hungary all of them belong to the latter group above – had just become independent, or were dreaming of independence, for the first time in their history. In other words, independence was by no means self-evident or consolidated at that stage. This means that although female suffrage in these countries was internally inclusive, there was an externally exclusive element involved: by giving women the right to vote, these new states tried to increase their internal cohesion. The entire society was harnessed for the common cause, that is, nation-building.

From today's perspective, the actual representation of women in politics may be more revealing, though. In the first columns of Table 3.7, we have inserted the percentage of seats held by women in the lower houses of European parliaments at the moment (spring 2005); the exclusion of the upper houses, where applicable, does not affect the overall picture. A geographical pattern is clearly visible. The areas influenced by Protestantism, the Nordic, Benelux, and Baltic countries, and German-speaking Central Europe have clearly more women in their parliaments than the rest of Europe.

It is hardly surprising that Turkey stands out as very 'non-European' when it comes to women's political participation. Although Turkish women had already received a right to vote in local elections by 1930, during the heydays of Kemalism, the percentage of women in the legislature – and, for that matter, also in the local and regional assemblies – is still on a very low level. Indeed, if we were to mention a single fact that should speak against Turkey's EU membership, one good candidate would certainly be the position of women in Turkish society and politics.

How can we then explain the clear differences between European countries – geography as such is no explanation – and what are their implications? A great deal has been written on how the proportional representation system (PR) generally favours women as opposed to the systems where single member constituencies are in use.[10] France, Britain and Ireland are clear examples of this. As shown in Table 3.7, in these countries the percentage of women in the European Parliament (EP) is much higher than in the national parliaments, because the PR system is in use in the EP elections. It has also been noted that the party list variant of PR is the electoral system most conducive to women's participation. Sweden's pole position can at least to some degree be explained by the use of party lists. Similar comments apply to the high percentage of women in the Spanish parliament, although the percentage is in any case quite remarkable, given the impression of machismo that is often attached to the country, and in comparison to such countries as Italy and France.

*Table 3.7: Women in European parliaments and the WEF 2005 ranking*

| | Elections (lower house) | Lower house total | Percentage of women in lower house | Percentage of women MEPs in the 2004 elected European Parliament | Percentage of women in 2004 EP minus per cent women in the national parliament | WEF ranking in 2005: rankings higher than 20 shaded |
|---|---|---|---|---|---|---|
| Sweden | 9/2002 | 349 | 45.2 | 57.9 | 12.7 | 1 |
| Denmark | 2/2005 | 179 | 37.9 | 35.7 | −2.2 | 4 |
| Finland | 3/2003 | 200 | 37.5 | 35.7 | −1.8 | 5 |
| Netherlands | 1/2003 | 150 | 36.7 | 44.4 | 7.7 | 14 |
| Spain | 3/2004 | 350 | 36.0 | 33.3 | −2.7 | 27 |
| Belgium | 5/2003 | 150 | 34.7 | 29.2 | −5.5 | 20 |
| Austria | 11/2002 | 183 | 33.9 | 38.9 | 5.0 | 28 |
| Germany | 9/2002 | 601 | 32.8 | 31.3 | −1.5 | 9 |
| Bulgaria | 6/2001 | 240 | 26.5 | – | – | 29 |
| Luxembourg | 6/2004 | 60 | 23.3 | 50.0 | 26.7 | 26 |
| Lithuania | 10/2004 | 141 | 22.0 | 38.5 | 16.5 | 12 |
| Croatia | 11/2003 | 152 | 21.7 | – | – | n.a. |
| Latvia | 10/2002 | 100 | 21.0 | 22.2 | 1.2 | 11 |
| Poland | 11/2001 | 460 | 20.2 | 13.0 | −7.2 | 19 |
| Portugal | 3/2002 | 230 | 19.1 | 25.0 | 5.9 | 23 |
| Estonia | 3/2003 | 101 | 18.8 | 33.3 | 14.2 | 15 |
| UK | 6/2001 | 659 | 18.1 | 24.4 | 6.3 | 8 |
| Czech Rep. | 6/2002 | 200 | 17.0 | 20.8 | 3.8 | 25 |
| Slovakia | 9/2002 | 150 | 16.7 | 35.7 | 19.0 | 21 |
| Cyprus | 5/2001 | 56 | 16.1 | 0.0 | −16.6 | n.a. |
| Greece | 3/2004 | 300 | 14.0 | 29.2 | 15.2 | 50 |
| Ireland | 5/2002 | 166 | 13.3 | 38.5 | 25.5 | 16 |
| Slovenia | 10/2004 | 90 | 12.2 | 42.9 | 30.7 | 22 |
| France | 6/2002 | 574 | 12.2 | 42.3 | 40.1 | 13 |
| Italy | 5/2001 | 616 | 11.5 | 19.2 | 7.3 | 45 |
| Romania | 11/2004 | 332 | 11.5 | – | – | 41 |
| Malta | 4/2003 | 65 | 9.2 | 0.0 | −9.2 | n.a. |
| Hungary | 4/2002 | 385 | 9.1 | 37.5 | 28.4 | 24 |
| Turkey | 11/2002 | 550 | 4.4 | – | – | 57 |
| Average | | | 21.8 | | | |
| Average EU | | | 22.7 | 30.3 | | |

*Note*: In its 2005 report, *Women's Empowerment: Measuring the Global Gender Gap* (co-authors: Augusto Lopez-Claros and Saadia Zahidi), the World Economic Forum (WEF) analyses women's rights in 58 countries. (This means that only Egypt scored worse than Turkey in this study.) The Gender Gap Ranking is based on five indicators: economic participation, economic opportunity, political empowerment, educational attainment, health and well-being.

*Source*: Inter-Parliamentary Union. PARLINE Database. Internet: www.ipu.org/parline-e/parlinesearch.asp; 15 February 2005.

The electoral system system is only a very imperfect explanation, however; it may in itself be a result of the ideological structures of society. In their interesting analysis, based on the *World Values Surveys*, Sheri

Kunovich and Pamela Paxton (2003) do note that the electoral system is significant, but general attitudes towards women[11] – in their terms, 'ideological explanations' – are nevertheless a clearly more important independent variable. There is a highly significant correlation between the number of women in the parliament and people's belief that 'men are better in politics'. From this perspective, the egalitarian traditions of the Nordic countries are the primary explanation for the fact that these countries excel on the list of women's political participation (explaining the origins of this egalitarianism goes beyond the scope of this book).

What is important, however, is that in many countries the number of women in parliaments is still remarkably low. The numbers have been increasing, both in Europe and globally, but not very fast; the situation could certainly be much better. The relationship between the European and national polities is interesting in this context. It is evident that in the majority of European countries, it has been easier for women to become member in the European Parliament than in the national parliament. Apart from Poland,[12] there is no country that would have significantly higher female representation in the national parliament. The European Parliament has thus become an alternative polity for women – and for other traditionally repressed groups, too. In the long run, this may change the political constellation at the nation-state level. As Niilo Kauppi (2005) has argued, in France it has already become an arena for women to collect such political capital that they later can make use of on the national level.

One might therefore expect women to be more positive about the European Union than men. But this does not seem to be the case. For example, in *Eurobarometer* 62 of 2004, 54 per cent of men – as opposed to 46 per cent of women – were positive about the Union. Women obviously do not perceive the European Union as an instrument of empowerment, even though they would have good reasons to do so. One possible explanation is that women attach particular importance to social security, health and education, issues not thought to be at the very top of the EU agenda. We will return to this issue as we talk about the nature of the Union in terms of individualism (cf. Table 7.8).

The final column of Table 3.7 adds a new dimension; a welfare ranking published by the World Economic Forum (see the legend of Table 3.7). The WEF ranking ties in neatly with our findings and may be seen as a validation of our admittedly crude measures. A different set of indicators would not necessarily yield a picture radically different from the one we have drawn. Finally, as we have talked a great deal about constitutions above, it is worth noting that in newer constitutions, unlike in older ones, equality between sexes is a self-evident constitutional clause, whereas in the older ones equality between sexes in not necessarily mentioned. In some cases, gender equality is specifically emphasised. In France, after the last amendment in 2000, the constitution now explicitly stipulates that 'Statutes shall promote equal access by women and men to elective offices and positions' (Article 3; cf. Freedman 2004). In reality, as Table 3.7 shows, this has only happened at the European level, but the situation may gradually be changing within French national politics as well.

The most important conclusion is, then, that Europeanisation has indeed meant more inclusive politics towards women. This can even be interpreted as one of the most positive achievements that the EU and other regional organisations have helped bring about.

## Death Penalty

The legality and legitimacy of the death penalty is a somewhat different indicator than the other three; the way in which it depicts the inclusiveness or exclusiveness of a state or society is much more indirect. It does, however, tell something about the relationship between the state and its citizens, about the extent to which the state respects its citizens; in this sense it can be also regarded as a measurement of inclusion. In other words, the acceptance of capital punishment indicates that the protection of the collective is a primary value; even human life can be sacrificed for its sake. This kind of collective also tends to be exclusive.

The history of the use of the death penalty contains a few noteworthy points. Although Europeans tend to believe that they are the frontrunners in human rights issues, they were by no means the first to abolish the death penalty for *all* crimes. Five Latin American countries came more than half a century before Europeans, namely Venezuela, Costa Rica, Ecuador, Uruguay and Colombia; they all had abolished the death penalty by 1910 (Anckar 2004, 17). Moreover, it has almost become common wisdom that attitudes to the death penalty are entirely different in the US and in Europe, but as Table 3.8 shows, still in the 1980s most European countries had the formal possibility to execute their citizens. It was not until that decade that the Council of Europe and a number of human rights organisations managed to make capital punishment a central human rights issue in the minds of the wider public.[13] At the moment, then, all European countries have abolished the death penalty for ordinary crimes, and only Latvia has not abolished it for all crimes. The ban on capital punishment may be a recent arrival in the package of 'common European values', but it is already a self-evident and important part. In contrast, elsewhere in the world, and particularly in Asia and Africa, the death penalty is still applied in a clear majority of countries (ibid. 12–16).

There is a clear geographical, and to some degree size, pattern in the first column of Table 3.8. The Nordic countries and other small countries like Austria and Portugal were the first to legally abolish the death penalty. As regards the time of last executions, it is much more difficult to find similar patterns, although the first two to abolish, Portugal and Sweden, belong to the above-mentioned group. Portugal's record is particularly noteworthy, for no one has been executed in the country since 1849. This means that the country was 100 years ahead of most other Western European states: most of them carried out the last execution only within the first two decades after the Second World War.

Table 3.8: Death penalty in Europe

| European countries whose laws do not provide for the death penalty for any crime | | | |
|---|---|---|---|
| | Date (A) | Date (AO) | Date (last ex.) |
| Austria | 1968 | 1950 | 1950 |
| Finland | 1972 | 1949 | 1944 |
| Sweden | 1972 | 1921 | 1910 |
| Portugal | 1976 | 1867 | 1849 |
| Denmark | 1978 | 1933 | 1950 |
| Luxembourg | 1979 | | 1949 |
| France | 1981 | | 1977 |
| Netherlands | 1982 | 1870 | 1952 |
| Germany | 1987 | | 1949/1981[1] |
| Romania | 1989 | | 1989 |
| Slovenia | 1989 | | 1957 |
| Croatia | 1990 | | 1973 |
| Czech Republic | 1990 | | 1989 |
| Hungary | 1990 | | 1988 |
| Ireland | 1990 | | 1954 |
| Slovakia | 1990 | | 1989 |
| Italy | 1994 | 1947 | 1947 |
| Spain | 1995 | 1978 | 1975 |
| Belgium | 1996 | | 1950 |
| Poland | 1997 | | 1988 |
| Bulgaria | 1998 | | 1989 |
| Estonia | 1998 | | 1991 |
| Lithuania | 1998 | | 1995 |
| UK | 1998 | 1973 | 1964 |
| Malta | 2000 | 1971 | 1943 |
| Cyprus | 2002 | 1983 | 1962 |
| Greece | 2004 | 1993 | 1972 |
| Turkey | 2004 | 2002 | 1984 |
| European countries whose laws provide for the death penalty only for exceptional crimes such as crimes under military law or crimes committed in exceptional circumstances, such as wartime crimes | | | |
| Latvia | | 1999 | 1996 |

*Note*: (1) FRG/GDR. *Abbreviations*: Date (A) = Date of abolition of death penalty for all crimes; Date (AO) = Date of abolition of death penalty for ordinary crimes; Date (last ex.) = Date of last execution.

*Sources*: Amnesty International (http://web.amnesty.org/pages/deathpenalty-abolitionist1-eng) and http://www.geocities.com/richard.clark32@btinternet.com/europe.html.

Apart from France and Turkey, all the countries that have executed their citizens after 1975 (shaded in the table) – the year when the Helsinki Final Act was signed, an act that raised human rights issues on the European political agenda in a new way – are former communist countries. The collapse of communism in 1989–91 ended this practice almost immediately; democratisation clearly meant Europeanisation in this respect.[14] It is worth noting, however, that in many of these countries public opinion is still clearly in favour of the death penalty. In many countries as much as two thirds of the population still support it, which is somewhat more than in the Western Europe. The views of the public and the political elites have thus differed significantly; elites can possibly be interpreted as more inclusive.[15]

Why have European states so unanimously abolished the death penalty, while the US and particularly its Southern states have not? An interesting recent analysis about the US is provided by Franklin E. Zimring (2003). He argues that the death penalty has survived in the country because of the fear of centralised power that the federal system of government generates. There is, in other words, a tension between the central and the local levels in the administration of justice, and the death penalty is a means to substantiate the power of the local level – to create a local community. Another explanation, also mentioned by Jennifer Culbert (2004), focuses on the racial relationships in the US that are, as is well known, particularly problematic in the Southern states. Viewed from this perspective, capital punishment is clearly a direct consequence of social exclusion.

It is obvious that no such factors exist in Europe. However, as many countries have gained new ethnic and religious communities, experienced as threatening to the traditional values, it is possible that the same type of racial mechanisms could prevail in Europe as well. There are some indications about this already. For example, van Koppen et al. (2002) report that support for capital punishment in fact increased in popularity in the 1990s, at least in some European countries. We, however, lack good comparative data for Western Europe – maybe because survey designers already think that the issue is no longer interesting or controversial.

The primary conclusion is thus that when it comes to such an individualistic human right as the right not to be executed, there are no longer any differences between European countries whatsoever; membership in the common European house has brought about a very significant harmonisation in this respect. We believe, furthermore, that if we had analysed some other 'individualistic' human rights issues, the picture would be fairly similar, even though abortion and euthanasia still raise much more controversy in the continent than the death penalty. The individual's life and rights are indeed well protected in today's Europe; the liberal-individualistic notion of human rights and democracy promoted by European regional organisations has had a major, and hopefully lasting, impact. We need to bear in mind that the legislators who drafted and enacted the laws, for example on the death penalty, are often more 'liberal' than the masses. Perhaps 'ordinary people' think more in terms of the collective and its protection than those who govern them.

## Concluding Remarks

The preceding analyses lead us to a number of general conclusions. The first and most important, though maybe somewhat trivial, conclusion is that European societies have indeed become more and more inclusive in recent years and decades, at least in terms of political citizenship. The countries of the continent consciously try to create mechanisms with which they can better involve new people in the activities of society and tolerate social and cultural differences; they constantly update their legislation, widen the variety of religious education, consider quotas for women in political bodies. From this perspective, ever more favourable conditions for deepening integration should exist. We have no reason to believe that other comparable indicators could have changed this general picture in any way.

The second central conclusion is closely related to the first one: measured in whatever way, European societies have become more and more similar to one another. The process of Europeanisation – or Westernisation – clearly dictates the development of these societies. There are, as we have shown, still a great number of more or less deep cleavages across the continent, but in many fields of life and politics it is not to possible find such cleavages. For example, the language requirement of naturalisation, possibly the most interesting aspect of 'citizenship' analysed in the chapter, does not seem to differentiate European countries to any significant degree. In the case of religion, the protective mechanisms of the dominant religion are often so subtle that it is virtually impossible to categorise these countries in any sensible manner geographically or culturally, although, admittedly, the Catholic states seemed somewhat more protective in constitutional terms. By contrast, the latter two indicators (women's political participation and death penalty) revealed a fairly clear geographical pattern; Scandinavia and some North-Western European countries score well in both these respects. They may be late-comers to the EU, but they are certainly not less 'European' by the standards of 'common European values'. Interestingly, and as analysed in the next chapter, this visible 'Europeanness' does not seem to correlate positively with support for integration.

All in all, European countries seem to be moving along an increasingly narrow tunnel, in legal, political, and even general cultural terms. There are differences, of course, but they have become smaller, or at least less conspicuous; the kind of politico-legal analysis from a bird's eye perspective that we have used here cannot unveil significant hidden socio-cultural differences. This similarity may be a sign of internal inclusion in itself. It is also important that there is no way we can assume that countries from Eastern, Western, Northern or Southern Europe would have profoundly differing patterns of inclusion/exclusion, or that we could find differences between the new and old member states. There is no a priori gap between East and West either; the legacy of communism has already lost much of its importance in this respect.

Simultaneously, however, and this is possibly the most important conclusion of this chapter, European nation-states still possess and seek to possess such a wide variety of more or less official mechanisms through which they construct and reconstruct their national identities, national communities and national togetherness, that they necessarily become exclusive to a certain degree. The language requirement of naturalisation is one such mechanism, but there are others, such as religious education, blasphemy laws and public holidays. It is particularly noteworthy that in some countries the mechanisms have become more exclusive in recent years; there is clearly a strengthening need to protect the traditional national community and its identity. Increasing inclusion is still the main trend but it also generates counterreactions of exclusion. The opposition that the European Draft Constitution encountered in the referenda of 2005 can undoubtedly be interpreted from this perspective.

Hence, to again resort to the metaphor above, in this increasingly narrow European tunnel, with a very limited amount of space around it, the necessity for making distinctions, of being different from others, has by no means become irrelevant; for some, it may even have become more important. This need to be different is possibly the ultimate similarity that defines the Europeanness of today.

What does all this mean from the perspective of the future of European integration, then, in addition to the fact that general conditions should be favourable? First of all, the question of integration becomes a question of resistance: to what extent the nation-states allow, by way of conscious political decisions, Europe to become part of their national entity is what ultimately determines how successful integration can be. We thus take a step further from Ole Wæver (2002, 25; cf. the notion of double structuration in Kauppi 2005) who argues that the primary question of European integration is not 'how the meaning of statehood or nationhood [...] has changed, it is the question of how the different states/nations in different ways have "Europe" integrated into their we's.'

The second answer requires a return to the main parameters that we took up in the theoretical part of this chapter, that is, the individual versus the collective level and the patterns of inclusion and exclusion. These two parameters can be cross-tabled in the following way (Table 3.9):

*Table 3.9: Possible consequences of inclusion and exclusion*

|  | Emphasis on the individual | Emphasis on the collective |
|---|---|---|
| Inclusion | Functioning rights for and mechanisms of participation; protection from any random social threats. | A community without permanent attributes; a community that is primarily defined by its willingness to include. |
| Exclusion | Limited rights; limited mechanisms of participation; limited protection from social threats (for some). | A community that is based on clearly defined, and therefore non-political, values and features. |

We believe that for integration to be successful in the long run, the European nation-states should be inclusive both at the level of individuals and the collective, that is, the nation-state. There is no doubt that from the individual's perspective, a reasonably high standard of inclusiveness has already been achieved; in this respect the rhetoric of common European values is indeed founded. At the collective level the existence of inclusive mechanisms or norms is more questionable, despite the overall trend towards increasing inclusion. Perhaps this is inevitable: it may be so difficult to define or codify the rights and limits of a given collective that mechanisms of exclusion are almost bound to emerge. But in spite of this, or perhaps precisely for this reason, we are inclined to conclude that the European nation-states should increasingly think of themselves in terms of what we call 'communities without permanent attributes' or 'communities that are primarily based on the idea of inclusion'. These kinds of communities must be profoundly aware of the randomness of their own values, and they are therefore always willing to enter into dialogue with others about the foundations of these values. If we, for example, seek to define the 'common European values' in as precise terms as possible, the risk – and it is only a risk, a horizon rather than reality – of exclusion inevitably increases. The German *Verfassungspatriotismus* may come closest to this kind of community without permanent attributes; the constitution is in fact an attribute that lies outside the community itself.

The more heterogeneous Europe becomes, the more important it becomes to promote these communities without permanent attributes. Ultimately this may even have happen at the European level: Europeans should learn to feel themselves members of a *demos* without attributes, and this may be a paradox indeed.

# NOTES

1. The authors wish to thank Ossi Piironen for his excellent research assistance for this chapter, and Pasi Saukkonen for his brilliant comments on an earlier version of it.

2. Many scholars have naturally paid attention to this linkage between the national and European levels; the linkage is highly dependent on the specific historical developments of each country. For example, Catherine Neveu (2000, 126) writes in the Spanish context: 'The Franco regime forged specific types of relationship between civil society and the state, which still have concrete consequences on the vision Spanish citizens have of citizenship, including at the European level.' The resistance to the notion of 'education to citizenship' clearly visible in the country can thus be seen as a legacy of the dictatorship.
3. The development of Western Christianity also played a major role in the evolution of this individualistic citizenship. Modern individualism was born with the in-worldly individuals that the Reformation helped create; it was *in* the world that the individual as an individual could show what capacities he or she possessed, not in an outworldly relationship with God (Dumont 1986; Vogt 2005).
4. Section 13 of the new German citizenship law states: 'A former German who has not settled in the domestic territory may upon his application be naturalised by the federal state of which he was previously a citizen if he meets the requirements of section 8 subsection 1 nos. 1 and 2; equivalent to a former German shall be any person *who is a descendant of* or has been adopted by a former German' (emphasis added; http://www.coe.int/T/E/Legal_Affairs/).
5. Indeed, as George Schöpflin has remarked: 'Without ethnicity it is difficult to secure democracy' (Schöpflin 2000, 6).
6. It was the Treaty of Maastricht, the foundation of the European Union, which formally introduced a European-level citizenship. It was mentioned already in the preamble of the Treaty in which the signers 'resolved to establish a citizenship common to nationals of their countries'.
7. A thorough discussion of the problems of citizenship data in Europe is provided by Clarke et al. (1998). Preuss et al. (2003) – and the issue of *Citizenship Studies* in which the article is published – discuss the extent to which citizenship is a politically and legally or a socially defined category in some Western European countries.
8. On the problems of the distinction between citizens and non-citizens – or between citizens, denizens, and helots – see Clarke et al. (1998, 44–5). Especially in Southern Europe, illegal immigration is a major problem, but the estimations of the numbers of these people vary a great deal, which is why we have not included them in our analysis.
9. In the 1999/2000 *European Values Study* surveys, conducted in most of the countries under scrutiny here, 43.7 per cent of respondents (N = 38 020) believed that the government should set 'strict limits on the number of foreigners [from less developed countries who come here to work]'; in Denmark this figure was 66.1 per cent and in the Netherlands 55.6 per cent. Moreover, 38.5 per cent would have let them come when 'jobs are available'. 'Anyone can come who wants to' was agreed on by a meagre 7.6 per cent and 'prohibit people coming here' by 10.2 per cent.
10. For example, Tinker (2004); Freedman (2004). Interestingly, Robert G. Moser (2001) has found that in post-communist Eastern Europe in the 1990s, PR did not seem to lead to high percentages of women; more women were in fact elected from single member districts. Moser explains this with party fragmentation, women's high level of education, and party structures.
11. Interestingly, Kunovich and Paxton (2003) do not make a distinction between men's and women's attitudes to women.
12. Malta and Cyprus cannot be counted because of the very low number of MEPs from these countries.
13. Protocol No. 6 to the European Convention on Human Rights from 1983 calls for unconditional abolishment of the death penalty in peacetime.
14. This rather simple conclusion is similar to that of Carsten Anckar (2004) who, in his large comparative and quantitative study on the death penalty in the world, notes that in Europe the degree of democracy and external pressure (in Eastern Europe) have been the most important determinants of the death penalty (in 1985 and 2000). On the world scale his conclusions do not sound surprising either: religion, degree of democracy, colonial heritage and history of slavery are the most important independent variables accounting for capital punishment at present.
15. In the only reasonably reliable comparative survey on support for the death penalty that we have been able to find, in six East Central European countries (Bulgaria, Czech Republic, Hungary, Lithuania, Poland, and Russia) the percentage of those who thought that their country should use the death penalty varied from 60 per cent in the Czech Republic to 79 per cent in Russia (in 2002). The survey was conducted by the Central European Opinion Research Group (www.ceorg-

europe.org). In Western Europe, support figures varied, according to van Koppen et al. (2002), between 16 per cent (Norway) and 50 per cent (the UK) in 2000.

## REFERENCES

Anckar, Carsten (2004), *Determinants of the Death Penalty. A comparative study of the world*, London and New York, Routledge.
Balibar, Étienne (2001), *Nous, citoyens d'Europe? Les frontières, l'État, le peuple*, Paris, Éditions La Decouverte.
Cederman, Lars-Erik (2001), 'Political Boundaries and Identity Trade-Offs', in Lars-Erik Cederman, ed., *Constructing Europe's Identity: The External Dimension*, Boulder and London, Lynne Rienner Publishers.
Clarke, James, Esbeth van Dam and Liz Gooster (1998), 'New Europeans: Naturalisation and Citizenship in Europe', *Citizenship Studies*, Vol. 2. No. 1.
Cochran, Molly (2000), *Normative Theory in International Relations: A Pragmatic Approach*, Cambridge, Cambridge University Press.
Culbert, Jennifer L. (2004), 'Why Still Kill. Reconsidering Capital Punishment in the United States', *Political Theory*, Vol. 32, No. 4.
Dumont, Louis (1986), *Essays on Individualism: Modern Ideology in Anthropological Perspective*, Chicago and London, The University of Chicago Press.
Freedman, Jane (2004), 'Increasing Women's Political Representation: The Limits of Constitutional Reform', *West European Politics*, Vol. 27, No. 1.
Heater, Derek (2004), *Citizenship: The Civic Ideal in World History, Politics and Education*, Manchester and New York, Manchester University Press.
Jurado, Elena (2002), *Complying with 'European' Standards of Minority Protection: Estonia's Relations with the European Union: OSCE and Council of Europe*, Doctoral dissertation, University of Oxford.
Kauppi, Niilo (2005), *Democracy, Social Resources and Political Power in the European Union*, Manchester and New York, Manchester University Press.
Koppen, Peter J. van, Dick J. Hessing and Christiane J. de Poot (2002), 'Public Reasons for Abolition and Retention of the Death Penalty', *International Criminal Justice Review*, Vol. 12, pp. 77–92.
Kunovich, Sheri and Pamela Paxton (2003), 'Women's Political Representation: The Importance of Ideology', *Social Forces*, Vol. 82, No. 1.
Lijphart, Arend (1969), 'Consociational Democracy', *World Politics*, Vol. 21, No. 2.
Meehan, Elisabeth (1993), *Citizenship and the European Community*, London, Sage.
Monnet, Jean (1997), *Muistelmat*, Helsinki, Edita (French original [1988]: *Mémoires*).
Moser, Robert G. (2001), 'The Effects of Electoral Systems on Women's Representation in Post-Communist States', *Electoral Studies*, Vol. 20, pp. 353–369.
Neveu, Catherine (2000), 'European Citizenship, Citizens of Europe and European Citizens', in Irène Bellier and Thomas M. Wilson, eds, *An Anthropology of the European Union. Building, Imagining and Experiencing the New Europe*, Oxford and New York, Berg.
O'Leary, Síofra (1996), *The Evolving Concept of Community Citizenship: From the Free Movement of Persons to Union Citizenship*, The Hague, London and Boston, Kluwer.
Panebianco, Stefania (2004), 'European Citizenship and European Identity: From Treaty Provisions to Public Opinion Attitudes', in Edward Moxon-Browne, ed., *Who are the Europeans Now?* Aldershot, UK and Burlington VT, USA, Ashgate.
Parisot, Françoise, coordonné par (1998), *Citoyennetés nationales et citoyenneté européenne*, Paris, Hachette.
Preuss, Ulrich K., Mehelle Everson, Mathias Koenig-Archibugi and Edwige Lefebvre (2003), 'Traditions of Citizenship in the European Union', *Citizenship Studies*, Vol. 7, No. 1.
Pocock, J.G.A. (1997), 'Deconstructing Europe', in Peter Gowan and Perry Anderson, eds, *The Question of Europe*, London and New York, Verso.

Saukkonen, Pasi (2003), 'The Political Organisation of Difference', *The Finnish Yearbook of Political Thought*, 2003.
Schöpflin, George (2000), *Nations, Identity, Power: The New Politics of Europe*, London, C. Hurst & Co.
Tinker, Irene (2004), 'Quotas for Women in Elected Legislatures: Do They Really Empower Women?', *Women's Studies International Forum*, Vol. 27, pp. 531–546.
Todorov, Tzvetan (2000), *Mémoire du bien, tentation du mal: enquête sur le siècle*, Paris, Laffont.
Verdery, Katherine (1999), *The Political Lives of Dead Bodies: Reburial and Postsocialist Change*, New York, Columbia University Press.
Vogt, Henri (2005), *Between Utopia and Disillusionment: A Narrative of the Political Transformation in Eastern Europe*, New York and Oxford, Berghahn Books.
Wæver, Ole (2002), 'Identity, Communities and Foreign Policy: Discourse Analysis as Foreign Policy Theory', in Lene Hansen and Ole Wæver, eds, *European Integration and National Identity: The Challenge of the Nordic States*, London and New York, Routledge.
Zielonka, Jan (2004), 'Challenges of EU Enlargement', *Journal of Democracy*, Vol. 15, No. 1.
Zimring, Franklin E. (2003), *The Contradictions of American Capital Punishment*, New York, Oxford University Press.

# 4. Support for the European Union

The European Union does not *qualify* for statehood. The federal authorities are a far cry from having monopolised power, and the Union thus fails to meet the classical criterion of statehood. The mental and physical borders of the Union are diffuse and, as we saw in the previous chapter, European citizenship carries but vague connotations among European voters. The low turnout in European Parliamentary elections throughout the Union (see Table 7.1) strongly suggests that the European level has not yet established itself as a relevant forum for grass-root mobilisation and participation.

All this notwithstanding, the European Union has almost all the trappings of a modern state. The crucial institutions and symbols are there; a federal government in the form of the European Commission, a bicameral parliamentary structure with the European Parliament representing the people and the European Council, an Upper House of sorts, representing the individual member states, a European Court of Justice, a common currency, a European flag, a European national anthem and most recently a European Draft Constitution. It is a union of European democracies with far-reaching political aspirations, including overcoming the so-called democratic deficit. This task will not be accomplished until the popularly elected European Parliament has been transformed into *the* key institution within the Union, making and unmaking governments, approving or rejecting the federal budget, and with overall responsibility for legislation. For a variety of reasons this is not likely to happen any time soon.[1] With respect to democracy, the EU is thus likely to remain ambivalent. It is open only to *bona fide* democracies; it has a record of promoting democracy within and beyond its own borders, but it is not yet willing to or capable of democratising itself all the way through.

Though not yet a full-fledged federal state, and nor, for that matter, a complete democracy, the European Union does qualify as an exceptionally well structured supra-national political system, ideally suited for the kind of systems analysis originally introduced by David Easton (1965a; 1965b) and subsequently elaborated upon by Pippa Norris (1999) and others. This is the perspective we will apply throughout this chapter. The focus will be on public support for the European Union in general and European institutions in particular as brought out by mass level survey data.

## Measuring Public Support for the EU

What does it take, Easton asked himself, for a political system to survive or persist? He is not primarily interested in democracies. His research interests are far more general, and in the process he identifies a set of key variables, presumably also of relevance for democratic political systems. Support is one of these key variables. It may be specific, an expression or feeling of gratitude for services rendered, or diffuse, generalised feelings of support often as a by-product of successful political socialisation. And it may be directed towards at least three different objects of support: the political community, the regime, and the authorities.

The political community represents the most fundamental level of support. It refers to the feeling that the members of a given society should have a common division of political labour because they are of the same nationality, speak the same language, and share a common history or whatever it is that holds them together. Support for the regime – its values and principles, its norms and its structure of authority – is almost equally fundamental. Just like the political community, the regime – whether democratic or not – normally benefits from a reservoir of diffuse support that has been built up over a number of years. This also makes it possible for the political system to tolerate even widespread dissatisfaction with its leaders or political authorities. But in the long run waning support for the authorities is likely to wear down the support for the regime beyond the critical level, and political leaders are therefore well advised to see to it that their decisions enjoy at least a minimum of support among the politically relevant members of the system (Easton 1965a; 1965b).

In a recent publication, Pippa Norris (1999) identifies no less than five objects and levels of support based on Easton's original model (see Figure 4.1). The political community and the authorities are carried over into the new typology virtually unchanged, whereas the regime gives rise to three new categories – regime principles, regime performance and regime institutions. The former is mentioned by Easton, who explicitly includes values and principles in his definition of the regime concept; and the concept of regime institutions is not that different from Easton's structure of authority. But Norris deserves praise for the crucial distinction between regime principles and regime performance. Support for regime principles represents a more fundamental level than support for regime performance; and we would expect dissatisfaction to make itself felt on the performance level before it spills over to the level of regime principles. But it probably makes good sense not to rule out any of the logical combinations. The kind of critical citizen, who is dissatisfied with the way democracy works, but nevertheless embraces democratic principles and ideals, should be an asset to any fledgling democracy (Klingemann 1999). Similar comments even apply to those, who look upon the principles of the democratic regime with suspicion, yet express satisfaction with the way the democratic regime actually works.

We have also opted for a systems framework, inspired by Norris and Easton. We will describe and analyse the European Union as a political system with different objects or dimensions of support. The choice of perspective is neither common, nor mainstream, but not that far removed from the notion of the EU as a system of internationalised governance (Niedermayer and Sinnott 1995).

*Figure 4.1: Objects and levels of political support*

Diffuse support ↑ ↓ Specific support

| Object | Characteristics of support |
|---|---|
| The political community | A basic attachment to the nation beyond the present institutions of government and a general willingness to co-operate together politically |
| Regime principles | Support for (for instance democracy) democracy as a principle or an ideal, i.e. as the most appropriate form of government |
| Regime performance | Support for the way the political system functions in practice, i.e. what the system delivers to its citizens |
| Regime institutions | Attitudes toward governments, parliaments, the executive, the legal system and police, the state bureaucracy, political parties and the military. Support for institutions rather than persons. For example, support for the presidency rather than support for the actual person occupying the presidency |
| Political actors | Specific support for particular political actors or authorities |

*Source:* Norris (1999, 10–12); cf. Linde and Ekman (2003).

Easton makes a strong case for the general applicability of his conceptual framework, but operates almost exclusively on the national level (Easton 1965b). Indeed – with all due respect – the term 'political community' seems to be tailor made for analyses of nation states. It is intrinsically interwoven with the notion of ethnically and/or historically defined societies. A coherent European society is at best only in the making, but it makes eminently good sense to examine the degree of identification with Europe among the citizens of the European Union. To that end, we need a set of indicators reminiscent of the standard items in this context.[2]

The ambivalent position adopted by the European Union on democracy in theory and actual practice made us exclude references to democracy from the items tapping support for EU regime principles. The three items singled out for attention all revolve around a perhaps even more fundamental dimension, attitudes towards the process of European integration in general and the European Union in particular (Table 4.1).

*Table 4.1: Indicators of public support for the EU*

| Objects | Indicators |
| --- | --- |
| The political community | In the near future, do you see yourself as [nationality] only, [nationality] and European, European and [nationality], or European only? |
| | Would you say you are very proud, fairly proud, not very proud or not at all proud to be European? |
| | People may feel different degrees of attachment to their town or village, to their region, to their country or to Europe. Please tell me how attached you feel to Europe? |
| Regime principles | In general, does the European Union conjure up for you a very positive, fairly positive, neutral, fairly negative or very negative image? |
| | What is your opinion on each of the following statements? Please tell me for each statement, whether you are for it or against it: Further enlargement of the European Union to include other countries in future years. |
| | Generally speaking, do you think that [our country's] membership of the European Union is a good thing, a bad thing, or neither good nor bad? |
| Regime performance | Taking everything into consideration, would you say that [our country] has on balance benefited or not from being a member of the European Union? |
| Regime institutions | Trust in the European Commission. |
| | Trust in the European Parliament. |
| Political actors | [No indicators available] |

The two following objects of support in Pippa Norris's modified version of Easton's model – regime performance and regime institutions – are tapped by items with face validity. Regime performance boils down to a question cast in truly instrumental terms. Have we – or have we not – benefited from EU membership? 'Regime institutions' confronts secondary survey researchers with an unusual, but pleasant, problem in the sense that there is a multitude of indicators available. This phenomenon is particularly pronounced in surveys focusing on the national level, but it also makes itself felt in the surveys commissioned by the European Union for the purpose of tapping attitudes towards the Union and its institutions. We are therefore well advised to concentrate on trust in or support for key institutions such as the European Parliament and the European Commission.

The last object of support – the political actors – poses a much more familiar problem. There are not any suitable indicators available. The *Eurobarometers* (EB), the *Central and Eastern Eurobarometers* (CEEB) and more recently the *Candidate Countries Eurobarometers* (CCEB) do feature occasional questions designed to gauge how knowledgeable respondents are about the European Union. This is admittedly an important dimension, but it has nothing to say about support for specific political actors, like Javier Solana and Romano Prodi. The general absence of such questions may in fact be seen as an artefact of the generally low-key approach of the European Commission to the political discourse within the member states. The European arena does not yet lend itself to the kind of actor-specific barometers familiar from national election studies; and we reluctantly have to proceed without paying further attention to the political actors.

In a national context, the political system derives the bulk of its diffuse support from what Norris refers to as the political community and the regime principles. But this is not necessarily the case within the European context. To the extent that Europeans are indeed moved by the notion of European unification, it is a phenomenon of relatively recent vintage. Sixty years ago Europe had just come out of a devastating world war; and fifteen years ago the European continent was still marked by the Cold War divisions. Since then Europe and, for that matter, the European Union have been politically redefined. We would therefore expect the European Union to have fewer stable sources of diffuse support than mainstream nation states.

The following mapping of support provides a solid empirical platform for further analyses in the second and third sections of this chapter, where we set out to account for variations within our sample of some 30 member countries, candidate countries and potential candidate countries in terms of divisions or cleavages structuring contemporary Europe (section 2) and in terms of a simple causal model for voter satisfaction with the European Union (section 3). The former calls for classical macro-sociological analysis; the latter for regression analyses, more spefically logit regressions, drawing on pooled Eurobarometer data from the early 1990s and onwards with a respectable 800 000 respondents.

**The political community**

Citizens of nation-states are inspired by a sense of political community based on the experiences and memories they share with fellow countrymen, past and present. Citizens of the European Union still cling to their respective national identities. The number of EU citizens who think of themselves as 'Europeans only' is very small indeed. Dual identities with a

European bias – people thinking of themselves primarily as Europeans but also as citizens of a nation-state – are also rare. Together the two categories occasionally add up to a sizeable proportion of the electorate. Luxembourg, Germany and France are cases in point. But one-digit numbers are far more common (Table 4.2).

*Table 4.2: National identity and European bias (%)*

|  | Nationality only (a) | Nationality and European (b) | European and Nationality (c) | European only (d) | European bias (c+d) |
|---|---|---|---|---|---|
| Great Britain | 64 | 24 | 4 | 3 | 7 |
| Finland | 58 | 36 | 4 | 1 | 5 |
| Greece | 53 | 41 | 3 | 3 | 6 |
| Sweden | 52 | 42 | 5 | 1 | 6 |
| Austria | 52 | 34 | 8 | 3 | 11 |
| Germany (east) | 50 | 37 | 7 | 3 | 10 |
| Portugal | 50 | 42 | 4 | 3 | 7 |
| Hungary | 49 | 46 | 4 | 1 | 5 |
| Ireland | 47 | 40 | 5 | 4 | 9 |
| Bulgaria | 46 | 46 | 6 | 2 | 8 |
| Netherlands | 45 | 44 | 7 | 3 | 10 |
| Belgium | 45 | 35 | 10 | 7 | **17** |
| Northern Ireland | 45 | 38 | 8 | 6 | 14 |
| Turkey | 45 | 47 | 5 | 3 | 8 |
| Lithuania | 44 | 42 | 11 | 3 | 14 |
| Czech Republic | 42 | 48 | 7 | 4 | 11 |
| Cyprus | 41 | 53 | 4 | 2 | 6 |
| Denmark | 38 | 50 | 7 | 3 | 10 |
| Latvia | 38 | 51 | 7 | 4 | 11 |
| Estonia | 35 | 51 | 9 | 5 | 14 |
| Poland | 34 | 56 | 9 | 2 | 11 |
| Spain | 33 | 52 | 8 | 3 | 11 |
| France | 33 | 49 | 9 | 6 | 15 |
| Slovakia | 32 | 51 | 12 | 5 | **17** |
| Malta | 31 | 62 | 6 | 1 | 7 |
| Romania | 31 | 56 | 7 | 5 | 12 |
| Germany (west) | 31 | 47 | 13 | 7 | **20** |
| Slovenia | 30 | 65 | 3 | 2 | 5 |
| Italy | 26 | 59 | 10 | 3 | 13 |
| Luxembourg | 20 | 45 | 11 | 21 | **32** |

Source: *Eurobarometer* 59 (March–April 2003) and *Candidate Countries Eurobarometer* 2003.4 (October–November 2003). The full question reads: 'In the near future, do you see yourself as (a) [nationality] only, (b) [nationality] and European, (c) European and [nationality], or (d) European only?'

The outcome is hardly surprising. It has taken the nation-states of Europe centuries to build up a solid reservoir of support for the political community. The European integration project has been running for less than half a century and under auspices radically different from those accompanying state and nation building also in contemporary Europe. The Soviet Union, for instance, used all the instruments of the modern state, including a great deal of coercion, in its attempts to integrate Estonia, Latvia and Lithuania into the USSR, but half a century clearly was not enough (Dellenbrant and Berglund 1987); the three Soviet Baltic republics seized the first opportunity to secede. Integration within the framework of the European Union relies on two entirely different concepts: consent by and continuous consultations with the participating member states. European institutions and political actors play a rather modest role and have limited visibility in the member states. This is obviously not the ideal setting for European identity politics.

*Table 4.3: Attachment to Europe (%)*

| Hungary | 92 | Malta | 66 |
|---|---|---|---|
| Romania | 89 | Portugal | 63 |
| Poland | 85 | Finland | 62 |
| Slovenia | 78 | Germany | 62 |
| Luxembourg | 76 | Ireland | 58 |
| Denmark | 73 | Latvia | 58 |
| Sweden | 72 | France | 57 |
| Bulgaria | 72 | Greece | 52 |
| Czech Republic | 68 | UK | 41 |
| Italy | 68 | Turkey | 41 |
| Belgium | 67 | Estonia | 41 |
| Slovakia | 67 | Lithuania | 38 |
| Spain | 67 | Cyprus | 34 |
| Austria | 66 | Netherlands | 29 |

Sources: *Eurobarometer* 60 (October–November 2003) and *Candidate Countries Eurobarometer* 2003.4 (October–November 2003). The full question reads: 'People may feel different degrees of attachment to their town or village, to their region, to their country or to Europe. Please tell me how attached you feel to Europe?' The figures in the table indicate the sum of 'very attached' and 'fairly attached'.

Yet the EU does seem to have an impact on identity formation. The six original co-signatories of the Treaty of Rome all have pronounced European biases. Luxembourg, (west) Germany and Belgium stand out as the most pro-European countries of the 29 actual and potential EU member states included in Table 4.2. With a pro-European bias of 10–15 per cent, the remaining three core countries – France, Italy and the Netherlands – are not trailing that far behind. But a long record as member clearly is not enough to promote European identity formation as evidenced by the national bias of the Northern periphery, including Britain with more than three decades within the Union.

Table 4.3 on attachment to Europe provides yet another community-level support indicator. The terms 'Europe' and the 'European Union' do not necessarily carry the same connotations – this may explain the low percentage of the Netherlands – but the outcome nevertheless suggests that the EU has a solid pro-European foundation to draw on. An overwhelming majority of member countries and soon-to-be member countries have scores of 60 per cent or more; and only half a dozen countries, including the UK, have scores of less than 50 per cent.

**Regime principles**

The principles upon which the European Union is built are elusive and to some extent contradictory. Though not itself a democracy, the EU is open to democratic states only and has made promotion of democracy into one of its main foreign policy objectives. The rule of law, civil and political liberties, political pluralism and other values familiar from the international democracy discourse have therefore become part of the all-inclusive ideological rhetoric uniting the 12, 15 or 25 member states (Beetham 1994); it is basically an uncontested dimension where federation and member states move hand in hand. The pledge to market economy and the free flow of capital and labour within the Union presumably constitutes yet another dimension, where the interests of the federal and national levels coincide and the treaties of Rome, Maastricht, and Nice, and more recently the Draft Constitution, may possibly lend themselves to the identification of further consensual dimensions.

Yet this is not the track we will pursue. We will focus exclusively on attitudes towards the European project of integration as such. We will start by taking a close look at the crucial question of enlargement.

The European Commission has operated with an open-ended definition of Europe and opened up the European integration project for new members in several consecutive enlargement waves, including the most recent and most dramatic wave of enlargement in May 2004 (Rose 1996; Berezin and Schain 2003). Figure 4.2 taps support for future enlargement among the voters in each of the EU countries as of May 2004, in two candidate countries, Bulgaria and Romania, scheduled to be part of the enlargement foreseen for 2007, and two potential EU members, Croatia and Turkey.

Those already in a prestigious club are not always in favour of opening up for new members, as each new member would make membership a little less exclusive. The strong endorsement of enlargement in the five non-member countries, including Turkey and Northern Cyprus, ties in very well with this logic (Figure 4.2). It would clearly be counterproductive for outsiders with an interest in climbing on board to call for an end to enlargement even before they have been accepted as full members. The countries with the lowest level of support for enlargement may also be seen to be acting in pursuit of narrow self-interest. Here we find eight countries; they are all part of the EU15 and include no less than three of the original six, Germany, Luxembourg and France, all three of them with scores that testify to more widespread feelings of unease about enlargement than manifested in the three Scandinavian countries with their long-standing record of conditional support for the EU, but nevertheless well ahead of Austria at the very bottom of the graph.

*Figure 4.2: In favour of future enlargements of the EU (%)*

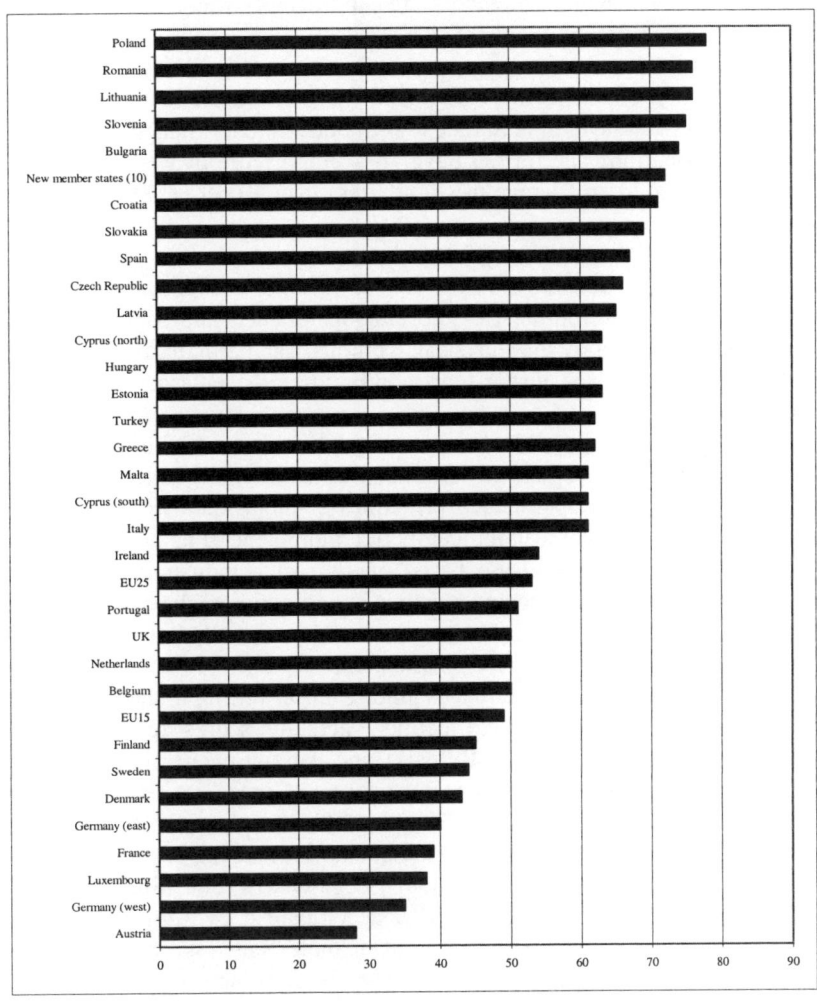

*Source: Eurobarometer* 62 (October–November 2004). The full question reads: 'What is your opinion on each of the following statements? Please tell me for each statement, whether you are for it or against it: Further enlargement of the European Union to include other countries in future years'. The bars in the figure indicate the share of respondents in each country who are in favour of future enlargements.

But narrow self-interest is not enough to make sense of the data. The strongly positive approach towards enlargement, prevalent in all ten enlargement countries as of May 2004, and, for that matter, in Spain, Greece and Italy, is in fact sufficient to refute the crude notion that insiders always have a strategic interest in keeping outsiders out. The country scores are largely a function of the timing of EU-membership, before or after 1 May 2004. The ten new members are significantly more open to further waves of enlargement than are the 15 pre-enlargement countries. The difference between the ten most recent members of the EU and the fifteen West European countries that had paved the way for the historic eastward enlargement of the Union is in fact so pronounced that it may work towards cleavage formation. The former have an average score of well over 70 per cent as opposed to an average of slightly less than 50 per cent for the EU15 (Figure 4.2).

Together the two groups of member countries produce an all-Union average somewhat above the 50 per cent level. It is a respectable aggregate measure of support for the flexible and open-ended approach to Europe traditionally adopted by the European Commission, particularly considering that polling took place just a few months after the enlargement of May 2004.

It is theoretically possible for individual EU citizens or individual EU member countries to oppose this and other kinds of enlargement, regardless of the pragmatic and open-ended principles of inclusion. We are therefore well advised to consider also indicators of a more general nature.

Figures 4.3–4.5 (below) are based on two such indicators. Figure 4.3 revolves around the positive and negative connotations of the EU in general. Figure 4.4 draws on a slightly more concrete, but nevertheless rather broad, question about the merits of EU membership. As may be expected, the EU conjures up strongly positive images among those waiting in the wings for a binding invitation to join. No country actually scores higher on this dimension than Romania, but Bulgaria and Turkey clearly belong to the same league. Ireland, Italy, Spain, Portugal and Greece are also among the countries with warm feelings for the EU along with Belgium and Luxembourg and two newcomers, Slovenia and Lithuania.

Seven countries stand out as distinctly negative. Here we find the UK, as always an outspoken critic of the EU, accompanied by Austria, the three Scandinavian EU countries and two out of three Baltic states, Estonia and Latvia. A similar geographical pattern may be discerned in Figure 4.4. EU membership tends to carry negative connotations in its northern periphery, including the UK, and positive connotations in Southern Europe, parts of continental Europe and Ireland.

By focusing on the other side of the coin, the negative rather than the positive evaluations of EU membership, Figure 4.5 makes the geographical contours of anti-EU currents somewhat sharper. Based as it is on time-series data from 1991 and onwards, the figure also provides a long-term perspective. Survey questions tapping the same underlying dimension are

Support for the European Union 69

sometimes phrased somewhat differently in different contexts. In this particular case, the *Eurobarometer* (EB) and the *Candidate Countries Eurobarometer* (CCEB) surveys are close but not identical (see sources under Figure 4.5); and thence our decision to present new and old EU countries separately.

*Figure 4.3: A positive image of the European Union (%)*

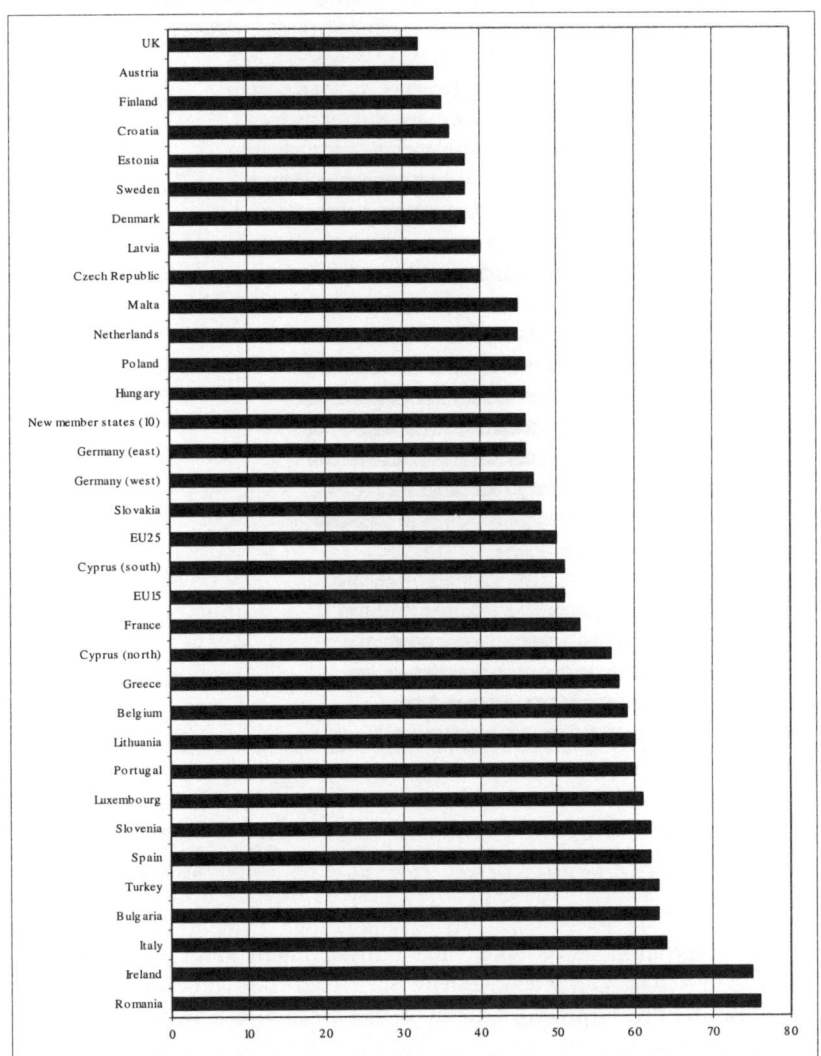

Source: *Eurobarometer* 62 (October–November 2004). The full question reads: 'In general, does the European Union conjure up for you a very positive, fairly positive, neutral, fairly negative or very negative image?' The bars in the figure indicate the sum of answers 'very positive' and 'fairly positive'.

*Figure 4.4: EU membership: a good thing? (%)*

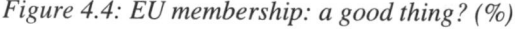

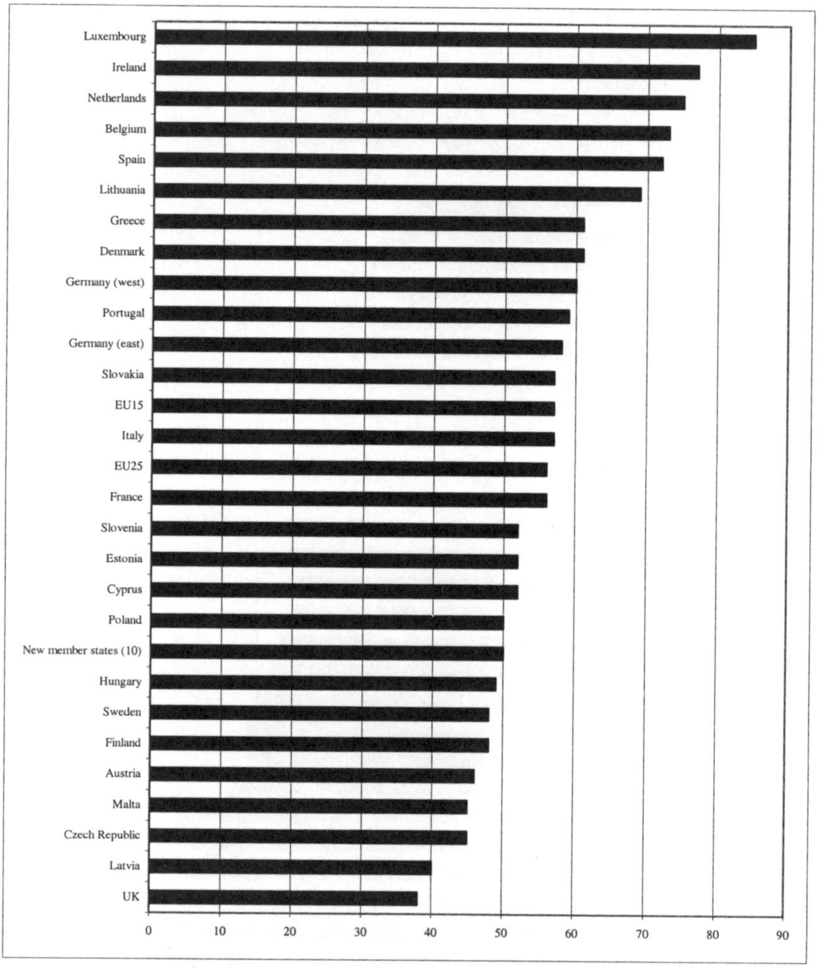

*Source: Eurobarometer* 62 (October–November 2004). The full question reads: 'Generally speaking, do you think that [our country's] membership of the European Union is a good thing, a bad thing, or neither good nor bad?' The bars in the figure indicate the share of respondents in each country who think that membership is 'a good thing'.

It may furthermore be noted that the maximum value reported in the figure is less than 35 per cent (Figure 4.5). That is good news for Brussels. Bad – but hardly surprising – news is that Britain, one of the key players within the EU, stands out as one of the pillars of union-wide anti-EU sentiments. Sweden's indisputably leading position within this camp, including Britain, Finland and Austria, is somewhat more surprising, but not entirely unexpected. In fact, with an average of almost 35 per cent of its voters over time describing EU membership as bad, Sweden beats neighbouring Norway, whose voters rejected EC/EU membership in a popular referendum, first in 1972 and then again in 1994 (Valen 1973; Valen and Ringdal 1998).

*Figure 4.5: EU membership: a bad thing, 1991–2004 (%)*

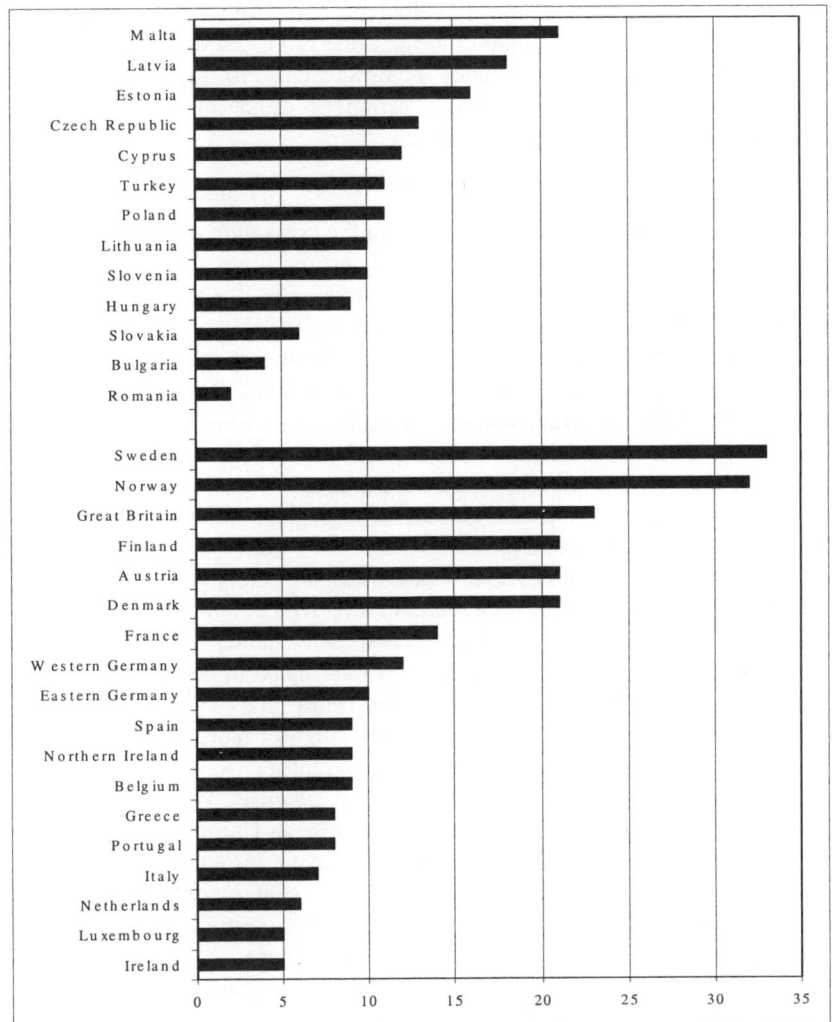

Sources: *Candidate Countries Eurobarometer* 2001; 2002; 2003.2; 2003.4; 2004.1; *Eurobarometer* 36 (autumn 1991) to 62 (autumn 2004). CCEB: 'Generally speaking, do you think that [our country's] membership of the European Union will be a good thing, a bad thing, or neither good nor bad?' EB 36–41: 'Generally speaking, do you think that [our country's] membership of the EC is a good thing, a bad thing, or neither good nor bad?' EB 42 and onwards: 'Generally speaking, do you think that [our country's] membership of the European Union is a good thing, a bad thing, or neither good nor bad?'

The new members also have a segment of the electorate evaluating EU membership as bad, but so far at least it has not reached the same level as in Western Europe (Figure 4.5). In Malta, the leading critic of the EU among the new members, a little more than two out of ten evaluate EU membership in negative terms, as opposed to almost four out of ten in Sweden. Anti-EU sentiments are less pronounced in Estonia and Latvia, but there is little doubt that these countries belong to the same group as Malta. The fit is not perfect, but Figure 4.5 nevertheless lends substance to the notion that there is a North–South, perhaps a centre–periphery, divide at work, structuring support for the European Union as such.

**Regime performance**

Few *Eurobarometer* items come closer to the crass *quid pro quo* dimension of European politics than the standard question about the benefits of EU membership as perceived by representative samples of voters in the various member countries. The full text reads: 'Taking everything into consideration, would you say that [our country] has on balance benefited or not from being a member of the European Union?' The question covers everything from material values such as macro-economic performance to immaterial values such as acceptance by the international community; and the question basically boils down to a politically correct version of the classical utilitarian query, though cast in aggregate, national terms: is there anything in it for my country?

Figure 4.6 provides an overview of the mood of the 25 EU members as of October–November 2004. The bars in the figure indicate the share of respondents in each country who feel that their country has benefited from being a member of the EU. The countries are listed in descending order of satisfaction, with Ireland at the very top (more than 85 per cent positive reviews) and Sweden at the very bottom (slightly more than 35 per cent positive evaluations). A total of seven countries – Ireland, Lithuania, Greece, Luxemburg, Belgium, Spain and Denmark – report levels of satisfaction with the performance of the European Union of 70 per cent or more. At the other end of the spectrum we have a group of eight countries with approval ratings in the range of 35–49 per cent, including Sweden, the United Kingdom, Cyprus, the Czech Republic, Austria, (east) Germany, Hungary and Finland. The remaining ten countries position themselves somewhere in-between these two groups, hovering between 50 and 70 per cent positive evaluations.

The citizens of the ten enlargement countries also pull in different directions. Some feel that EU membership has made a huge positive difference; others adopt a more sceptical attitude. The former prevail in Lithuania, Slovakia, Slovenia, Estonia and Poland, and just barely in Malta and Latvia; the latter dominate in Cyprus, the Czech Republic and Hungary. On the average, however, the overall impact of the ten enlargement countries is negligible. The ten new members, the 15 pre-enlargement countries and the current EU25 all land on averages slightly above the 50 per cent mark.

*Figure 4.6: Positive evaluation of EU membership (%)*

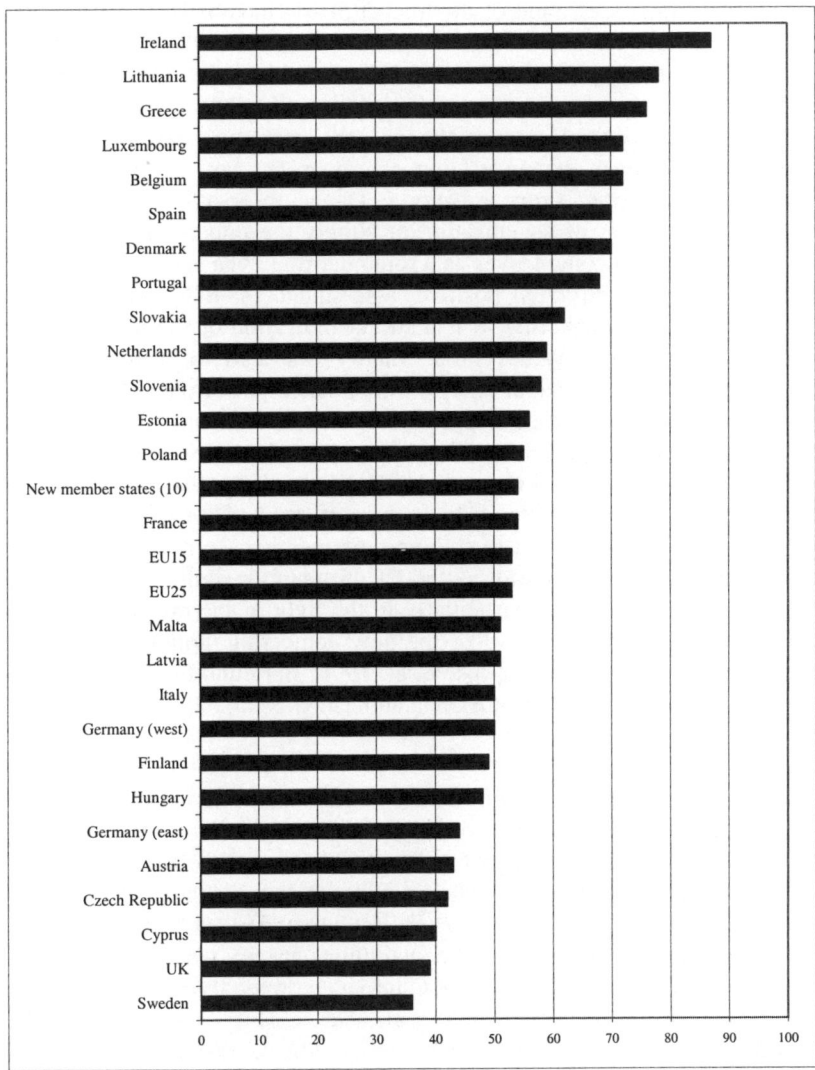

Source: *Eurobarometer* 62 (October–November 2004). The bars in the figure indicate the share of respondents in each country who feel that their own respective country has benefited from being a member of the EU.

The six core members of the European Union – the Benelux countries, France, Italy and the western parts of Germany – tend to evaluate EU membership in positive terms, the three former – Belgium, Luxemburg and the Netherlands – more strongly so than the three latter (Figure 4.6). Former EFTA members tend to be overrepresented among the countries with a negative overall assessment of the impact of EU membership. Sweden, the UK and Austria all end up in this group.[3] But, with 70 per cent of the electorate evaluating EU membership in favourable terms, Denmark, also a former EFTA member with well known reservations about the supranational aspects of the European Union, lands squarely among the top seven countries. Whatever the underlying causes might be – a tribute to the responsiveness of the European Union to Danish reservations, the long-term effects of a process of socialisation or simply the impact of geographical proximity – the outcome serves as a reminder that even stable patterns may be broken.[4] The strongly positive assessment of EU membership in Lithuania is also noteworthy. It is a strong indication of the importance of symbolic, immaterial values in a country that had to pledge itself to dismantle its major source of energy – the nuclear power plant of Ignalina – to be admitted to the European Union (Duvold and Jurkynas 2004).

To the extent that the 'benefit' item taps satisfaction with the European Union at work, the overall impression is indeed quite positive. Roughly two countries out of three tend to evaluate the performance of the EU in positive terms, and so do the voters of the ten new member countries, the 15 pre-enlargement countries as well as the EU25 member countries. This is not only good, it is excellent, particularly in the light of the rather widespread dissatisfaction with the record of the new democratic political regimes in Central and Eastern Europe (Rose et al. 1998; Berglund et al. 2001; Linde and Ekman 2003; Linde 2004; Ekman and Linde 2005).

**Regime institutions**
The items tapping support for or trust in regime institutions take us close to, but not all the way to, the men and women actually responsible for running these very institutions. Support for the presidency – the office of President of the Republic within the sphere of competence vested in it by the constitution – does not necessarily spill over on the incumbent. This is why presidential and semi-presidential constitutions specify what to do when the incumbent violates the constitution. Conflicts between the executive and the legislature are rarely cast in such terms, but standoffs with constitutional ramifications are not unheard of as brought out by the ill-fated presidency of Rolandas Paksas (2002–03) in Lithuania and the truncated second term of US President Richard Nixon, who resigned in the summer of 1974 to avoid impeachment.

The relationship between the incumbent and the office may also work the other way around. A popular president does not necessarily boost support for the presidency as laid down in the constitution unless he/she sets out to do so; and in the event that the incumbent pledges himself to constitutional reform, he may very well succeed. Charles de Gaulle – who successfully edged France from the weak and largely ceremonial presidency of the Fourth Republic to the strong presidency of the Fifth Republic – is a case in point. The transition from democracy to dictatorship in most countries of Central and Eastern Europe during the interwar era, including Germany, also fits into the same category.

*Figure 4.7: Trust in the European Commission (%)*

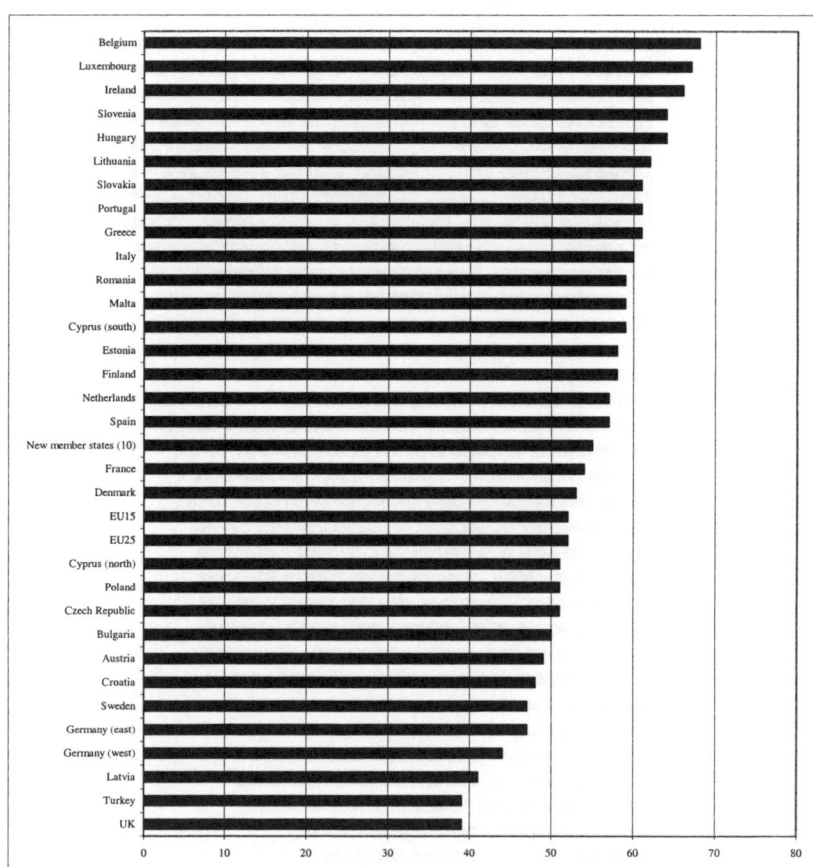

Source: *Eurobarometer* 62 (October–November 2004). Respondents are asked if they tend to trust or tend not to trust the European Commission. The bars in the figure indicate the share of respondents in each country who 'tend to trust' the Commission.

We are thus well advised to treat the trust items at face value and refrain from shaky inferences on the individual level. However tempting it may be, we must use the data we have on trust in the European Commission (Figure 4.7) and trust in the European Parliament (Figure 4.8) sparingly and not as a springboard for far-flung speculations about the legitimacy of the men and women currently serving these very institutions. The almost rosy picture that emerges in both instances suggests that European citizens are overwhelmingly supportive of the two key institutions of the European political system: the federal government (Figure 4.7) and the popularly elected European parliament (Figure 4.8).

*Figure 4.8: Trust in the European Parliament (%)*

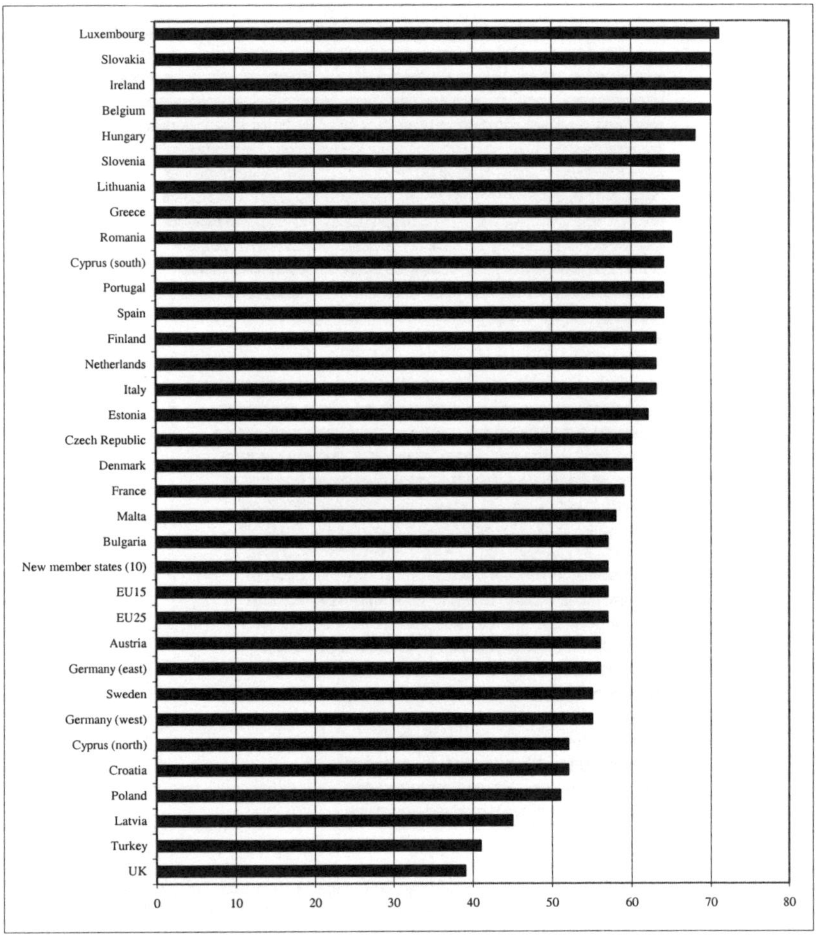

Source: *Eurobarometer* 62 (October–November 2004). Respondents are asked if they tend to trust or tend not to trust the European Parliament. The bars in the figure indicate the share of respondents in each country who 'tend to trust' the Parliament.

But the member states are by no means interchangeable, and the between-country variations may possibly have something to say about the underlying logic, particularly in the event that the geographical and political pattern ties in with the inferences we have made as we have moved from one level of support to another in Norris's elaboration upon Easton's basic model of the political system.

There is a gap of some 40 percentage points between the United Kingdom, at the very bottom of both tables, and Belgium and Luxembourg, two countries at the very top of Figures 4.7 and 4.8, respectively. With averages of less than 50 per cent, eight countries tend not to trust the European Commission, but only three of them – Latvia, Turkey and the UK – stand out as distinct from the mainstream. In Figure 4.8, these three countries land not only at the bottom of the scale but in an exclusive group of three, tending to distrust rather than trust the European Parliament. It is a truly heterogeneous group that testifies to the UK's non-committal and awkward position within the European Union, more than to anything else.

The ten countries at the very top of the two graphs represent the familiar mixture of old and new member countries. Here we find core members like Belgium and Luxembourg, but also a number of countries from consecutive waves of enlargement like Ireland, Greece and Portugal along with an array of eastward enlargement countries. Four of the latter – Slovenia, Slovakia, Hungary and Lithuania – consistently count among the seven countries with the highest scores for trust in the European Commission and the European Parliament.

So, the good news is that there is a pattern to the between-country variations, but the bad news is that we cannot make sense of it by invoking the standard macro-political indicators at hand. Trust in European institutions is not just a function of long-term commitment to and socialisation into European politics. If it were, Belgium and Luxembourg would not be the only co-signatories of the Treaty of Rome to make it to the top ten of Figures 4.7 and 4.8. Trust in European institutions may possibly be related to state and nation building, but the relationship clearly is not linear. If it were, we would not find Latvia, Lithuania, the Czech Republic and Slovakia, four countries sharing a short and – to some extent – troubled record of state and nation building, occupying positions so far apart from one another; Lithuania and Slovakia among the top seven countries; Latvia among the three countries least inclined to trust the European Commission and the European Parliament; and the Czech Republic among the many EU countries positioning themselves somewhere in the middle of the scale.

Similar comments apply to the old Cold War divide. The eight East European enlargement countries of May 2004 and the two countries of South-Eastern Europe scheduled to join in 2007 make surprisingly little difference as evidenced by the small variations between them and the mainstream West European democracies (see the respective group averages displayed in Figures 4.7 and 4.8). The North–South divide and the EFTA connection seem to be two somewhat more promising dimensions. Southern Europe, including West European countries like Greece, Portugal and Spain, but also East European countries like Slovenia and Romania, tend to be more favourably disposed towards the European Commission and the European Parliament than the countries of the Northern tier like Germany and the Scandinavian countries. In a similar vein, it may be noted that former EFTA countries like the UK, Sweden and Austria tend to be rather critical of the European Commission as well as the European Commission.

It is tempting to conclude this mapping expedition by launching the tentative hypothesis that attitudes towards European institutions reflect the overall assessment of the European integration project – itself a by-product of idiosyncratic collective and individual decision-making processes.

**The Macro-level Revisited**

The data we have presented thus far not only suggest that there are general dimensions at work structuring support for the EU and its institutions. The findings also testify to the presence of country-specific factors shaping the overall approach towards the European Union, in some cases for decades. We will return to some of the more conspicuous outliers later on in this section, but only after having put the tentative hypotheses of the previous section to a test.

When adapting Norris's model of the political system to the European Union and discussing the indicators at hand, we suggested that the EU was likely to have experienced difficulties in mobilising diffuse support. There is no strong sense of political community; the regime principles are elusive and hard to differentiate from regime performance, and EU institutions often have low visibility. The subsequent mapping of support for the EU in the member and candidate countries suggests that our educated guesses were not that far off the mark and the two correlation matrices lend additional support to our tentative conclusions (Tables 4.4 and 4.5).

The raw data for EB 62, the first post-enlargement *Eurobarometer*, had not been released as we were drafting this chapter. Tables 4.4 and 4.5 therefore draw on pre-enlargement surveys commissioned by the European Union, EB 59.1 (2003) and CCEB 2003:4, respectively. This is somewhat unfortunate as it forces us to divide the current EU25 into the two pre-enlargement groups, EU15 and the ten candidate countries as of early 2004. The two tables pull in the same direction and highlight the importance of two distinct, though not entirely related, clusters of variables. Items with a strong element of evaluation – good/bad, positive/negative, benefit/no benefit – tapping support for regime performance or regime principles form one distinct cluster, just as they should given the assumption of a blurred borderline between 'performance' and 'principles'.

*Table 4.4: Support for the EU among the EU15: off-diagonal correlation matrix of seven indicators of public support. Pearson's r ($r_{xy}$)*

|  | Membership: good/bad | Membership: benefit | EU image: positive/ negative | Feeling European | Trust in the EP | Trust in the Commission | Trust in Council of Ministers |
|---|---|---|---|---|---|---|---|
| Membership: good/bad |  | 0.63 | 0.64 | 0.28 | 0.43 | 0.44 | 0.42 |
| Membership: benefit |  |  | 0.57 | 0.24 | 0.40 | 0.41 | 0.40 |
| EU image: positive/negative |  |  |  | 0.27 | 0.46 | 0.46 | 0.45 |
| Attachment: feeling European |  |  |  |  | 0.19 | 0.19 | 0.18 |
| Trust in European Parliament |  |  |  |  |  | 0.81 | 0.74 |
| Trust in the Commission |  |  |  |  |  |  | 0.77 |

Source: *Eurobarometer* 59.1 (2003). All correlations are significant at the 0.01 level.

*Table 4.5: Support for the EU among the ten enlargement countries as of May 2003: off-diagonal correlation matrix of seven indicators of public support. Pearson's r ($r_{xy}$)*

|  | Membership: good/bad | Membership: benefit | EU image: positive/ negative | Feeling European | Trust in the EU | Trust in the EP | Trust in the Commission |
|---|---|---|---|---|---|---|---|
| Membership: good/bad |  | 0.74 | 0.67 | 0.26 | 0.66 | 0.57 | 0.56 |
| Membership: benefit |  |  | 0.63 | 0.22 | 0.68 | 0.57 | 0.55 |
| EU image: positive/negative |  |  |  | 0.29 | 0.63 | 0.53 | 0.52 |
| Attachment: feeling European |  |  |  |  | 0.26 | 0.22 | 0.22 |
| Trust in the European Union |  |  |  |  |  | 0.73 | 0.71 |
| Trust in European Parliament |  |  |  |  |  |  | 0.85 |

Source: *Candidate Countries Eurobarometer* 2003.4 (2003). All correlations are significant at the 0.01 level.

In a similar vein, it may be noted that the items tapping trust in the key European institutions – the European Parliament, the Commission, and the Council of Ministers – form a distinct cluster in both tables. Feeling

European – the only item we have presumably tapping identity formation or diffuse support within the European Union – finally stands out as something of a deviant case, with relatively low correlation coefficients (Tables 4.4 and 4.5). All in all, however, the correlation matrices lend support to the assumption or expectation, subsequently turned into the tentative hypothesis, that the lack of diffuse support makes the EU a more vulnerable political system than the mainstream nation-state.

The underlying pattern in the tables and figures in the previous section frequently lent itself to interpretations in terms of the historical record of the individual member countries in the current process of European integration. The six co-signatories to the Treaty of Rome – Belgium, France, Germany (west), Italy, Luxembourg and the Netherlands – have a special position as founding fathers of the European Union. They initiated the process and opened up for expansion by inviting a number of West European countries to join. The West European waves of enlargement brought a number of former EFTA members into the European Union, including the UK, Denmark, Portugal, Austria, Finland and Sweden. Previous commitment to a competing trade organisation with much more mainstream long-term objectives than the EU may in fact go a long way towards accounting for the rather detached approach towards the EU prevalent in the Nordic countries.

The following tables (Tables 4.6–4.8) set out to test one of the hypotheses formulated in the previous section, namely the hypothesis that the timing of EU membership somehow have an impact on the attitudes to the European Union (EU: good thing/bad thing). Member states and applicant countries have been sorted according to the actual or foreseen timing of their acceptance as full members of the European Union. Together the three tables offer a telling tribute to the importance of history.

*Table 4.6: Support for the EU by wave of enlargement: 10 per cent cut-off*

| Support for EU | Original six | 1970s–1980s | 1990s | 2004–2007 |
|---|---|---|---|---|
| Critical voices: 10 per cent or less | Belgium Italy Netherlands Luxembourg | Spain Northern Ireland Greece Portugal Ireland | Germany (east) | Lithuania Slovenia Hungary Slovakia Bulgaria Romania |
| Critical voices: above 10 per cent | France Germany (west) | Great Britain Denmark | Sweden Finland Austria | Malta Latvia Estonia Czech Republic Cyprus Turkey Poland |

*Source* [Tables 4.6–4.8]: *Eurobarometer* 62 (October–November 2004). The full question reads: 'Generally speaking, do you think that [our country's] membership of the European Union is a good thing, a bad thing, or neither good nor bad?' The classification of countries is based on the proportion of voters who think that membership is a 'bad thing'.

The three tables represent variations on a theme in the sense that we deliberately allow the cut-off to shift from very stringent (10 per cent critical voices), to somewhat less stringent (15 per cent critical voices) and to even less stringent (20 per cent critical voices). The term 'critical voices' refers to respondents who think the EU is a 'bad thing'. With a 10 per cent cut-off as in Table 4.6, 90 per cent or more of the respondents have to say they perceive the European Union as a good thing for their respective countries to be listed in the first of the two rows. Four of the six founding fathers – Belgium, Italy, Luxembourg and the Netherlands – may be seen to meet this rather stringent criterion, while France and Germany (west) fail to do so (Table 4.6).

*Table 4.7: Support for the EU by wave of enlargement: 15 per cent cut-off*

| Support for EU | Original six | 1970s–1980s | 1990s | 2004–2007 |
| --- | --- | --- | --- | --- |
| Critical voices: 15 per cent or less | France Germany (west) Belgium Italy Netherlands Luxembourg | Spain Northern Ireland Greece Portugal Ireland | Germany (east) | Czech Republic Cyprus Turkey Poland Lithuania Slovenia Hungary Slovakia Bulgaria Romania |
| Critical voices: above 15 per cent | | Great Britain Denmark | Sweden Finland Austria | Malta Latvia Estonia |

*Table 4.8: Support for the EU by wave of enlargement: 20 per cent cut-off*

| Support for EU | Original six | 1970s–1980s | 1990s | 2004–2007 |
| --- | --- | --- | --- | --- |
| Critical voices: 20 per cent or less | France Germany (west) Belgium Italy Netherlands Luxembourg | Spain Northern Ireland Greece Portugal Ireland | Germany (east) | Latvia Estonia Czech Republic Cyprus Turkey Poland Lithuania Slovenia Hungary Slovakia Bulgaria Romania |
| Critical voices: above 20 per cent | | Great Britain Denmark | Sweden Finland Austria | Malta |

82    *The Making of the European Union*

But it only takes a moderate liberalisation of the cut-off criterion to bring France and Germany (west) in among the four other co-signatories of the Treaty of Rome in 1957 (Table 4.7). A further relaxation of the cut-off criterion to, say, 20 per cent critical voices, reduces the number of critical countries in the union to a total of six, Malta and the former EFTA countries Britain, Denmark, Austria, Finland and Sweden. Portugal is in fact the only former member of EFTA not to end up squarely among the EU critics (Table 4.8).

*Table 4.9: Support for the EU by region: 10 per cent cut-off*

| Support for EU | Southern and Continental Europe | Northern and Non-Continental Europe | Central and Eastern Europe | Baltic Region |
|---|---|---|---|---|
| Critical voices: 10 per cent or less | Spain Belgium Greece Portugal Italy Netherlands Luxembourg | Northern Ireland Ireland | Germany (east) Slovenia Hungary Slovakia Bulgaria Romania | Lithuania |
| Critical voices: above 10 per cent | Malta Cyprus France | Sweden Norway Great Britain Finland Denmark | Austria Germany (west) Czech Republic Poland | Latvia Estonia |

*Source* [Tables 4.9–4.11]: *Eurobarometer* 62 (October–November 2004). The full question reads: 'Generally speaking, do you think that [our country's] membership of the European Union is a good thing, a bad thing, or neither good nor bad?' The classification of countries is based on the proportion of voters who think that membership is a 'bad thing'.

*Table 4.10: Support for the EU by region: 15 per cent cut-off*

| Support for EU | Southern and Continental Europe | Northern and Non-Continental Europe | Central and Eastern Europe | Baltic Region |
|---|---|---|---|---|
| Critical voices: 15 per cent or below | France Spain Belgium Greece Portugal Italy Netherlands Luxembourg Cyprus | Northern Ireland Ireland | Germany (east) Germany (west) Czech Republic Poland Slovenia Hungary Slovakia Bulgaria Romania | Lithuania |
| Critical voices: Above 15 per cent | Malta | Sweden Norway Great Britain Finland Denmark | Austria | Latvia Estonia |

The alignments within the EU lend themselves to interpretations in terms of geographical regions. Table 4.9 identifies four such regions, already familiar from the previous analysis, and classifies the countries within the regions in terms of the relative presence or absence of 'critical voices'. The table is based on a 10 per cent cut-off and provides a clear and straightforward pattern which is reinforced by the two subsequent tables as the cut-off moves to 15 (Table 4.10) and finally to 20 per cent (Table 4.11).

*Table 4.11: Support for the EU by region: 20 per cent cut-off*

| Support for EU | Southern and Continental Europe | Northern and Non-Continental Europe | Central and Eastern Europe | Baltic Region |
|---|---|---|---|---|
| Critical voices: 20 per cent or below | France Spain Belgium Greece Portugal Italy Netherlands Luxembourg Cyprus | Northern Ireland Ireland | Germany (east) Germany (west) Czech Republic Poland Slovenia Hungary Slovakia Bulgaria Romania | Latvia Estonia Lithuania |
| Critical voices: Above 20 per cent | Malta | Sweden Norway Great Britain Finland Denmark | Austria | |

There is an obvious North–South divide, visible already in Table 4.9 and very prominent in Table 4.11. Southern and Continental Europe are distinctly more supportive than the countries of the Northern tier, including Britain. There are no indications of a lingering East–West Cold War divide. We know from the previous section that enlargement has had but a minor impact on EU average scores, and we can now see that the ten enlargement countries do not constitute a homogeneous group. Some of them are more supportive of the European Union than others, a characteristic they share with their more established partners in Western Europe.

Quite a few of the new members and candidate countries are recent arrivals, not only to Brussels, but also to state- and nationhood. Estonia, Latvia and Lithuania had been part of the Soviet Union for half a century when they regained independence in the early 1990s. With the exception of an interlude during the Second World War, Slovakia and the Czech Republic had co-existed within one state from the very beginning in 1919 until the Velvet Divorce of 1992 (Deegan-Krause 2004; Mansfeldová 2004). The disintegration of Yugoslavia, also in the early 1990s, paved the way for several new state formations, including Slovenia, now in the Union, and Croatia, impatiently waiting for an invitation to climb on board. Cyprus has been divided into a Greek and Turkish state since the 1970s, but the division of the island and the Turkish state formation have never been recognised by the international community, and questions of state and nation building loom large in the background. State and nation building revolves around fundamental issues such as the rule of law, the principles of inclusion and exclusion, and 'good governance', crucial issues that might conceivably deflect attention from the European Union and undermine commitment to it. New states invariably have to settle unsolved questions of state and nation building, and we would therefore expect them to be less inclined than others to support the EU.

*Table 4.12: Support for the EU in new and old states: 20 per cent cut-off*

| Support for EU | Stateness: an issue | Stateness: not an issue |
| --- | --- | --- |
| Critical voices: 20 per cent or less | Latvia<br>Estonia<br>Czech Republic<br>Cyprus<br>Lithuania<br>Slovenia<br>Slovakia | France<br>Germany (east and west)<br>Spain<br>(Northern Ireland)<br>Belgium<br>Greece<br>Portugal<br>Italy<br>Netherlands<br>Luxembourg<br>Ireland<br>Turkey<br>Poland<br>Hungary<br>Bulgaria<br>Romania |
| Critical voices: above 20 per cent | | Sweden<br>Norway<br>Great Britain<br>Finland<br>Austria<br>Denmark<br>Malta |

*Source: Eurobarometer* 62 (October–November 2004). The full question reads: 'Generally speaking, do you think that [our country's] membership of the European Union is a good thing, a bad thing, or neither good nor bad?' The classification of countries is based on the proportion of voters who think that membership is a 'bad thing'.

But, as may be gauged from Table 4.12, this is not the case. It is rather the other way around. All the seven countries, where stateness is an issue, have relatively few 'critical voices', 20 per cent or less, and end up in the first row. Three of them – Lithuania, Slovakia and Slovenia – actually qualify for the 10 per cent cut-off and two more – Cyprus and the Czech Republic – for the 15 per cent cut-off.

A short summary of our findings thus far is now in order. Our initial expectations about levels and types of support have been borne out by the data in the two first sections of this chapter. Diffuse support is in relatively scarce supply in the EU. Europeans have almost no sense of political community; very few Europeans identify with Europe; and 'regime principles' and 'regime performance' overlap to such an extent that the two levels frequently cannot be differentiated from one another.

We have solid evidence documenting the special position of the founding fathers within the Union, the lingering negative impact of EFTA on support for the EU, and, somewhat surprisingly, the positive impact on the EU of member states with stateness problems. We have compelling evidence of a North/South divide, and hardly any evidence supporting the notion of a remaining East/West Cold War divide.

Few scholars would deny the presence of country-specific factors shaping long-term attitudes for or against the EU. Country-specific conditions come in handy as some kind of residual factors when we have squeezed all the information we possibly can out of the original explanatory variables. If we have nothing else at hand, why not attribute the outcome to British, Swedish or, for that matter, Lithuanian mentality? The UK, Sweden and Lithuania occupy extreme positions, the two former among the EU critics and the latter among the pro-EU countries, and models cast in general terms may not be sufficient to account for their behaviour. So in that sense references to mentality, custom or traditions represent a step forward. But it will be no more than an idle and tautological exercise unless we take the time to specify what we mean by, say, British mentality, and try to translate as much as possible of this new factor into generally applicable variables.

The following multivariate analyses of pro-EU sentiments over time may be seen as a step in that direction. With it, our perspective shifts from aggregate and macro to individual and micro and from recent or very recent data to long-term trends. In the final analysis, though, countries will remain our primary objects of classification.

## A Multivariate Analysis of Support

In an attempt to identify long-term determinants of support for the EU, we will now exploit the analytical potential of all the *Eurobarometers* at hand from 1990 to 2003. This gives us a pooled dataset with a limited number of key variables (see Table 4.1.3 and Table 4.1.4, Appendix 4.1) and a very large number of respondents, in some cases almost 800 000, from the member and candidate countries, and a number of states devolved from the Soviet Union and the defunct Yugoslav federation, all in all 36 states. With the open-ended vision of Europe applied by the European Commission, some of the eleven states outside the current borders of the Union may become members in subsequent waves of enlargement. Opinions about and attitudes towards the European Union prevalent in these countries are therefore of no minor importance, and the pooled data set gives us an opportunity to take them into account, albeit to a limited degree.

The two previous sections have told us that the EU enjoys only limited diffuse support. This makes specific or *quid pro quo* support, given as it were in exchange for favours rendered, all the more important. We have therefore decided to focus on the question – familiar from the previous parts of this chapter – about what benefits, if any, EU membership entails. Respondents, who think their respective countries benefit or are likely to benefit from EU membership or from good relations with the Union, implicitly express support for the performance of the Union. This will be our dependent variable in this part of the chapter.[6]

*Table 4.13: Percentage of respondents who think their respective countries benefit from the EU*

| Country | Benefit (%) | N | Country | Benefit (%) | N |
|---|---|---|---|---|---|
| Albania | 92 | 2 716 | Denmark | 73 | 28 194 |
| Ireland | 92 | 29 623 | Italy | 71 | 18 296 |
| Bulgaria | 87 | 2 944 | Czech Republic | 70 | 3 232 |
| Romania | 87 | 4 179 | Armenia | 68 | 2 531 |
| Lithuania | 87 | 3 163 | Belgium | 68 | 25 305 |
| Croatia | 82 | 1 634 | Slovenia | 65 | 3 964 |
| Greece | 81 | 28 532 | Belarus | 63 | 2 180 |
| Netherlands | 81 | 27 755 | Spain | 61 | 25 564 |
| Portugal | 81 | 28 371 | Kazakhstan | 61 | 2 300 |
| Luxembourg | 80 | 14 266 | Yugoslavia | 61 | 855 |
| Latvia | 78 | 3 232 | France | 60 | 26 073 |
| Hungary | 78 | 3 134 | Germany (east) | 55 | 18 758 |
| Georgia | 78 | 1 706 | Germany (west) | 53 | 32 848 |
| Ukraine | 77 | 2 287 | Finland | 50 | 19 642 |
| Republic of Macedonia | 77 | 2 546 | Norway | 50 | 7 761 |
| Estonia | 75 | 3 371 | Austria | 49 | 16 270 |
| Northern Ireland | 75 | 5 640 | UK | 48 | 28 400 |
| Slovakia | 74 | 3 608 | Russia | 47 | 2 281 |
| Poland | 73 | 2 392 | Sweden | 31 | 15 029 |

Table 4.13 provides information about the relative number of citizens who feel that their own country benefits from the EU as members, or for non-members, their present relation to the organisation. In most countries, two out of three or more of the respondents feel that their respective countries have benefited from the EU connection. The geographical distribution of this explicitly instrumental form of support follows well-known historical patterns, largely documented in the two previous parts of the chapter. We now get a more complete picture, including information

about the number of respondents (N) by country in the pooled data set. In a deliberate effort to avoid redundancies, we make a point of focusing on aspects not raised earlier.

The countries may be seen to break down into three large groups. The first group includes four of the original six member states, all of them part of Stein Rokkan's city belt, the Netherlands, Belgium, Luxembourg and Italy, smaller West European democracies like Denmark and Ireland, and all the new East European member states, except for Slovenia. Most East European countries not yet accepted as members, Bulgaria and Romania, slated for membership in 2007, Croatia, the Republic of Macedonia, Albania, Ukraine, and even Georgia and Armenia also land in this group (Table 4.13; Lipset and Rokkan 1967; see also Chapter 2).

The second group includes countries more divided with respect to the benefit item, with affirmative replies in the range of 51–66 per cent. This group is dominated by major West European actors within the EU such as France and Germany. But here we also find non-member states with slim chances of membership in the near future, the Republic of Serbia and Montenegro, Kazakhstan and, last but not least, Belarus. These are countries with complex and troubled relations with the EU, marked not only by promises of political and economic cooperation but also by fundamental differences on fundamental values such as human rights and the rule of law, adding a new dimension to the evaluation of the Union.[7]

We finally have a third group of countries where less than 51 per cent think the country has benefited from its relations with the EU. In this group we find a number of former members of EFTA who remained members of this organisation even after the core country, the UK, had left for EU membership together with Denmark and Ireland in 1973. Russia is also in this group, sharing some of the characteristics of Kazakhstan and Belarus in the second group.

The general impression is nevertheless positive. Only five countries, three member and two non-members, fail to judge the EU as beneficial, and just one country, Sweden, has a large Eurosceptical majority. At this stage of the investigation, we make it our primary objective to unravel the dynamics of this distribution beyond the macro-historical level, and this clearly cannot be done unless we take the functions of the EU into consideration. As we see it, the EU has two major functions, at least when approached from a citizens' perspective: to provide for a better economic future and to secure democracy as a form of government in the member countries (Berglund et al. 2001, 119–46; Berglund 2003). We thus need two independent variables tapping satisfaction with political and economic development in the respective member or would-be member countries.

*Table 4.14: Countries sorted by percentages satisfied with democracy and the development of household financial situation (%)*

| Country | Better financial situation than last year (%) | N | Satisfied with democracy or development of democracy in own country (%) | N |
|---|---|---|---|---|
| Denmark | 57.5 | 2 268 | 80.6 | 21 838 |
| Luxembourg | 63.2 | 788 | 77.7 | 10 112 |
| Norway | 52.7 | 1 696 | 76.7 | 8 798 |
| Netherlands | 48.0 | 2 375 | 71.9 | 21 861 |
| Ireland | 42.4 | 2 545 | 69.9 | 20 854 |
| Sweden | Missing data | 0 | 65.6 | 9 776 |
| Austria | Missing data | 0 | 65.1 | 9 648 |
| Finland | Missing data | 0 | 61.1 | 13 736 |
| UK | 35.5 | 3 321 | 58.5 | 23 177 |
| Germany (west) | 41.2 | 2 073 | 58.1 | 27 248 |
| Portugal | 52.1 | 2 529 | 55.8 | 21 222 |
| Belgium | 42.4 | 2 168 | 55.0 | 21 455 |
| Spain | 42.4 | 2 290 | 54.5 | 21 306 |
| France | 28.9 | 2 722 | 52.9 | 21 819 |
| Albania | 78.6 | 4 655 | 50.1 | 6 057 |
| Czech Republic | 30.6 | 4 304 | 48.2 | 7 701 |
| Northern Ireland | 41.9 | 745 | 46.2 | 4 506 |
| Croatia | 31.0 | 1 131 | 45.1 | 1 871 |
| Poland | 22.2 | 4 570 | 44.0 | 6 429 |
| Republic of Macedonia | 23.1 | 3 272 | 42.9 | 4 885 |
| Georgia | 35.4 | 2 983 | 41.7 | 3 842 |
| Lithuania | 23.5 | 4 081 | 41.3 | 5 962 |
| Slovenia | 29.9 | 2 961 | 40.8 | 5 714 |
| Yugoslavia | 52.3 | 660 | 40.6 | 927 |
| Greece | 24.9 | 3 194 | 40.6 | 21 748 |
| Romania | 31.7 | 4 671 | 39.5 | 6 995 |
| Estonia | 33.2 | 4 225 | 38.1 | 6 125 |
| Germany (east) | 59.1 | 3 207 | 36.5 | 14 414 |
| Latvia | 22.9 | 4 245 | 29.7 | 6 171 |
| Slovakia | 24.9 | 3 776 | 27.6 | 6 277 |
| Italy | 36.8 | 2 197 | 26.5 | 22 504 |
| Hungary | 8.8 | 4 582 | 24.8 | 7 003 |
| Bulgaria | 17.1 | 6 079 | 24.1 | 7 800 |
| Kazakhstan | 16.7 | 2 311 | 18.8 | 2 728 |
| Ukraine | 11.1 | 4 987 | 18.8 | 5 332 |
| Belarus | 18.3 | 3 956 | 15.4 | 4 531 |
| Armenia | 20.9 | 3 814 | 14.1 | 4 731 |
| Russia | 21.4 | 4 757 | 11.8 | 5 824 |

*Note*: Percentages and number of observations (N) reported in the table refer only to those who are satisfied with the development of household situation and with democracy as defined below.

The *Eurobarometers* contain a couple of standard items assessing satisfaction with democracy, and an array of questions pertaining to the economic prospects of the country and, for that matter, the individual respondents. In the surveys conducted in Western Europe satisfaction with democracy is tapped by the following straightforward question: 'On the whole, are you very satisfied, fairly satisfied, not very satisfied or not satisfied at all with the way democracy works in [our country]?' The East European surveys feature a similar item, but cast in somewhat different terms: 'On the whole, are you very satisfied, fairly satisfied, not very satisfied or not satisfied at all with the way democracy is developing in [our country]?' Functionally, however, the two items are interchangeable and will be treated as such; 'very' and 'fairly satisfied' are coded '1'; 'not very' and 'not at all satisfied' are coded '0'.

As for the economy, we have chosen a question asked in the *Eurobarometers* about the respondents' houshold financial situation. As may be gauged from Table 4.14 and Tables 4.1.3–4.1.4 in Appendix 4.1, this item was used only sparingly and in some cases not at all. The question reads as follows: 'Compared to 12 months ago, do you think that the financial situation of your household has; (1) got a lot better, (2) got a little better, (3) stayed the same, (4) got a little worse or (5) got a lot worse?' We have dichotomised the variable by taking 'a lot better' and 'a little better' as a positive response and giving them the code '1'; the categories 'a little worse' and 'a lot worse' are seen as negative; their code is '0'. 'Stayed the same' does not quite fit into the dichotomy and is therefore omitted.[8] This reduces the number of observations (N), in some cases even drastically.

Table 4.14 reports the percentage answering that the financial situation is better[9] and the percentage expressing satisfaction with democracy or democratic development. The countries have been ranked according to satisfaction with democracy. The immediate impression is that the two items are correlated across countries when we use them as attributes of the national units. This is, however, a tendency not without exceptions.

We have also examined the interaction between these variables and their impact on the perceived benefits from the EU to own country. We have tested four alternative combinations of the two dichotomised independent variables, constructing a table with four columns (Table 4.15). In two of the cases – the first column (group 1) and the last column (group 4) – the variables pull in the same direction with consistently negative or positive values ('0' versus '1'). In the two remaining groups, we have a mixed picture with a positive value on one of the variables and a negative value on the other, or vice versa. The four alternative combinations may serve as crude instruments of prediction based on the data at hand.

Testing the data this way, we find that more than two thirds of European citizens satisfied with democracy and the development of household finances (group 4) believe that the EU is beneficial to their country, the only exceptions being Belarus (64.8 per cent), Great Britain (62.2 per cent) and

Norway (59.8 per cent). If all Europeans were *either* satisfied with democracy *or* satisfied with the development of their own financial situation (columns 2 to 4 in Table 4.15), the EU would have been appreciated by more than two thirds of Central and East Europeans, from the Baltic to the Black Sea.

*Table 4.15: Percentage of respondents who think their country benefits from the EU (respondents grouped in terms of their democratic and financial satisfaction and/or dissatisfaction)*

| Country | Group 1: Respondents who are dissatisfied with financial situation *and* dissatisfied with democracy | Group 2: Respondents who are dissatisfied with financial situation *and* satisfied with democracy | Group 3: Respondents who are satisfied with financial situation *and* dissatisfied with democracy | Group 4: Respondents who are satisfied with financial situation *and* satisfied with democracy |
|---|---|---|---|---|
| France | 41.5 | 66.0 | 58.8 | 80.7 |
| Belgium | 55.4 | 72.1 | 75.5 | 88.4 |
| Netherlands | 66.0 | 86.2 | 81.9 | 91.0 |
| Germany (west) | 37.3 | 56.4 | 55.9 | 75.6 |
| Italy | 64.0 | 81.6 | 81.0 | 83.8 |
| Luxembourg | 66.7 | 73.8 | 72.1 | 82.2 |
| Denmark | 50.5 | 76.5 | 59.3 | 79.8 |
| Ireland | 78.1 | 89.8 | 88.0 | 93.7 |
| Great Britain | 33.0 | 47.1 | 52.0 | 62.2 |
| Northern Ireland | 69.3 | 73.3 | 78.2 | 88.4 |
| Greece | 77.0 | 89.1 | 87.8 | 95.6 |
| Spain | 31.8 | 56.8 | 58.2 | 77.5 |
| Portugal | 59.7 | 82.2 | 80.9 | 92.9 |
| Germany (east) | 45.2 | 65.5 | 57.5 | 76.9 |
| Norway | 41.2 | 53.1 | 59.8 | 59.8 |
| Albania | 73.4 | 97.0 | 94.3 | 95.9 |
| Armenia | 68.0 | 65.7 | 65.3 | 69.7 |
| Belarus | 59.5 | 62.8 | 69.2 | 64.8 |
| Bulgaria | 83.0 | 87.7 | 88.1 | 90.1 |
| Croatia | 74.3 | 84.3 | 76.4 | 86.6 |
| Czech Republic | 49.7 | 75.4 | 65.1 | 86.6 |
| Slovakia | 67.7 | 76.7 | 72.9 | 75.2 |
| Estonia | 70.2 | 73.7 | 74.5 | 84.3 |
| Georgia | 70.0 | 73.9 | 70.8 | 86.7 |
| Hungary | 72.2 | 84.6 | 87.4 | 89.3 |
| Latvia | 68.2 | 78.8 | 78.8 | 87.6 |
| Lithuania | 84.2 | 88.6 | 86.6 | 92.6 |
| Macedonia | 67.3 | 79.7 | 73.6 | 87.6 |
| Poland | 61.0 | 74.7 | 72.3 | 82.0 |
| Romania | 80.3 | 91.2 | 85.2 | 94.8 |
| Russia | 42.3 | 64.4 | 52.7 | 70.2 |
| Slovenia | 53.4 | 67.7 | 64.0 | 78.4 |
| Ukraine | 75.2 | 82.3 | 74.0 | 84.5 |
| Kazakhstan | 56.1 | 68.3 | 67.0 | 69.8 |
| Yugoslavia | 50.4 | 74.4 | 57.6 | 74.5 |
| Mean | 61.2 | 74.9 | 72.1 | 82.3 |

Similar comments apply to the citizens of Belgium, the Netherlands, Luxembourg, Italy, Portugal and Ireland. In fact, the second column (group 2) and the third column (group 3) in Table 4.15 reveal almost identical patterns, with some exceptions, like Denmark, the Czech Republic, Russia and Yugoslavia. In these countries, the level of support for the EU remains high among satisfied democrats with a perceived worsening financial situation (group 2), but lower among dissatisfied democrats with brightening economic prospects (group 3).

Citizens unhappy with democracy *as well as* the financial situation can be found in the first column in Table 4.15. Here we get an indication of who the diehard supporters of the European Union are. The Baltic states, most of the Balkan countries, Hungary, Slovakia, Georgia and Ukraine stand out, all in Eastern Europe, alongside Ireland and Greece in Western Europe. The citizens of these countries are ready to support the European Union regardless of other political and economic considerations.

The data at hand lead us to two observations of general importance. First, in big countries with considerable economic clout such as Spain, France, Germany and Russia, only citizens who are *both* satisfied with how democracy works *and* have improved their financial situation unequivocally see the EU as beneficial to their own country. For this group, the two proposed independent variables immediately seem to be necessary but not sufficient in order to produce high levels of specific support. The rejection of the EU constitution in the French referendum in late May 2005 has widely been seen as a by-product of high levels of unemployment and a less than popular president. This ties in nicely with our assumption that voters expect the EU to promote not only democracy but also prosperity. Second, the presence of a group of diehard EU supporters suggests that we should not only continue the investigation but also consider additional variables.

To reach beyond the limited information found above, we propose a multivariate analysis based on logistic regression with the benefit item as the dependent variable. Logistic regression is appropriate, since the dependent dummy variable measures the log odds of a dichotomy as a function of the independent variables, while OLS regression may predict probabilities outside the permissible range of 0.00–1.00. The general formula for the natural log (logit) estimation on a dependent variable $i$, for $k$ independent variables is (cf. Bohrnstedt and Knoke 1988):

$$\hat{L}_i = \alpha + \beta_1 X_{1i} + \beta_2 X_{2i} + ... + \beta_K X_{Ki}$$

When $i$ is a dummy variable with values 0 and 1, the antilog of $\hat{L}_i$ is:

$$\frac{p_{Y=1}}{p_{Y=0}} = e^{\alpha + \beta_1 X_1 + \beta_2 X_2 + ... \beta_K X_K}$$

Logit regressions may seem harder to interpret than OLS regressions, since the coefficients refer to a dependent variable measured as the logarithm of the odds of two probabilities. The basic understanding of the coefficients is that positive or negative signs indicate increasing or decreasing log odds of positive benefit evaluations, respectively, controlling for other variables in the equation. In order to increase the intuitive explanatory power, all variables have been recoded into dichotomies. This allows us to express the effects in probability terms. That is, the net effect of an independent variable on the probability of a positive benefit evaluation is found by multiplying the variance of the dependent variable by the estimated regression coefficient. A hypothetical example might be used to illustrate the dynamics of the method: if 60 per cent of respondents in a given country score positively on the EU benefit item, the proportion is 0.600 and the variance $(0.600)*(1-0.600) = 0.240$. Assume a logistic regression coefficient from the independent dummy variable 'satisfaction with democracy' of 1.117. The net probability effect of satisfaction with democracy on the EU benefit item is $(1.117)*(0.240) = 0.280$ for respondents of the country in question. The interpretation of this effect is that satisfaction with democracy increases the likelihood of positive evaluation of the EU by a ratio of 0.280 or 28 per cent relative to non-satisfaction with democracy, controlling for other variables in the equation. Due to the intuitive appeal of operating with such net probability effects instead of logistic coefficients, the following tables and figures will be based on calculated net effects significant at least at the 0.05 level, while lists of regression coefficients are placed in Appendix 4.1 (see Table 4.1.1).

Figure 4.9 presents the full model, which introduces two new independent variables in addition to satisfaction with democracy, and household financial situation: type of community and age. In the *Eurobarometer* surveys, type of community is registered as 'rural/village', 'small town' or 'big town'. In order to capture the possible effects of living in an urban context, we have dichotomised the variable by giving respondents the value '1' (urban) for answering 'small town' or 'big town', while 'rural/village is given the value '0'. We would expect city dwellers to be more dependent on the global economy than villagers, and therefore more inclined to view the EU as beneficial. In addition, the rural periphery has frequently supported nationalist and regionalist ideologies often in collusion with agrarian or Christian democratic movements, and more recently, in Central and Eastern Europe, with nostalgic and nationally oriented communist forces, not particularly enthusiastic about the idea of European integration (Lipset and Rokkan 1967; Urwin 1980). The EU is therefore particularly likely to be hailed with limited enthusiasm in new member states and candidate countries with a large rural sector, concerned about the prospect of competition with high-tech West European agriculture.

*Figure 4.9: Multivariate logistic regression model of EU benefit item on young age, urban context, satisfaction with democracy and with development of household financial situation*

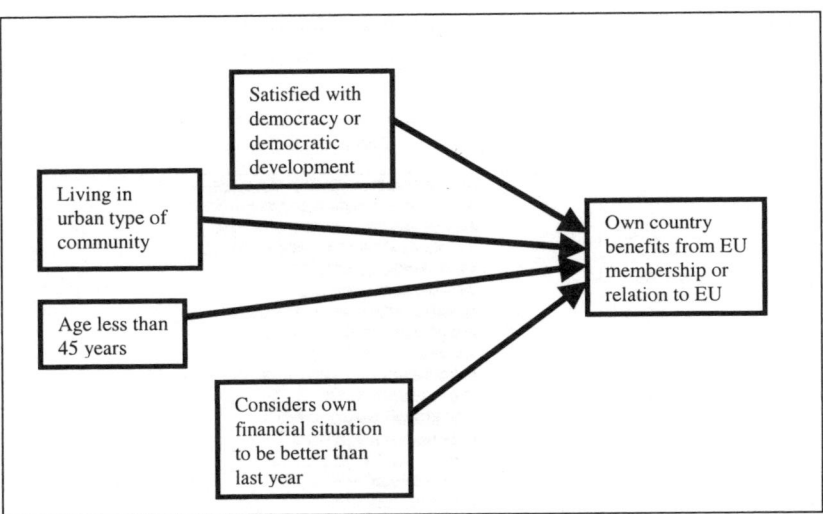

Age has also been included as a dichotomised independent variable by giving respondents below 45 years of age the value '1', whereas respondents 45 years of age or older are given the value '0'. We generally expect younger persons to be more inclined to see the future as promising, including the prospect of further European integration. Moreover, younger citizens living in recently non-democratic polities should be expected to be less inclined to nationalistic or communist nostalgia (cf. Ekman and Linde 2005). Young age also means 'no past', particularly in many new member states and applicant countries; EU membership may therefore feature as a idealistic vision appealing to younger more than to older citizens of these countries. By including these two additional independent variables, we arrive at the model presented in Figure 4.9. In the boxes we find the variable categories we expect will yield logistic net probability effect.

The net probability effects from this causal model are shown graphically as stacked histograms in Figure 4.10; the exact values are given in Table 4.1.1 (Appendix 4.1). The countries have been sorted by the sum of all net effects. Independent variables with statistically non-significant net probability effects have been treated as a zero-effect for the variable in question. The top half of the histogram contains mainly countries already in the EU prior to the most recent extension. For these countries, the model yields results for at least two of the independent variables. The countries in the bottom half of the figure are predominantly non-member countries, some of whom are applicant countries today. For the countries in this group, only one or two of the independent variables have a significant net probability effect on perceived benefits from EU membership (Figure 4.10).

*Figure 4.10: Net effects of a multivariate logistic regression model of EU benefit item on young age, urban context, satisfaction with democracy and financial situation*

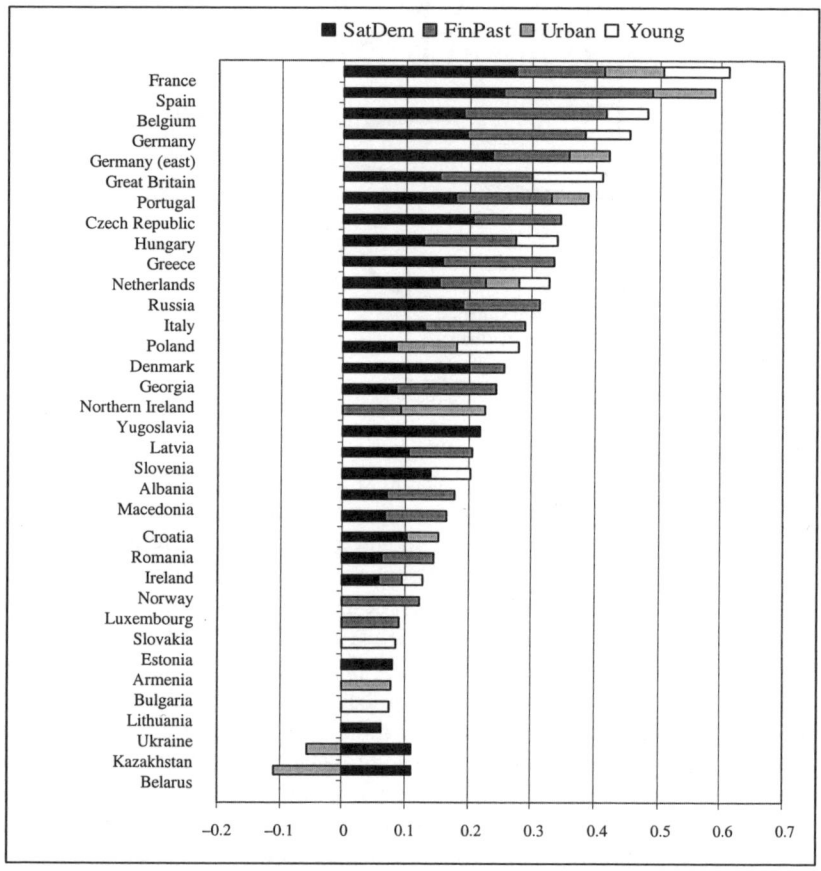

Some features are noteworthy. Though not a member of the EU, Russia has a profile similar to that of an established member like Italy; in both countries satisfaction with democracy and household financial situation are significant determinants of voter evaluations of the EU. Three other former Soviet republics also stand out as interesting. The citizens of Belarus have different opinions about the benefits of the EU, but these differences are not significantly accounted for by any of the independent variables in our model. The citizens of Ukraine and Kazakhstan, who are satisfied with the development of democracy in their respective countries, also tend to view the country's relationship with the EU as beneficial. But this effect is partly offset by the failure to win the large rural population for the cause of the EU. The combined net probability effects are therefore lower than the net effect of satisfaction with democracy. This testifies to the presence of a contradiction between two perspectives, possibly indicative of a certain frustration among the citizens of Ukraine and Kazakhstan: a contradiction between evaluations of the EU from a democratic perspective and from the perspective of everyday life.

*Figure 4.11: Geographical distribution of net probability effect of young age (less than 45) in a multivariate logistic regression model of EU benefit item on young age, urban context, satisfaction with democracy and a positive assessment of own financial situation*

In Figures 4.11 through 4.13 we have documented the net probability effect for each independent variable on a separate map. The darkest shade indicates a strong impact of the independent variable; when the latter changes from 0 to 1, this increases the probability of a positive evaluation of the EU by a fraction of 0.2 to 0.299. The lighter shades indicate similar probability shifts, from 0.1 to 0.199 and from 0 to 0.099, respectively. No colour indicates that there are no data for the country (this applies to Iceland, Sweden, Finland, Switzerland, Bosnia, Moldova and Turkey for all four maps) or that the independent variable has no significant impact (for the rest of the countries).

*Figure 4.12: Geographical distribution of net probability effect of* urban location *in a multivariate logistic regression model of EU benefit item on young age, urban context, satisfaction with democracy and a positive assessment of own financial situation*

Given the other three independent variables, the impact of young age is not strong anywhere (Figure 4.11). It is moderately strong in the United Kingdom and France, and has a slight impact in the Low Countries, Germany, Ireland, Poland, Slovakia, Hungary, Slovenia and Bulgaria. This outcome might seem somewhat counterintuitive considering the absence of a significant impact in the less developed part of Europe with the exception of Bulgaria. The result is largely an artefact of interaction between youth and satisfaction with democracy. Young people, less tainted than others by the authoritarian past, are likely to be more satisfied with the democratic development of their respective countries. In some of the older and richer member states there seems to be a positive impact of youth beyond the general satisfaction with democracy and the financial situation.

*Figure 4.13: Geographical distribution of net probability effect of a positive assessment of household financial situation in a multivariate logistic regression model of EU benefit item on young age, urban context, satisfaction with democracy and a positive assessment of own financial situation*

Much of the same applies to urban location (Figure 4.12). It exerts a relatively moderate independent influence only in Spain and a slight influence in Portugal, France, the Netherlands, Poland, Croatia and Armenia. As mentioned above, urban location has a negative impact in Ukraine and Kazakhstan. Generally speaking, the effect of urban location and young age seems to be absorbed by satisfaction with democracy and household financial situation. To the extent that these demographic factors have an independent positive effect, this occurs mainly in some of the more developed economies. For urban location, there is an independent negative impact in two of the less developed economies, Armenia being an exception.

The impact of the respondents' financial situation compared to last year is strong or moderately strong in all EU member states except Ireland, the Netherlands and Denmark (Figure 4.13). In Ireland the effect is weakened by an independent effect of young age, in the Netherlands by an independent effect of urban location and in Denmark by a very strong concentration of effects from satisfaction with democracy. In Norway a moderate effect of 'financial situation' seems to be dominant. Eurosceptic Norway is in fact the only West European country where satisfaction with household financial situation takes precedence over all other independent variables.

In the new member states of Eastern Europe household financial situation does not seem to make much of a difference.[10] Among the East European non-member countries, Belarus, Ukraine and the countries devolved from the former Yugoslavia follow the same pattern as the new member states; in this group of countries, Russia stands out as a notable exception featuring a moderately strong impact of household financial situation, along with Albania and Georgia. In Romania this variable also has a slight impact (Figure 4.13).

The overall picture is that financial situation has an independent impact throughout the EU. Two non-member countries, both important in their own right, also have citizens who tend to evaluate the benefits of the EU in terms of their own financial situation – small but energy-rich Norway and large raw-material producing Russia.

In Figure 4.14, we find the independent variable with the strongest impact. Satisfaction with democracy is strong or moderately strong in all present EU member states except Ireland, Poland, Lithuania and Estonia, as well as Slovakia, where it has no significant impact at all. As for non-member states, there is a relatively strong impact in the Federation of Serbia and Montenegro, a moderate impact in Russia, Ukraine and Kazakhstan, and a slight impact in Romania, Macedonia, Albania and Georgia. For some non-members, including Norway, Belarus, Bulgaria and Armenia, satisfaction with democracy has no impact. This is an interesting set of countries; they have at least one factor in common, however. Satisfied and dissatisfied democrats alike know that membership in the EU is a remote possibility. In Bulgaria, age seems to be more important than satisfaction with the way democracy works. The general impact of this variable is thus fairly similar to that of the previous independent variable, with the important proviso that satisfaction with democracy seems to be the key predictor in many Central and East European countries. A grand conclusion might therefore be that democracy stands out as the more universally valid predictor of specific support for the EU (Figure 4.14).

*Figure 4.14: Geographical distribution of net probability effect of* satisfaction with democracy *in a multivariate logistic regression model of the EU benefit item on young age, urban context, satisfaction with democracy and a positive assessment of own financial situation*

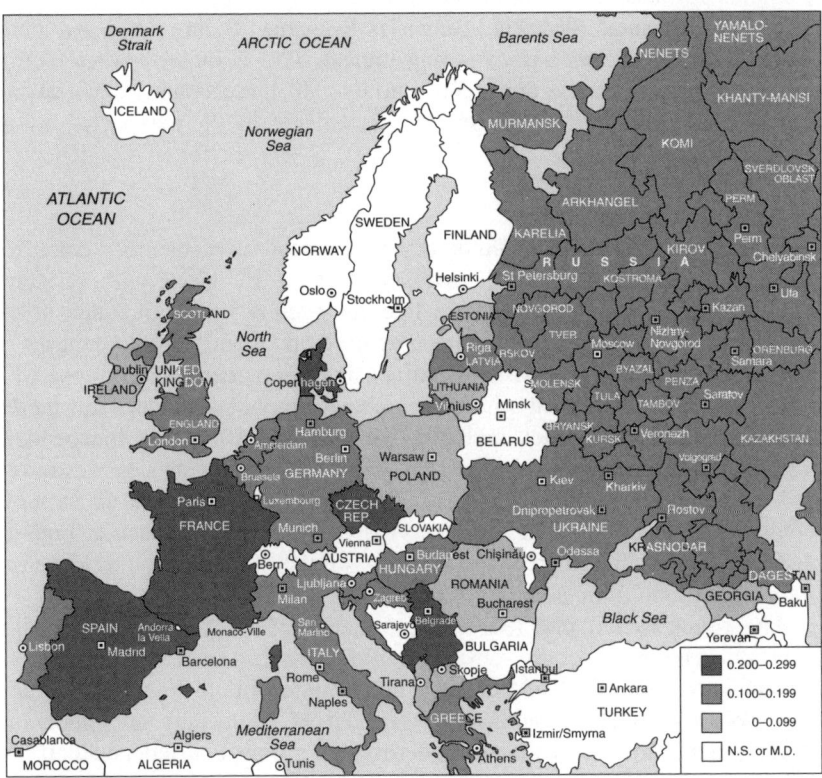

All in all, an attitudinal indicator like support for the EU and related attitudinal items seem to carry more weight in Europe than demographic predictors. Satisfaction with democracy is a powerful determinant by itself or *in combination with* positive evaluations of the household financial situation. West and Central Europeans are particularly sensitive to the combined effect of these two variables. Satisfaction with democracy without pronounced optimism about economic prospects is the pattern among the smaller former EFTA members who have joined the EU, a pattern shared with Ukraine and the countries devolved from the former Yugoslavia.

But there are some countries where satisfaction with democracy is less important than other factors in determining attitudes towards the EU. Improving financial situation stands out as the dominant determinant of support in very marginal countries to the extension process such as Albania, Georgia and Macedonia, as well as, maybe not surprisingly, Norway. In Poland and Northern Ireland, demographic context plays a more important role than attitudes. For a set of countries as diverse as Luxembourg, Ireland, Estonia, Lithuania, Slovakia, Bulgaria, Romania, Belarus and Armenia, none of the predictors have a strong impact. This is mostly an artefact of lacking variation in the dependent variable. In these countries voters are either overwhelmingly optimistic or pessimistic in their expectations or fears about the EU.

**A simplified model**

Does popular support for democracy in the respective member countries have an impact on the overall assessment of the EU along with variables tapping the demographic structure like age (young versus old) and urban versus rural? To that end, we have classified and identified all countries in the scatter plot in Figure 4.15 by juxtaposing the percentages of those who view the EU as beneficial with the combined impact not of the full model but of a simplified model, including all but one of the four independent variables in Figure 4.9. The question about household finances was asked rather sparingly (Tables 4.1.3–4.1.4, Appendix 4.1) and not at all in some countries of obvious relevance in the EU context, notably Austria, Finland and Sweden. At this stage of the analysis, we therefore decided to leave the item on household finances out of the model.

The countries fall into four categories defined by the quadrants of the diagram (Figure 4.15). In some countries (Group 1) a clear majority of respondents (more than 65 per cent) consider the EU to be beneficial and *they do so irrespective* of their assessment of democracy or democratic development in their own country, across age groups and independently of where they live; together these factors account for less than one fifth of the variation in the logistic regression model. Not surprisingly, this group contains many non-member countries, with populations eager to join the EU and situated in the vicinity of present member countries: Ukraine, Romania, Bulgaria, the Republic of Macedonia, Croatia, Albania and more remote Georgia and Armenia. Furthermore, this group contains some new members with populations still enthusiastic and hopeful of potential benefits to come from the EU; like Slovakia, Slovenia, Latvia and Lithuania. Two older member countries, Ireland and Greece, two indisputable winners in the process of European integration, can also be found in this group.

Luxembourg, a small city-belt country with little by way of demographic segmentation, also belongs here.

*Figure 4.15: Share of respondents who say their country has benefited or will benefit from EU membership by the impact of all the independent variables in the simplified model*

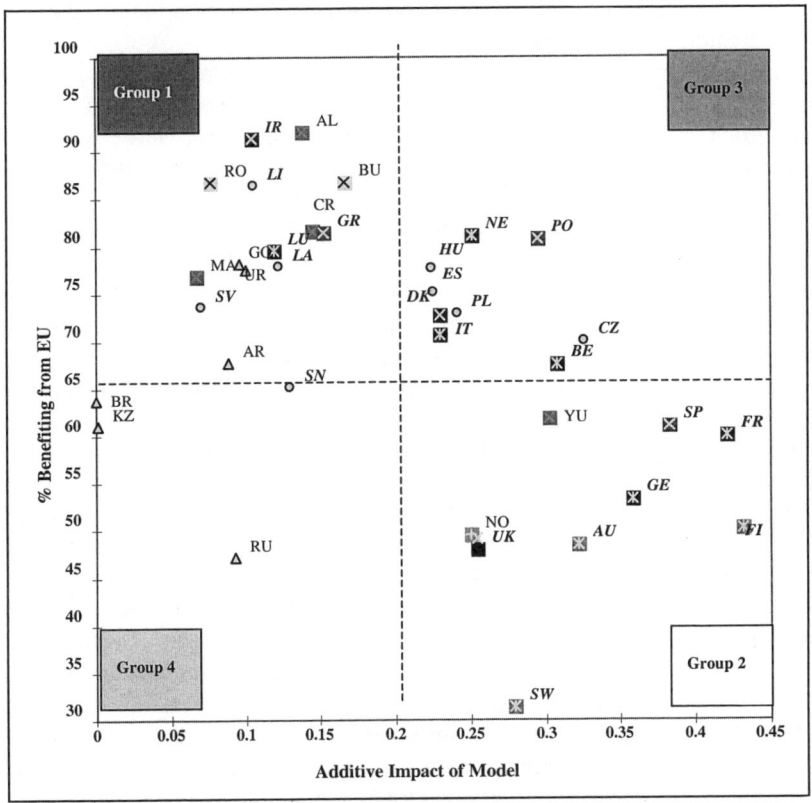

*Note*: Data from Table 4.13 and Table 4.1.2 in Appendix 4.1.

In the opposite corner, we have another group of countries (Group 2) where a minority or a marginal majority see the EU connection as an asset and where satisfaction with democracy, young age and urban location *have a combined impact which differentiates* among citizens. This group contains the major powers within the EU: Germany, France and the UK. Perhaps it stands to reason that citizens, who have traditionally looked upon their respective countries as 'a great power', will find it difficult to see something beneficial about a supranational organisation intruding on the territory of the nation-state. Spanish voters also seem to have adopted this attitude. Sweden and Austria, also former empire states, belong to the same group. Finland and Norway, both with a relatively short record of independence and wary of supranational commitments, land squarely in the same group. The former Yugoslavia, today the Federation of Serbia and Montenegro, may seem an odd case in the group, but it is probably psychologically difficult for many Serbs to consider joining an organisation featuring many of its enemies in a recent military conflict.

Group 3 counts only member countries with strong majority support for the EU as *beneficial* and where *citizens are differentiated* by variations in support for democracy and demographic position. Here we find 'sophisticated' old member states from the city belt: the Netherlands, Belgium and Italy; as well as the best adjusted of the new members: Poland, the Czech Republic, Hungary and Estonia – and two not-so-new members, Portugal and Denmark, sharing a past as former EFTA members. In the final analysis, however, the EFTA past probably weighs less heavily on them than their respective experiences within the EU. Portugal is in a sense easy to account for. It has a record an indisputable net winner of the flow of money within the Union. Denmark has a far more complicated relationship with the EU, marked by a series of referenda on about just every turning point in the history of the European Union, most recently about the Maastricht Treaty, which was first rejected by the Danish voters in a referendum of 2 June 1992 and then accepted in a new referendum on 18 May 1993, but only after the treaty had been renegotiated to allow the Danes to remain outside the Monetary Union for as long as they see fit. Danish referenda on binding international commitments such as the Maastricht Treaty are constitutionally mandatory; and barring constitutional amendments, there is no way that Danish governments could avoid them even if they would want to. In the long run, however, the recurring referenda may very well have contributed towards the high level of model differentiation in this particular case. Constantly recurring campaigns over EU-related issues leave their mark on long-term political commitments.

The last group (Group 4) comprises Russia, Belarus and Kazakhstan. Belarus's placement is almost self-explanatory, this being the only European country where transition to democracy has been put on hold. Relations between Belarus and the EU are currently marked by mutual suspicion, and Byelorussians know that EU membership will be out of reach at least for the duration of the current regime. Russia's and Kazakhstan's placement this low on perceived benefits from potential EU-membership can also be interpreted as a sign of political realism on part of their citizens. Satisfaction with democracy has a considerable impact on how Russians and Kazakhs perceive the EU, but this effect is almost totally eliminated by the opposite effect of urban residence. Ties with the EU are less likely to be perceived as an asset in the urban environment. The generally negative approach to the EU among Russians and Kazakhs actually makes perfect sense in the light of the proverbial story about the Fox and the Cherries: 'They are hanging too high and they are probably sour as well'.

## By Way of Conclusion

Citizens' evaluation of EU institutions is not a major consideration in the everyday politics of the EU. Normally the political initiative lies with the governmental elites of the Council, the elected representatives of the Parliament, the bureaucratic dons of the Commission and the legal minds of the Court. Whether this is good or bad largely depends on the perspective applied. Some Europeans are clamouring for more direct influence on the EU from its citizens. They complain about 'the democratic deficit' and advocate referenda as a mechanism for decision-making. Others are staunch believers in representative democracy and do not mind that decisions are made in the European Parliament, if they are Federalists, or support the present powers of the European Council or the Council of Ministers, if they prefer a Europe of Nations.

However, when referenda are held, the citizens' evaluation of institutional change is the very theme on the ballot. Some countries, notably Denmark and Ireland, have constitutions that require mandatory referenda in cases when institutional changes in the EU may infringe on national sovereignty as defined by the national constitution. Thus, Denmark and Ireland have held several referenda as the EU has undergone institutional change and the citizens of both countries are renowned for having rejected one treaty each. Countries where referenda are not mandatory, have occasionally resorted to referenda usually in order to gain additional legitimacy for institutional change. Often this strategy works, but occasionally it backfires; the Swedish referendum about adopting the Euro is a case in point. The ongoing ratification process for the European Constitution has been waylaid because if was rejected at the polls in the Netherlands and France in non-mandatory and advisory referenda.

More often than not when institutional changes in the EU are defeated at the polls, the results are explained in terms of the domestic political and/or economic situation. Thus, Dutch and French voters have not 'really' rejected the Constitution, but have merely seized the opportunity to express their dissatisfaction with, for example, the French President, high unemployment or Muslim immigration. Be that as it may, Figure 4.15 (above) may help us identify countries likely to question and mobilise against Brussels on the basis of dissatisfaction with democracy or the democratic development within each country. In our view, Groups 2 and 3 constitute high-risk groups in terms of ratification by referenda. Whatever the general level of specific support for the EU, the voters in these groups of countries combine their evaluation of EU benefits with their assessment of democracy at home. Dissatisfaction with the way democracy works at home may spill over on the evaluation of the EU. Political forces negative to institutional change may easily take advantage of this. If demographic factors such as age or urbanisation have additional effects, so much more the merrier for the opponents of European integration. It is noteworthy that countries which at one time or another have voted 'no' to membership or to institutional change include Norway, Denmark, Sweden, France and the Netherlands, all belonging to Groups 2 and 3. Moreover, in these two groups we also find countries where referenda have not been held, but where opinion polls have indicated popular majorities against the Constitution, the euro or both. Cases in point are Germany and the UK. In contrast, there is only one country with a historical 'no' vote in Group 1, Ireland. In this case we might add that the Irish 'no' to the Nice Accord was based on exceptionally low turnout and that the Irish reversed their decision in a later referendum (see Appendix: Chronology of European Integration). No wonder, then, that most countries in Groups 2 and 3 have a preference for ratification of new treaties with the European Union by parliament without asking the voters for guidance in popular referenda. This may of course be seen as defending the principle of representative democracy, but it may also be a virtue born out of necessity.

## NOTES

1. Many member states are reluctant to transfer authority to a federal parliament, where they account for just a small fraction of the MPs. There is also a fair amount of opposition within the union against the notion of a United States of Europe (see Chapter 7).
2. Some of the standard identification and attachment indicators have an implicit European dimension; others could easily be adapted to the European level. The standard pride item (proud of own country) could thus be transformed into an indicator tapping pride in Europe (proud of being European).
3. There is admittedly a great deal of variation within this group. With almost 50 per cent positive evaluations of the impact of EU membership, Finland is more than somewhat removed from predominantly negative Sweden.
4. Of the three factors listed, only proximity to the European continent differentiates Denmark from Great Britain. Sweden, Austria and Finland are more recent EU members than Denmark. The difference between the three former and the latter would thus seem to be a function of the duration of EU membership, early versus very recent.
5. Commitment to the premature closing and dismantling of Lithuania's most important source of energy, the nuclear power plant of Ignalina, was a steep price to pay for membership of the European Union (Duvold and Jurkynas 2004).
6. The wording of standard *Eurobarometer* questions like the benefit item of particular interest to us vary somewhat from one set of surveys to another (cf. Tables 4.1 and 4.4–4.5). Citizens of member states are asked: 'Taking everything into consideration, would you say that [our country] has on balance benefited or not from being a member of the European Union?' And respondents can say whether they feel they have benefited or not. Most surveys in non-member countries feature a similar item but with a different wording: 'Who do you think benefits the most out of the relationship between [our country] and the European Union? Is it the European Union, [our country] or do both equally benefit?' In our pooled dataset, quite a few countries have moved from

being non-members to becoming members throughout the period under investigation. In coding the data, we have tried to harmonise the responses by creating a dummy variable where citizens of member countries have been given the code '1' for answering that their country has benefited from EU membership and '0' if this is not the case. For citizens of non-member countries the responses that 'our country' and 'both our country and the EU' have benefited from the country's relationship to the EU have been coded as '1', whereas the response that 'the EU' (and therefore, not the country of which the respondent is a citizen) has benefited is coded as '0'.
7. Slovenia is also classified in this group, albeit as the highest-ranking member and very close to belonging to the first group of countries.
8. There is a special problem related to the response 'stayed the same'. The response 'stayed the same' can carry different connotations depending on the economic situation in the country at the point in time when the question was posed to the respondent. In a situation of economic decline, 'stayed the same' might well be a positive response, whereas in a situation of general economic growth the same response might be rather negative. Since economic growth and decline vary across countries and over time during the decade and a half of our investigation, we have chosen to omit respondents who have given this answer.
9. It is a weakness that there are no data available for Sweden, Austria and Finland. As mentioned above, these three countries are rather important since their citizens are among those who are the least inclined to see the EU as beneficial for their respective countries. We have therefore opted for two separate but related models – a model, including the question about financial situation and excluding the countries where this question was not part of the survey, and another model, also referred to as the simplified model including Sweden, Austria and Finland to the detriment of the question about finances, no longer in the model.
10. The Czech Republic, Latvia and Hungary are exceptions with a moderate impact of financial situation.

# REFERENCES

Beetham, David (1994), *Defining and Measuring Democracy*, London, Sage Publications.
Berezin, Mabel and Martin Schain, eds, (2003), *Europe without Borders: Remapping Territory: Citizenship and Identity in a Transnational Age*, Baltimore and London, The Johns Hopkins University Press.
Berglund, Sten (2003), 'The Consolidation of Democratic Governance in East Central Europe', *Journal of Japanese Political Science*, autumn 2003.
Berglund, Sten, Frank Aarebrot, Henri Vogt and Georgi Karasimeonov (2001), *Challenges to Democracy: Eastern Europe Ten Years after the Collapse of Communism*, Cheltenham, UK and Northampton, MA, USA, Edward Elgar.
Bohrnstedt, George W. and David Knoke (1988), *Statistics for Social Data Analysis*, 2nd edn, Itasca, Ill., F.E. Peacock Publishers.
*Candidate Countries Eurobarometer* 2001, 2002, 2003.2, 2003.4, 2004.1, Machine-readable data files and codebooks, Brussels, European Commission.
Degan-Krause, Kevin (2004), 'Slovakia', in Sten Berglund, Joakim Ekman and Frank Aarebrot, eds, *The Handbook of Political Change in Eastern Europe, Second Edition*, Cheltenham, UK and Northampton, MA, USA, Edward Elgar.
Dellenbrant, Jan-Åke and Sten Berglund (1987), 'The Baltic Republics: Years of Integration 1940-1980', Åbo, Åbo Akademi.
Duvold, Kjetil and Mindaugas Jurkynas (2004), 'Lithuania', in Sten Berglund, Joakim Ekman and Frank Aarebrot, eds, *The Handbook of Political Change in Eastern Europe, Second Edition*, Cheltenham, UK and Northampton, MA, USA, Edward Elgar.
Easton, David (1965a), *A Framework for Political Analysis*, New York, Prentice-Hall.
Easton, David, (1965b), *A Systems Analysis of Political Life*, New York, London and Sydney, John Wiley & Sons.

Ekman, Joakim and Jonas Linde (2005), 'Communist Nostalgia and the Consolidation of Democracy in Central and Eastern Europe', *Journal of Communist Studies and Transition Politics*, Vol. 21, Nr. 3, September 2005 issue, pp. 354–74.

Klingemann, Hans-Dieter (1999), 'Mapping Political Support in the 1990s: A Global Analysis', in Pippa Norris, ed., *Critical Citizens: Global Support for Democratic Governance*, Oxford, Oxford University Press.

Linde, Jonas (2004), *Doubting Democrats: A Comparative Analysis of Support for Democracy in Central and Eastern Europe*, Örebro, Örebro Studies in Political Science.

Linde, Jonas and Joakim Ekman (2003), 'Satisfaction with Democracy: A Note on a Frequently Used Indicator in Comparative Politics', *European Journal of Political Research*.

Lipset, Seymour Martin and Stein Rokkan, eds (1967), *Party Systems and Voter Alignments: Cross-National Perspectives, International Yearbook of Political Behavior Research 7*, New York, Free Press.

Mansfeldová, Zdenka (2004), 'The Czech Republic', in Sten Berglund, Joakim Ekman and Frank Aarebrot, eds, *The Handbook of Political Change in Eastern Europe, Second Edition*, Cheltenham, UK and Northampton, MA, USA, Edward Elgar.

Norris, Pippa (1999), 'Introduction: The Growth of Critical Citizens', in Pippa Norris, ed., *Critical Citizens: Global Support for Democratic Governance*, Oxford, Oxford University Press.

Rose, Richard (1996), *What is Europe? A Dynamic Perspective*, New York, Harper Collins Publishers.

Rose, Richard, William Mishler and Christian Haerpfer (1998), *Democracy and Its Alternatives: Understanding Post-Communist Societies*, Baltimore, The Johns Hopkins University Press.

Urwin, Derek W. (1980), *From Ploughshare to Ballotbox: The Politics of Agrarian Defence in Europe*, Oslo and New York, Universitetsforlaget, distributed by Columbia University Press.

Valen, Henry (1973), 'Norway: "No" to EEC', *Scandinavian Political Studies*, Vol. 8.

Valen, Henry and Kristen Ringdal (1998), 'Structural Divisions in the EU Referendums', in Anders Todal Jenssen, Pertti Pesonen and Mikael Giljam, eds, *To Join or not to Join*, Oslo, Scandinavian University Press.

## Appendix 4.1

*Table 4.1.1: Net logistic probability effects of a multivariate logistic regression model of EU benefit item on young age, urban context, satisfaction with democracy and a positive assessment of own financial situation*

| Country | N | Net logistic effects for the independent variables | | | |
|---|---|---|---|---|---|
| | | Sat. dem. | Pos. finsit. | Urban cmt. | Young age |
| France | 1 705 | 0.275 | 0.138 | 0.093 | 0.105 |
| Spain | 1 502 | 0.254 | 0.235 | 0.101 | n.s. |
| Germany (east) | 1 645 | 0.235 | 0.122 | 0.064 | n.s. |
| Yugoslavia | 572 | 0.218 | n.s. | n.s. | n.s. |
| Czech Republic | 915 | 0.207 | 0.138 | n.s. | n.s. |
| Denmark | 1 643 | 0.202 | 0.055 | n.s. | n.s. |
| Germany (west) | 1 093 | 0.195 | 0.187 | n.s. | 0.070 |
| Belgium | 1 375 | 0.192 | 0.222 | n.s. | 0.067 |
| Russia | 1 069 | 0.191 | 0.120 | n.s. | n.s. |
| Portugal | 1 782 | 0.178 | 0.151 | 0.059 | n.s. |
| Greece | 2 207 | 0.159 | 0.176 | n.s. | n.s. |
| Netherlands | 1 563 | 0.154 | 0.073 | 0.052 | 0.049 |
| Great Britain | 2 173 | 0.153 | 0.147 | n.s. | 0.111 |
| Slovenia | 1 012 | 0.140 | n.s. | n.s. | 0.064 |
| Italy | 1 439 | 0.129 | 0.159 | n.s. | n.s. |
| Hungary | 1 183 | 0.128 | 0.147 | n.s. | 0.064 |
| Ukraine | 983 | 0.111 | n.s. | –0.057 | n.s. |
| Kazakhstan | 1 076 | 0.110 | n.s. | –0.110 | n.s. |
| Latvia | 1 060 | 0.106 | 0.101 | n.s. | n.s. |
| Croatia | 901 | 0.102 | n.s. | 0.052 | n.s. |
| Georgia | 946 | 0.086 | 0.157 | n.s. | n.s. |
| Poland | 889 | 0.084 | n.s. | 0.097 | 0.099 |
| Estonia | 1 048 | 0.079 | n.s. | n.s. | n.s. |
| Albania | 1 463 | 0.070 | 0.107 | n.s. | n.s. |
| Macedonia | 974 | 0.066 | 0.100 | n.s. | n.s. |
| Lithuania | 872 | 0.061 | n.s. | n.s. | n.s. |
| Romania | 1 345 | 0.061 | 0.084 | n.s. | n.s. |
| Ireland | 1 787 | 0.057 | 0.038 | n.s. | 0.033 |
| Luxembourg | 529 | n.s. | 0.089 | n.s. | n.s. |
| Northern Ireland | 477 | n.s. | 0.092 | 0.135 | n.s. |
| Norway | 840 | n.s. | 0.123 | n.s. | n.s. |
| Armenia | 1 239 | n.s. | n.s. | 0.077 | n.s. |
| Belarus | 893 | n.s. | n.s. | n.s. | n.s. |
| Bulgaria | 991 | n.s. | n.s. | n.s. | 0.076 |
| Slovakia | 1 096 | n.s. | n.s. | n.s. | 0.085 |

Sign.: p > 0.05

*Table 4.1.2: Net logistic probability effects of a multivariate logistic regression mode of EU benefit item on young age, urban context and satisfaction with democracy*

| Country | N | Net logistic effects for the independent variables | | |
|---|---|---|---|---|
| | | Sat. Dem. | Urban cmt. | Young age |
| Spain | 11 827 | 0.263 | 0.050 | 0.070 |
| Czech Republic | 1 973 | 0.246 | n.s. | 0.080 |
| Germany (west) | 14 012 | 0.245 | 0.032 | 0.081 |
| Austria | 3 173 | 0.242 | n.s. | 0.08 |
| France | 11 720 | 0.239 | 0.066 | 0.116 |
| Denmark | 13 181 | 0.230 | n.s. | n.s. |
| Germany (east) | 8 256 | 0.229 | 0.047 | 0.059 |
| Yugoslavia | 827 | 0.221 | n.s. | 0.082 |
| Belgium | 11 614 | 0.197 | 0.026 | 0.085 |
| Russia | 1 506 | 0.192 | −0.099 | n.s. |
| Sweden | 3 022 | 0.187 | 0.092 | n.s. |
| Portugal | 12 790 | 0.184 | 0.038 | 0.073 |
| Finland | 5 848 | 0.180 | 0.123 | 0.129 |
| Hungary | 1 875 | 0.178 | n.s. | 0.046 |
| Italy | 11 981 | 0.161 | n.s. | 0.069 |
| Netherlands | 12 645 | 0.156 | n.s. | 0.095 |
| Greece | 13 045 | 0.155 | −0.019 | 0.017 |
| Norway | 4 368 | 0.143 | 0.107 | n.s. |
| Great Britain | 12 914 | 0.133 | n.s. | 0.121 |
| Slovenia | 2 461 | 0.130 | n.s. | n.s. |
| Latvia | 2 003 | 0.123 | n.s. | n.s. |
| Luxembourg | 5 981 | 0.120 | n.s. | n.s. |
| Macedonia | 1 600 | 0.116 | n.s. | -0.049 |
| Poland | 1 933 | 0.116 | 0.072 | 0.054 |
| Albania | 1 741 | 0.112 | n.s. | 0.027 |
| Kazakhstan | 1 436 | 0.106 | −0.105 | n.s. |
| Georgia | 1 402 | 0.101 | n.s. | n.s. |
| Estonia | 2 183 | 0.100 | 0.076 | 0.049 |
| Bulgaria | 1 762 | 0.099 | n.s. | 0.068 |
| Ukraine | 1 296 | 0.096 | n.s. | n.s. |
| Croatia | 1 588 | 0.094 | 0.051 | n.s. |
| Northern Ireland | 2 634 | 0.087 | 0.061 | 0.05 |
| Ireland | 12 881 | 0.086 | n.s. | 0.019 |
| Romania | 2 510 | 0.077 | n.s. | n.s. |
| Lithuania | 1 783 | 0.062 | 0.044 | n.s. |
| Armenia | 1 731 | n.s. | 0.089 | n.s. |
| Belarus | 1 315 | n.s. | n.s. | n.s. |
| Slovakia | 2 294 | n.s. | n.s. | 0.071 |

Sign.: p > 0.05

*Table 4.1.3: The availability of variables used in this study from the Eurobarometer trends and the CCEB datasets*

| Variables | West European trend | East European trend | CCEB 2001 1 | CEEB 2002 2 | CCEB 2003 1 | CCEB 2003 2 | CCEB 2003 3 | CEEB 2003 4 |
|---|---|---|---|---|---|---|---|---|
| Respondent age | X | X | X | X | X | X | X | X |
| Type of community | X | X | X | X | X | X | X | X |
| Country benefits from EU membership | X | | | | | | | |
| EU relation: who benefit | | X | | | | | | |
| Financial situation compared to last year | X | X | | | | | | |
| Statisfaction with democracy | X | X | | | X | | | |
| Satisfaction with democratic development | | X | | | | | | |

*Table 4.1.4: The availability of variables used in this study from some additional Eurobarometer datasets*

| Variables | EB 52 | EB 53 | EB 54 | EB 55 | EB 56 | EB 57 | EB 58 |
|---|---|---|---|---|---|---|---|
| Respondent age | X | X | X | X | X | X | X |
| Type of community | | | | X | X | X | X |
| Country benefits from EU membership | X | X | X | X | X | X | X |
| EU relation: Who benefit | | | | | | | |
| Financial situation compared to last year | | | | | | | |
| Statisfaction with Democracy | X | X | X | | X | | X |
| Satisfaction with democratic development | | | | | | | |

# 5. Support for Deeper Political Integration: The External Dimension

Foreign and security policies have traditionally belonged to the most vital tasks of nation-states. They have not been willing to give away too much of their power in these fields. This vitality is what justifies this chapter: if Europeans are willing to cooperate in foreign and security policy, they are presumably also willing to deepen their cooperation in other fields. Indeed, the development of the Union's external and security dimensions – and people's attitudes to them – establishes the outer limits of integration, perhaps more clearly than any other policy dimension.

Public opinion generally defines the acceptable boundaries of politics, and stakes out the space within which political elites can resolve controversies (Dalton 1988, 2; 2002; Sinnott 1995, 11). As regards the EU's external dimension, the crucial issue is in what way public opinion constrains or shapes the possibilities to create a Union that can act with one voice in world politics. This would entail a Union that balances the global ambitions of the US, Russia and China, and – ideally – a Union that promotes development, democratic values and respect for human rights throughout the world. It would also entail a common European foreign and security policy identity. As we saw in the previous chapter, the emergence of such a common identity is by no means self-evident. Even a rather vaguely defined unifying identity for the EU member states has proven hard to cultivate (cf. Duchesne and Frognier 1995). Or rather, we found a basic attachment to 'Europe', but national interests nevertheless persist – and usually dominate.

Like the previous chapter, the present chapter draws on the major European cross-national public opinion surveys, above all the *Eurobarometers* and the *Candidate Countries Eurobarometers* and explores the overall support for the European Union as a global political actor from a bottom-up or citizens' perspective.[1] It is noteworthy that this kind of perspective has been to a large extent neglected in the literature, although the external affairs of the Union have generated a great deal of scholarly interest in recent years (Soetendorp 1999; Smith 1999; 2003; Holland 2004;

Smith 2004; Christiansen and Tonra 2004). This may, of course, be seen as a reflection of the traditionally elite-driven nature of foreign and security policies. Given the problems that the EU has had with its democratic record, however, it seems self-evident to us that the views of 'ordinary' Europeans should matter much more than they currently do in this respect.

The analysis breaks down into four sections, each of which focuses on a different external policy field of the EU, although there is also some overlap between these fields; the global role and the foreign policy of the EU are not always separate issues. The first section briefly reviews the development of the EU's common foreign policy and proceeds with an empirical analysis of how people see it. The second section deals with European defence and security policy. The US and transatlantic relations are covered in the third section, while enlargement and the borders of the EU are analysed in the fourth part. In the concluding section, we explore the implications of people's common foreign policy attitudes in terms of diffuse and specific support for the EU as a political system.

**A Common Foreign Policy?**

In 1991, at the outbreak of the war in the former Yugoslavia, Luxembourg's Foreign Minister Jacques Poos declared that 'the hour of Europe' had dawned (as opposed to the hour of the Americans). The Cold War had come to an end, and from now, 'Europe' would take care of its own business; it was Europe's task to bring about a ceasefire in the Balkans. This optimism proved premature, however. Almost four years of failed peace negotiations would follow, the full outbreak of war, ethnic cleansing and mass killings – and 'Europe' was unable to stop it. Not until the United States chose to enter the stage could the war come to an end. A *Pax Americana* (the Dayton Agreement) was concluded in November 1995. The EU had failed, or in any case showed the world that 'Europe' was not yet a force to be reckoned with in international affairs. Europe could not 'speak with one voice' and it did not have the (military) means to back up its will (cf. Silber and Little 1996, 159; George and Bache 2001, 399; Bale 2005, 253).

This failure reinforced the need to create a Common Foreign and Security Policy (CSFP) at the European regional level. Only a few months after the outbreak of the Bosnian war, this policy was initiated in the Treaty of the European Union (1992) in a very unambiguous manner (section 5, article 11, paragraphs 1 and 2): 'The Union shall establish and conduct a common foreign and security policy that comprises all areas within foreign and security policy [...] The member states shall in an active and unconditional manner support the Union's foreign and security policy in a spirit of loyalty and mutual solidarity'. The CFSP has subsequently been reinforced through the introduction of more coherent instruments and more efficient decision-making (in the Amsterdam Treaty and the Nice Treaty).

The EU also has a High Representative for the Common Foreign and Security Policy, a post currently held by Mr Javier Solana (cf. Soetendorp 1999; Smith 2004). In 1999, the EU also assumed a more explicitly military dimension into its sphere of activities, by initiating the European Security and Defence Policy (ESDP).

In reality, however, these policy instruments have not fulfilled the expectations attached to them. For example, the EU was incapable of decisive action in February 1996, when Greece and Turkey quarrelled over the Imia islands in the Adriatic; and again in the 1997 refugee crisis following Albania's economic collapse. Furthermore, the crisis in Kosovo in 1998–99 saw NATO and UN action, while the EU appeared weak, far from the image of the EU as an influential actor in world politics envisaged in the Maastricht Treaty (cf. Bale 2005, 259–62). The biggest blow came in the spring of 2003, however, when the campaign against Iraq seriously undermined the ability of EU leaders to join forces and speak with one voice in world politics. Tony Blair and José Maria Aznar broke ranks with Gerhard Schröder and Jacques Chirac, and supported US President Bush in his plans to invade Iraq. The remaining EU member states were divided on this issue. Some countries, like Italy, the Netherlands and Denmark supported the war, while Sweden, for example, opposed an armed conflict. The then candidate countries were generally more favourably disposed towards US action than the 15 countries already in the Union; thence the distinction between 'new' and 'old' Europe promoted by the Bush administration.

The war on Iraq – just like the Balkan wars – demonstrated the present limitations of the EU as a global actor. The member states of the EU have successfully managed to stick together when it comes to economic issues (i.e. trade), perhaps even showing solidarity on environmental issues and aid.[2] But 'high politics' remains a difficult issue (Bomberg and Stubb 2003, 195–213; Holland 2004; Christiansen and Tonra 2004). Above all, it remains unclear what 'European foreign policy' actually stands for, since it (for the time being, anyway) seems to encompass almost all of what the EU *and* its member states do or say in world politics (Hill 1996; 1998; Bretherton and Vogler 1999; Peterson and Smith 2003, 196–98; Smith 1999; 2003; McCormick 2002; Bale 2005, 259–62).

However, in recent efforts to redesign the Union and its institutions, foreign and security policies and the Union's global agenda more generally, have played an essential role, much more so than in the negotiations that led to the Treaty of the European Union. The EU's determination to shoulder a larger share in the responsibility for global security has become more and more evident, and it seeks to further strengthen its position in various global regimes. The Draft Constitution clearly reflects these ambitions. The Constitution gives the EU competence to define and implement a common foreign and security policy as well as a common defence and security policy. This policy should be based on 'mutual political solidarity' among the member states, that is, identification of common interests and convergence of actions. Also, the idea is to create a Union with a common strategy in world politics. Articles 4 and 5 of the Draft state:

> In its relations with the wider world, the Union shall uphold and promote its values and interests. It shall contribute to peace, security, the sustainable development of the Earth, solidarity and mutual respect among peoples, free and fair trade, eradication of poverty and the protection of human rights, in particular the rights of the child, as well as to the strict observance and the development of international law, including respect for the principles of the United Nations Charter. [...] The Union shall pursue its objectives by appropriate means commensurate with the competences which are conferred upon it in the Constitution.

In institutional terms, the Constitution makes two particularly significant amendments to the provisions of earlier treaties: the creation of a new institution, a Minister of Foreign Affairs, and the creation of a European External Action Service. The Minister of Foreign Affairs will de facto become the voice of the CFSP – if and when the Constitution is ratified.

**Public support for a common foreign policy**
What about public opinion, then? Do Europeans in general appreciate the need for a common European foreign policy; do they accept that issues like security, defence and foreign policy are transferred from the national to the European level? Table 5.1 lists the 15 old EU member states, the 10 new member states, and the remaining candidate countries – Turkey, Bulgaria, and Romania – with respect to public support for and opposition to a common European foreign policy in 2004.

At first glance, a rather diverse picture seems to emerge. The UK stands out as the most sceptical country in the sample, with 39 per cent explicitly against the notion of a common foreign policy for the EU members, and only 39 per cent in favour. The Nordic countries – Sweden, Denmark, and Finland – score high on the Eurosceptical dimension as well. Still, a majority – 65 per cent of the respondents in the old EU member countries – is in fact *in favour* of a common EU foreign policy; only 22 per cent are against it. Among the core EU countries – France, Germany, Italy and the Benelux countries – the percentages 'in favour' range between 66 and 77 per cent (Table 5.1). It may also be noted that the average support for a common foreign policy has stayed at about the same level since 1994, although the share of critical respondents has increased somewhat (cf. *Eurobarometer* 61).

Also in the new EU member states, the majority of citizens (68 per cent) is in favour of a common EU foreign policy. There are significant cross-national differences, however: in the Czech Republic, Estonia and Malta, almost 25 per cent of respondents are explicitly *against* a common foreign policy; in Slovakia and Slovenia, around 75 per cent are explicitly in favour of it. In the two post-communist countries left outside the 2004 expansion wave – Bulgaria and Romania – 74 per cent of respondents are 'in favour'. In Cyprus, the corresponding figure is 81 per cent. Not surprisingly, Turkey has a large share of undecided citizens, with 47 per cent 'in favour' and 17 per cent 'against' (Table 5.1).

*Table 5.1: Opinions on a common foreign policy (%)*

| 15 old EU member states | 2004 EU member states | Remaining EU candidates | Against | In favour |
|---|---|---|---|---|
| Sweden | | | 44 | 49 |
| UK | | | 39 | 39 |
| Denmark | | | 39 | 50 |
| Finland | | | 36 | 55 |
| | Malta | | 24 | 50 |
| | Czech Republic | | 23 | 57 |
| | Estonia | | 23 | 62 |
| France | | | 22 | 66 |
| Austria | | | 21 | 62 |
| Netherlands | | | 21 | 69 |
| Portugal | | | 18 | 62 |
| | | Turkey | 17 | 47 |
| | Latvia | | 17 | 67 |
| Spain | | | 17 | 69 |
| Belgium | | | 17 | 71 |
| Ireland | | | 16 | 66 |
| | Poland | | 16 | 70 |
| Germany | | | 16 | 74 |
| | Hungary | | 14 | 70 |
| | Slovakia | | 14 | 74 |
| | Slovenia | | 14 | 76 |
| Greece | | | 14 | 78 |
| Luxembourg | | | 13 | 77 |
| Italy | | | 12 | 77 |
| | Lithuania | | 10 | 61 |
| | Cyprus | | 9 | 81 |
| | | Bulgaria | 6 | 74 |
| | | Romania | 6 | 74 |

Sources: *Eurobarometer* 61 (February–March 2004) and *Candidate Countries Eurobarometer* 2004.1 (February–March 2004). The full question reads: 'What is your opinion on the following statement? Please tell me whether you are for it or against it: One common foreign policy among the member states of the European Union, towards other countries'.

All in all, a majority of all respondents support the idea of a common EU foreign policy, in the old as well as in the new EU member states, but there are marked differences between the countries. What is more, the differences seem to form a pattern reminiscent of that in Figure 4.5 in the previous chapter. The figure provides a summary of generalised opposition to EU membership in the 15 old member states (1991–2004), in the 10 new member states and the candidate countries (2001–2004). We found that the older member states in Western Europe – the Benelux countries and Germany and France, alongside Southern Europe (Italy, Spain, Portugal, and Greece) and Ireland (including Northern Ireland), harboured relatively few opponents to EU membership. The Eurosceptics were basically found in non-continental Europe – in Great Britain, the Nordic countries (Denmark, Sweden, Norway, and Finland) as well as in Austria. As for the new member states, a more diverse picture was found. The most Eurosceptical voices were found in Malta, Latvia, Estonia and the Czech Republic. In the remaining countries, articulate opposition was not particularly widespread.

Returning to Table 5.1, we find that hesitation regarding a European foreign policy is most common in countries that are generally Eurosceptical – Finland, Denmark, Sweden and the UK (cf. Figure 4.5). Conversely, 'pro-common-foreign-policy' attitudes seem to be combined with a general pro-EU stance. This indicates that support for a common European foreign policy – and perhaps support for an active EU in world politics as well – correlates with respondents' general attitudes towards the EU. This, in turn, might arguably be seen as an outcome of actual experience with European integration.

Is the same pattern valid for the new EU member states and the candidate countries? Arguably, yes (cf. Fawn 2003). The most Eurosceptical countries among the new EU members – Malta, Latvia, Estonia and the Czech Republic – are found at the higher end of the 'against-the-common-foreign-policy' continuum in Table 5.1. The expected pattern is admittedly somewhat obscured by Latvia's 'middle' position. Furthermore, we would have expected somewhat less support for a common European foreign policy in Cyprus, and perhaps a little more support in Turkey, given the outcome in Figure 4.5. But all things considered, the outcome is not inconsistent with the formula presented above: support for a Union speaking and acting as one in world affairs seems to be closely related to generalised support for the EU as such.

Table 5.2 provides some empirical evidence about this relationship in the old member states. We have simply cross-tabulated survey items measuring attitudes towards the EU with questions dealing with the international role of the EU. The first item is basically the same item as in Table 5.1 (although we have had to use somewhat older surveys): support for a common foreign policy among the member states of the EU. In the 15 old EU member states, a total of 67 per cent are in favour (spring 2003). Controlling for pro/contra EU attitudes, we find that among those EU citizens who feel that membership of the EU is 'a good thing', as many as 79 per cent are in favour of a common foreign policy. The corresponding figure for the second item is 82 per cent (support for a common defence and security policy). The third item – 'the European Union being responsible for matters that cannot be effectively handled by national, regional and local governments' – gives basically the same result. Respondents who find membership in the EU to be 'a good thing' are also inclined to support a Union with significant global influence.

*Table 5.2: Attitudes towards the EU as an international actor by support for EU membership in EU15 (%)*

|  |  | Membership of the EU | | |
| --- | --- | --- | --- | --- |
|  |  | ...a good thing | ...a bad thing | Total |
| A common foreign policy? (CFSP) | For | 79 | 39 | 67 |
|  | Against | 13 | 48 | 20 |
| A common defence and security policy? (ESDP) | For | 82 | 44 | 70 |
|  | Against | 12 | 45 | 18 |
| More responsibility to the EU? | For | 75 | 44 | 65 |
|  | Against | 13 | 39 | 18 |

Source: *Eurobarometer* 59.1 (March–April 2003). The full column question reads: 'Generally speaking, do you think that our country's membership of the European Union is a good thing, a bad thing, or neither good nor bad?' Note that the categories 'neither good nor bad' and 'don't know' have been excluded. The full row question reads: 'What is your opinion on each of the following statements? Please tell me for each statement, whether you are for it or against it: One common foreign policy among the member states of the European Union, towards other countries; A common defence and security policy among European Union member states; The European Union being responsible for matters that cannot be effectively handled by national, regional and local governments.' N = 16 307.

The outcome is thus in one respect very clear, even surprisingly clear: it seems that more than three-quarters of those citizens who find membership of the EU to be 'a good thing' also support the efforts to create a common foreign policy for Union members. However, it is interesting to see that those who are in principle against EU membership easily assume what can possibly be interpreted as a pragmatic approach towards EU foreign policy. Almost half of them seem to think that 'as our country has decided to cooperate in the Union context, a common foreign and security policy is a natural part of this cooperation'.

**Public Support for a Common Defence Policy**

Intuitively, we could expect the European Security and Defence Policy (ESDP) to be the most sensitive part of the CFSP for EU citizens; security and defence have traditionally been *the* core function of the nation-state. It is thus not surprising that the ESDP is a latecomer on the Union agenda. We need to remember, however, that security cooperation within the European integration process has been of secondary importance until fairly recently. NATO has been, ever since it was founded in 1949, the primary mechanism of military cooperation in Europe. After the end of communism, it was equally, if not more, important for the countries of Eastern Europe to join the transatlantic framework as it was to join the EU.

The idea of a common European security system had already emerged during the early years of the Cold War. In 1948, France, the UK and the Benelux countries signed the Treaty on Economic, Social and Cultural Collaboration and Collective Self-Defence in Brussels. The Treaty developed into the Western European Union, founded by these countries, Italy and West Germany in 1954. The idea of common security policy then survived within the WEU and later within the framework of the informal European Political Cooperation (EPC), launched in 1970.

But it was not until the crisis in Yugoslavia in the early 1990s that the question re-emerged (cf. Howorth and Keeler 2003; Bale 2005, 258). In St Malo in 1998, France and the UK officially decided to bring military issues on to the EU agenda, after decades of British resistance. Only a year later, in the Helsinki Summit of December 1999, the Council decided to start developing 'the Union's military and non-military crisis management capability as part of a strengthened common European policy on security and defence' (www.iss-eu.org). The Union also decided to create its own rapid reaction forces of some 60 000 troops. The first EU-led military operation was carried out in Macedonia in 2003.

*Table 5.3: Share of respondents per country 'against' a common defence and security policy*

| 0–10 per cent | 11–24 per cent | 25 + per cent |
|---|---|---|
| Cyprus (2) | Czech Republic (11) | Austria (28) |
| Romania (3) | Greece (12) | UK (28) |
| Bulgaria (4) | Germany (12) | Denmark (31) |
| Italy (7) | Estonia (13) | Finland (35) |
| Hungary (7) | Spain (13) | Sweden (38) |
| Slovakia (7) | Slovenia (14) | |
| Lithuania (8) | Belgium (14) | |
| Luxembourg (10) | Portugal (14) | |
| Poland (10) | France (16) | |
| Latvia (10) | Netherlands (16) | |
| | Turkey (16) | |
| | Malta (18) | |
| | Ireland (21) | |

Sources: *Eurobarometer* 61 (February–March 2004) and *Candidate Countries Eurobarometer* 2004.1 (February–March 2004). The full question reads: 'What is your opinion on the following statement? Please tell me whether you are for it or against it: A common defence and security policy among the European Union member states'.

In Table 5.3, we have summarized the share of critical respondents concerning the ESDP in the 28 EU member states and candidate countries. The overall picture is clear: public opposition to a European defence policy is not particularly pronounced within the Union today. The level of criticism is basically at the same low level as in the case of the CFSP. Thus, 72 per cent of the citizens in the old member states and 79 per cent of the citizens of the new member states support the notion of a common European defence and security policy (*Eurobarometer* 61; *Candidate Countries Eurobarometer* 2004.1). This may seem surprising at first sight but there are several rather evident explanations for it: owing to NATO and its convincing military capacity, military cooperation across the continent is seen as 'normal' and the role of the EU still appears insignificant. Moreover, as this survey was conducted during the controversial war in Iraq, we could wonder to what extent the hope that an alternative to NATO – or to the US – would emerge is reflected in their answers.

The cross-national pattern of scepticism that we have encountered before is manifest here as well, however. The Eurosceptical countries are – as expected – found to be the most critical countries: Austria, Sweden, Finland, Denmark, and the UK. It is noteworthy that the three first of these countries have a long tradition of neutrality/non-alignment, which clearly has made their citizens critical about giving away their independent military decision-making power. On the other hand, in the generally Eurofriendly countries – for example, Romania, Bulgaria, Italy, Luxembourg and Slovakia – we find very few critical voices. Ireland is the most obvious deviant case. Despite being one of the most Eurofriendly countries within the Union today (cf. Figure 4.5), as many as 21 per cent of the Irish respondents are against a common European defence policy (Table 5.3). In the absence of a better explanation, this may owe to the long tradition of non-alignment that has obviously served the country well.

It is also interesting to note that Eurosceptical Estonia and Latvia have rather few opponents to a common defence policy. In both countries, only some 10 per cent are against the ESDP, but twice as many think of their country's EU membership in negative terms (Figure 4.5). The delicate geo-politics of these two countries may go a long way towards accounting for this popularity. Two points are noteworthy. First, the Russian-speaking minorities – many of the Russians are still non-citizens – remain a significant problem in this part of Europe, a problem that Russian authorities often refer to in their negotiations with the EU.[3] Second, the eastward enlargement of the EU has unavoidably contributed to Russia's new and complicated geo-political situation; the feelings of insecurity and fear that Russia traditionally inspires in the small Baltic states are therefore not likely to lose momentum and abate any time soon.

The opinion surveys utilized here contain a few more items, which may be used to assess levels of support for a common defence policy within EU25. For example, when asked about whether the national governments, NATO or the EU should make the final policy decisions regarding European defence, the Union turned out to be the most trusted actor. 46 per cent of 'old' Europe opted for the EU, 25 per cent for their respective governments, and 14 per cent for NATO. The 10 new members are somewhat less enthusiastic about the EU (40 per cent), and somewhat more supportive of their respective national governments (27 per cent) and NATO (18 per cent).

## Support for 'one voice' in world politics

The empirical investigation in the first part of this chapter demonstrated that – for the time being – a clear majority of EU citizens in all member countries seem to accept the notions of common European foreign, defence and security policies. As we have seen, differences between countries may to some extent be attributed to citizens' overall assessments of the EU, and other country-specific factors. The small differences between 'old' and 'new' Europe stand in stark contrast to the rather significant differences in official policy that became visible during the Iraq crisis in 2002–03.

*Table 5.4: Support for a common European voice in world politics (%)*

| Elements | 15 old EU member states | 10 new EU member states |
| --- | --- | --- |
| When an international crisis occurs, EU member states should agree a common position | 81 | 83 |
| The EU should guarantee human rights in each member state, even if this is contrary to the wishes of some member states | 79 | 80 |
| EU foreign policy should be independent of United States foreign policy | 77 | 75 |
| The EU should work to guarantee human rights around the world, even if this is contrary to the wishes of some other countries | 76 | 67 |
| The EU should have a rapid military reaction force that can be sent quickly to trouble spots when an international crisis occurs | 70 | 72 |
| The EU should have its own seat in the United Nations Security Council | 65 | 62 |
| The EU should have its own Foreign Minister, who can be the spokesperson for a common EU position | 64 | 61 |

Sources: *Eurobarometer* 61 (February–March 2004) and *Candidate Countries Eurobarometer* 2004.1 (February–March 2004). The full question reads: 'The European Union already has a Common Foreign and Security Policy and a European Security and Defence Policy. There is now a debate how much further these should be developed. Do you tend to agree or tend to disagree with each of the following statements?' The percentages indicate the share of affirmative respondents.

In Table 5.4, we continue the analysis of the differences between these groups of countries by using a battery of questions tapping people's attitudes to a common European voice in world politics. As a rule, the table confirms our previous findings; differences are not pronounced. On one item after another, citizens in the east as well as in the west lend support to various elements of a common European foreign policy.

It is particularly interesting that eight out of ten EU citizens agree that an international crisis justifies a common EU position. When it comes to the specific implementation of such a common position, the EU citizens are a bit more hesitant. Still, a respectable 64 per cent (EU15) and 61 per cent (in the new member states) agree that the EU should have its own Foreign Minister, and approximately as many that the EU should have its own seat in the United Nations Security Council. Over 70 per cent of the EU citizens accept a European military reaction force.

Some 80 per cent of the respondents feel that the EU has a responsibility to guarantee human rights within the Union, even if this should be contrary to the wishes of individual member states. Opinions are more divided when it comes to the EU's global responsibility to promote human rights. Seventy-six per cent of citizens in the old member states and 67 per cent in the new member states agree that the EU has such a responsibility. Finally, about three-quarters (75–77 per cent) of EU citizens think that EU foreign policy should be independent of US foreign policy. Thus, the overall conclusion here is that Europeans' are clearly in favour of an active role for the Union in the world. At the same time, as made evident by the last item mentioned here, this role should be different from that of the current United States. This will be the topic of the next empirical section.

Before we move on, however, the findings of this section should be put into context by drawing attention to the relative importance of a common foreign and security policy. In the standard *Eurobarometer* surveys, respondents are regularly asked about the most important issues facing their own country at the moment. When polled in the autumn of 2004, unemployment (46 per cent), the economic situation (27 per cent) and crime (24 per cent) were the most common answers. No more than 2 per cent identified defence/foreign policy as a timely issue (*Eurobarometer* 62). It would thus seem that foreign policy, in the minds of most citizens, is a fairly abstract or remote policy field. From this perspective, public support for the CFSP and the ESDP may very well be labelled as uninformed support. It is possible that citizens lend support for these particular policy fields without knowing (or caring) too much about them (cf. Manigart 2001).

Still, the foreign policy dimension is not totally void of meaning. When asked about what the EU means to the respondents personally, the item 'a stronger say in the world' was picked by a respectable 26 per cent of citizens in the new member states, and by 28 per cent of citizens in the old member states. The top ranking among the new member states were freedom of movement (62 per cent), the euro (45 per cent), and peace (37 per cent). The corresponding figures for the old members were 51 per cent, 50 per cent and 31 per cent, respectively (*Eurobarometer* 61; *Candidate Countries Eurobarometer* 2004.1). Thus, it does make sense to measure public opinion on foreign policy issues; but we are all the same well advised to use the figures cautiously.

**The EU and the US**

Following the Second World War, the United States helped re-build Western Europe. The communist threat from the east justified a continued American presence on the continent. For the US and NATO, it was always a matter of 'keeping the Russians out, the Germans down and the Americans in' (cf. Lundestad 1998). The West European governments warmly welcomed this military – and ideological – presence, with the exception of France perhaps. A transatlantic community was established.

This US presence was, of course, regularly contested over the years. For example, in the late 1960s anti-American sentiments spread throughout Western Europe along with the ideas of the New Left, the criticism of capitalism and liberal democracy in general and the Vietnam War in particular. The peace- and environmental movements of the 1970s and 1980s in many respects inherited this anti-American platform, although as it became more and more apparent that the US was to win the Cold War, these sentiments gradually waned. However, the collapse of the communist regimes in Central and Eastern Europe in the late 1980s and early 1990s quickly changed the whole security constellation in Europe, which led many to ask whether the US presence in the continent was still justified.

In the spring of 1999, the NATO bombings of the former Yugoslavia again fuelled US-critical voices in Europe, although most European governments actually backed the NATO action. The Iraq war in 2003, then, brought the transatlantic relations into a deep crisis (Peterson and Pollack 2003; Markovits 2005). Even if some EU leaders, above all Tony Blair, sided with the Bush administration, critical voices were raised all over Europe at the time, among political elites as well as among ordinary citizens, and across the whole left–right political spectrum. The anti-war-on-Iraq demonstrations of 15 February 2003 gathered several million people in the main squares of the European capitals. Today (2005), these anti-American feelings still appear strong, although the most difficult phase is probably over. The crucial question for the future is in any case whether the post-war transatlantic friendship is slowly coming to its end (cf. Heilbrunn 1996; Fulbrook 1999, 168–9, 208–9; Janning 1999, 345–9; Markovits 2005; Bale 2005, 251).

## The US as a threat?

So how widespread have the anti-American sentiments been among the European publics in the aftermath of 9/11 and the Iraq war? The *Flash Eurobarometer* 151 – conducted in the autumn of 2003 in the 15 old EU member states – included a question tapping respondents' perceptions of threats to world peace: 'For each of the following countries, tell me if in your opinion, it presents or not a threat to peace in the world?' In Table 5.5, we have listed the affirmative percentages for each given country. The outcome should of course be treated with caution, but it nevertheless gives us a general idea about perceived threats among the EU citizens, from the mental horizon of October 2003.[4]

*Table 5.5: Countries perceived as a threat to peace in the world (%)*

|  | SP | SE | GR | F | I | A | FIN | B | DK | G | P | UK | IRL | L | NL | EU 15 |
|---|---|---|---|---|---|---|---|---|---|---|---|---|---|---|---|---|
| Israel | 56 | 52 | 61 | 55 | 48 | 69 | 60 | 63 | 64 | 65 | 55 | 60 | 62 | 66 | 74 | 59 |
| Iran | 41 | 44 | 26 | 55 | 58 | 49 | 48 | 54 | 55 | 57 | 56 | 54 | 54 | 62 | 64 | 53 |
| North Korea | 37 | 49 | 30 | 49 | 42 | 69 | 57 | 49 | 63 | 65 | 59 | 59 | 66 | 65 | 70 | 53 |
| United States | 61 | 54 | 88 | 52 | 43 | 63 | 63 | 59 | 52 | 45 | 53 | 55 | 60 | 55 | 64 | 53 |
| Iraq | 42 | 41 | 27 | 50 | 55 | 45 | 53 | 54 | 50 | 57 | 59 | 54 | 54 | 56 | 61 | 52 |
| Afghanistan | 36 | 36 | 23 | 50 | 58 | 40 | 44 | 48 | 47 | 54 | 54 | 49 | 55 | 54 | 61 | 50 |
| Pakistan | 38 | 41 | 23 | 53 | 49 | 53 | 39 | 46 | 46 | 52 | 48 | 44 | 50 | 57 | 58 | 48 |
| Syria | 25 | 29 | 17 | 44 | 41 | 36 | 25 | 37 | 35 | 35 | 40 | 41 | 37 | 44 | 51 | 37 |
| Libya | 24 | 29 | 13 | 42 | 27 | 33 | 34 | 37 | 33 | 39 | 42 | 43 | 40 | 42 | 52 | 36 |
| Saudi Arabia | 32 | 23 | 25 | 44 | 37 | 33 | 29 | 40 | 38 | 31 | 45 | 34 | 38 | 41 | 43 | 36 |
| China | 27 | 27 | 28 | 24 | 27 | 32 | 31 | 29 | 36 | 26 | 39 | 40 | 37 | 36 | 43 | 30 |
| India | 13 | 22 | 14 | 20 | 18 | 26 | 23 | 23 | 24 | 22 | 26 | 28 | 27 | 28 | 34 | 22 |
| Russia | 19 | 19 | 23 | 20 | 16 | 24 | 29 | 21 | 23 | 19 | 30 | 27 | 31 | 27 | 25 | 21 |
| Somalia | 6 | 11 | 7 | 15 | 19 | 15 | 10 | 11 | 13 | 17 | 24 | 20 | 17 | 20 | 20 | 16 |
| EU | 9 | 11 | 14 | 6 | 5 | 3 | 6 | 8 | 9 | 4 | 13 | 18 | 12 | 6 | 7 | 8 |

*Source*: Flash Eurobarometer 151 (2003a) 'Iraq and Peace in the World'. The item reads: 'For each of the following countries, tell me if in your opinion, it presents or not a threat to peace in the world?'

*Notes*: Spain (SP), Sweden (SE), Greece (GR), France (F), Italy (I), Austria (A), Finland (FIN), Belgium (B), Denmark (DK), Germany (G), Portugal (P), United Kingdom (UK), Ireland (IRL), Luxembourg (L), Netherlands (NL), and the average for the 15 old member states (EU15).

Among the old EU member states, 53 per cent see the US as a threat, hardly flattering for the Bush administration. The country is on a par with Iran and North Korea (53 per cent, respectively), and ironically, actually scores higher than both Iraq (52 per cent) and Afghanistan (50 per cent). Only Israel, a close ally of the US, is seen as a bigger threat. In all countries, save Italy, a *majority* of citizens feel that Israel is a threat to peace in the world – not surprisingly given the recent media coverage on killings, suicide bombings, and the building of the so-called security wall on the West Bank.

The traditional Cold War enemies and nuclear weapon states – Russia

(21 per cent), China (30 per cent) and India (22 per cent) – stand out as rather moderate threats to peace in the world, according to this opinion survey. The only Sub-Saharan African country included here – Somalia – is perceived as a threat by a meagre 16 per cent of the citizens of the EU. The Middle East countries Syria, Libya and Saudi Arabia score higher (around 36 per cent), doubtless an effect of 9/11 and the perceived threat of terrorism.

Greece, Spain, Finland and Sweden are the most US-sceptical countries in the Union, but even in allied countries in the Iraq war, a majority of citizens share the opinion that the US poses a threat to peace in the world: in Spain 61 per cent, and in the UK 55 per cent. In fact, only Germany and Italy have majorities of the opposite opinion: 52 per cent of Germans and 55 per cent of Italians do *not* perceive the US as a threat, which is somewhat surprising given the strong opposition to the Iraq war in these countries. In Germany, this opposition even made possible for Chancellor Gerhard Schröder to renew his mandate in the parliamentary elections of autumn 2002.

All in all, it seems that people's country-related threat perceptions are indeed heavily influenced by the war on Iraq and the threat of international terrorism. When polled in the spring of 2003, international terrorism was at the top of the EU citizens' 'fear list'. Eight out of ten Europeans in the 15 old member states claimed to fear international terrorism (*Eurobarometer* 59.1). In the same *Flash Eurobarometer* that we have used in Table 5.5, respondents were explicitly asked about the righteousness of the war. No less than 68 per cent of EU citizens were of the opinion that the military intervention was not justified.

**The US as a global actor**
In the autumn of 2003, another *Flash Eurobarometer* survey was conducted in the 15 old member states, dealing with the issue of (economic) globalisation, defined as 'the general opening-up of all economies, which leads to the creation of a truly world wide market'. The respondents were presented with this definition in the survey moment, and subsequently asked to assess the influence of a number of actors on the globalisation process.

Three out of four EU citizens feel that the US exercises too much influence on the process of globalisation. The corresponding figures for multinational corporations and financial circles are lower (62 per cent and 59 per cent, respectively), in spite of the fact that most Europeans certainly see globalisation as primarily an economic phenomenon. By contrast, the majority of respondents hope that consumer associations (66 per cent), trade unions (55 per cent) and their own respective countries (54 per cent) would have more influence on the global economic situation and the principles of world trade; there is apparently a widespread wish in Europe that globalisation be regulated better than at the moment. As for the EU itself,

37 per cent of the respondents feel that the Union has about the right level of influence on the world economy, and almost the same number would be willing to increase its influence (Table 5.6). We shall return to the theme of globalisation in Chapter 7.

Table 5.6: *Perceived influence on the globalisation process (%)*

|  | Just the right level of influence | Too much influence | Not enough influence |
|---|---|---|---|
| The European Union | 37 | 21 | 34 |
| National governments | 32 | 24 | 37 |
| Our country | 32 | 10 | 54 |
| International institutions | 32 | 24 | 34 |
| Political parties | 27 | 30 | 35 |
| Anti-globalisation movements | 25 | 15 | 49 |
| Trade unions | 23 | 15 | 55 |
| Financial circles | 23 | 59 | 11 |
| Consumer associations | 22 | 8 | 66 |
| Multinationals | 21 | 62 | 11 |
| The United States | 14 | 75 | 7 |

*Source: Flash Eurobarometer* 151 (2003b) 'Globalisation', p. 16. The full question reads: 'For each of the following actors, tell me if it has/they have too much, not enough, or just the right level of influence on the process of globalisation'. (The figures for 'don't know' and 'no answer' are not shown in the table.) Approximately 7 500 respondents.

In Figure 5.1, we have summarized public attitudes towards the US, drawing on the standard *Eurobarometer* (spring 2003). Respondents are asked to assess the role of the United States in the world, with respect to five different topics: the fight against terrorism, growth of the world economy, peace in the world, the fight against poverty in the world and the protection of the environment. As for the fight against terrorism, 45 per cent of the West European citizens think that the US plays a positive role. In the UK, Denmark, Sweden, the Netherlands and Ireland, over 50 per cent appreciate the US efforts. The explanation for these positive views may be simple: many people certainly think that the cause is justified, but not the means. In Greece, by contrast, 80 per cent disapprove of Washington's post-9/11 crusade.

The four remaining items in Figure 5.1 suggest that people are truly critical towards the role of the US in world politics. Most EU citizens remain unimpressed by US efforts to fight poverty or protect the environment. When it comes to promoting economic growth, the views are more balanced: 37 per cent are critical and 34 per cent positive. In the maintenance of peace, the US obtains a negative judgement from 58 per cent of all respondents. Again, the Greeks stand out as particularly US-sceptical with 91 per cent choosing the 'negative' alternative, followed by the eastern part of Germany (78 per cent), France (73 per cent), and Spain and Finland (69 per cent, respectively). At the less anti-American end of the spectrum, we find Denmark (35 per cent negative) and the UK (32 per cent negative). Given that these two countries are generally known to belong to the Eurosceptic cluster of EU member states, one may wonder whether some of their citizens perceive support for the EU and support for transatlantic relations as mutually exclusive concepts.

*Figure 5.1: The image of the role played by the US in the world among EU citizens (%)*

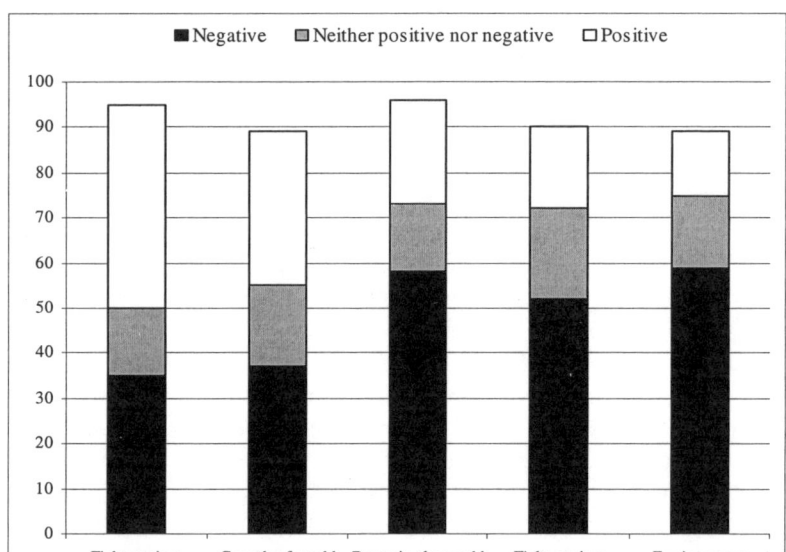

Source: *Eurobarometer* 59.1 (March–April 2003). The full question reads: 'In your opinion, would you say that the United States tend to play a positive role, a negative role or neither a positive nor a negative role regarding the fight against terrorism / growth of the world economy / peace in the world / the fight against poverty in the world / protection of the environment?' Note that the percentages for 'don't know' have been excluded. N = 16 307.

It has been argued that the inclusion of the former communist states into the EU will make the Union friendlier towards the United States. Post-communist citizens supposedly believe that they owe their freedom to the US, the country that stood up against the Soviet Union and communism during the Cold War and eventually emerged as the victor in the ideological battle. However that may be, it is true that the eastward enlargement has brought in a number of new NATO members into the Union, and with them more widespread feelings of pro-Americanism in Europe. The US still enjoys credibility as a safeguard against Russian imperialist aspirations, especially in the Baltic states (cf. Stent and Shevtsova 2002; Wiatr 2004; *Radio Free Europe/Radio Liberty* 26 April 2004).

Unfortunately, we do not have access to all the items in Figure 5.1 for all the 10 new member states. In the *Eurobarometer* 62 (autumn 2004), however, respondents throughout EU25 were asked to evaluate the global role of the US with respect to peace in the world and the fight against terrorism.

As for the role of the US and peace in the world, a majority of all respondents in EU25 were more critical (58 per cent) than supportive (22 per cent). In fact, only three of the countries which participated in the *Eurobarometer* 62 survey had a predominantly positive perception of the US as a promoter of world peace: Romania (53 per cent), the Czech Republic (47 per cent), and Lithuania (43 per cent). The most critical voices were found in Greece, Cyprus, France, Belgium and Turkey.

The east–west divide was more evident as the US fight against terrorism was assessed. A relative majority (46 per cent) of Europeans in the 15 old member states believed that the US plays a predominantly *negative* role in the world in this respect. Among the new member states, it was rather the other way around: 53 per cent of the respondents thought *positively* of the US for combating terrorism. Pro-American sentiments were especially manifest in the Czech Republic (67 per cent), Romania (66 per cent), and Lithuania (61 per cent). Citizens in the new member states thus seemed slightly less anti-American than citizens in the old member states – not, however, to the extent that the US-related distinction between 'new' and 'old' Europe would be entirely justified.

In conclusion, the US indeed has a tarnished image in Europe in the mid-2000s. The negative image is reconstructed almost daily: drastic reports of American mistreatment and torture of Afghan and Iraqi prisoners of war and the failure to achieve stability in Iraq, despite heavy American military presence, dominate news coverage in Europe. It is hard to tell how much impact the war in Iraq and its aftermath will have on Europe's foreign policy, but there is no doubt that it will rather strengthen the efforts to create a common European foreign policy than to weaken them. In the long run, European political elites may very well become more explicitly critical of the US, which would have serious consequences for the global system of multilateral governance.

**The EU and the Borders of Europe**

Let us now turn to an analysis of public opinion and the borders of the EU. The breakdown of both communism and the Soviet Union changed the political map of Europe profoundly. In a bold move designed to bridge the gap between East and West, the EU responded by opening its doors to the new democracies of Central and Eastern Europe (cf. Berglund et al. 2004; Linde 2004). These countries were all deemed to meet the 1993

Copenhagen criteria, that is, having more or less stable democratic institutions, the rule of law, respect for human rights and protection of minorities, as well as a functioning market economy and a basic readiness to adopt EU legislation (Wallace and Wallace 2000; George and Bache 2001; Craig and de Búrca 2003).

The rhetoric was often poetic. According to the official homepage of the EU (www.europa.eu.int), the May 2004 enlargement entailed 'a historical opportunity to unite Europe peacefully after generations of division and conflict'. The expansion would 'extend the EU's stability and prosperity to a wider group of countries, consolidating the political and economic transition that has taken place in Central and Eastern Europe since 1989'. European Commission President Romano Prodi's speech in honour of the largest expansion wave in the history of integrated Europe is also a good example:

> It took courage, determination, and a lot of effort from the peoples and political forces in the new member states to get this far. It took vision and generosity from the peoples and the leaders in the current European Union. Five decades after our great project of European integration began, the divisions of the Cold War are gone, once and for all. And we live in a united Europe (*Radio Free Europe/Radio Liberty* 1 May 2004).

Enlargement also brought new problems to the agenda of the EU. It gave the Union a number of new neighbours, for example Croatia, Belarus and Ukraine, some of whom had questionable democratic credentials, and thus also raised the question of the final borders of Europe. Moreover, the Union's relationship with Russia became an even more acute issue than before.

We cannot go into the details of these issues here. Instead, we will just briefly review the views of European citizens about the 2004 and possible future enlargements. Who are considered to be part of the European family – the insiders – and who are the unwelcome outsiders?

**Views of EU15**

In Table 5.7, we have summarised attitudes towards the enlargement of the EU in the 15 old EU member states. Two different survey items have been used: in the first column, the respondents have been asked to evaluate the May 2004 enlargement of the EU; the second column is based on the respondents' attitudes towards a future enlargement in general. It is noteworthy that the first item was used in a different context in Chapter 4. However, unlike Figure 4.2 displaying positive attitudes towards enlargement, Table 5.7 shows the share of negative or disapproving respondents. Also, the table is based on opinion surveys from early spring 2004, just before the May 1 enlargement, whereas the data used in Figure 4.2 was collected towards the end of that year.

In general, support for the 2004 enlargement was not overwhelming in the old EU member states. On average, 39 per cent were against it, while 42 per cent were in favour. Here, overall Euroscepticism or Eurofriendliness do not explain the cross-national differences in any straightforward manner. Eurosceptical countries often hold positive attitudes towards enlargement. Eurosceptics in Scandinavia presumably reckon that the enlargement of the Union will work as an obstacle to intensified and deepened integration, and therefore do not oppose enlargement. Conversely, the large share of negative respondents in Germany, Luxembourg, Belgium, France and the Netherlands could be interpreted as a wish to deepen integration within a more narrowly defined European Union (Table 5.7). For these countries, it is also a matter of tradition and fear for losing influence within the Union. As members of the original six, their influence within the Union has always been more significant than their size would lead us assume.

*Table 5.7: Opposition to enlargement in EU15 (%)*

|  | Enlargement of the EU in 2004: against | Further enlargement of the EU: against |
|---|---|---|
| Germany | 56 | 60 |
| Austria | 52 | 59 |
| Luxembourg | 51 | 53 |
| Belgium | 49 | 49 |
| France | 47 | 52 |
| Netherlands | 45 | 43 |
| Finland | 44 | 55 |
| UK | 40 | 40 |
| Sweden | 37 | 48 |
| Denmark | 31 | 43 |
| Portugal | 27 | 28 |
| Italy | 25 | 28 |
| Ireland | 22 | 30 |
| Greece | 19 | 23 |
| Spain | 18 | 17 |
| EU15 | 39 | 37 |

*Source*: *Eurobarometer* 61 (February–March 2004). The first item reads: 'Please tell me whether you are for or against it: the enlargement of the European Union to include ten new countries this May'. The second item reads: 'Please tell me whether you are for or against it: the enlargement of the European Union to include new countries'. The percentages indicate the share of negative respondents.

But there are other dimensions that matter as well. The least enthusiastic respondents in Table 5.7 are found in Germany and Austria, that is, the countries bordering the old 'Eastern Europe'. Here, enlargement has been perceived by many as a potential threat to social welfare. In the spring of 2004, tabloids in Germany (and throughout Western Europe) wrote a lot about the 'social benefit tourists' soon to invade the Union. No wonder, then, that the recent *Eurobarometers* have registered fears of losing jobs and social benefits among citizens in Western Europe, as a result of immigrant flows from post-communist Europe. When polled in the spring of 2004, 72 per cent of the respondents in the 15 old member states feared that the enlarged EU would entail 'the transfer of jobs to other member countries which have lower production costs'. The loss of social benefits was feared by 53 per cent of the respondents (*Eurobarometer* 61).

The second column in Table 5.7 displays the share of respondents who are against any further enlargements of the Union. It is interesting to see that a majority of citizens in the old member states oppose the idea: 43 per cent are against it, while 37 per cent support further enlargement and 20 per cent express no opinion at all. Again, Germans and Austrians are the most disapproving (around 60 per cent). Though not explicitly stated, this seems to indicate – as we discussed in some detail in Chapter 3 – that Turkey, the Balkan countries and Orthodox Eastern Europe are not self-evident members of the European family in the eyes of West European citizens (cf. Lundgren 1998; Hettlage 1999; Hansen 2000; Kohli 2000).

**Views of new member states**
Support for enlargement is more pronounced in the ten new member states. We have seen that a majority of citizens support their own countries' respective membership (cf. Chapter 4). When polled in February–March 2004, as many as 71 per cent of the respondents in the new member states generally supported the 2004 enlargement; this is a remarkably higher percentage than that among the old member states (42 per cent). The most widespread support was found in Cyprus and Slovakia (80 per cent supportive respondents in both countries), while outright opposition was most visible in Estonia (20 per cent against) and Malta (17 per cent against). Furthermore, 60 per cent of the respondents in the ten new member states were in favour of further enlargements of the EU (*Candidate Countries Eurobarometer* 2004.1). These views clearly seemed to echo the views of political elites. For example, to celebrate the big bang of 1 May 2004, many Central European Presidents and Prime Ministers spoke about 'returning to where we belong' (Estonian Prime Minister Juhan Parts), 'returning to Europe' (Hungarian Prime Minster Peter Medgyessy), 'making history' and 'returning to [the] European family' (Polish President Aleksander Kwasniewski).

Once inside the Union, the new members will have to take sides in the debate about the relative merits of breadth versus depth of integration. It is not unlikely that the initial 'Europhoria' will be replaced by a more pragmatic approach. It may soon become evident that even a Union of 25 members necessarily involves a number of structural and efficiency problems; and further enlargements might also diminish the amount of economic benefits now gained from the Union. Czech President Vaclav Klaus had already referred to this potential pragmatism in his speech on the eve of the 1 May 2004 enlargement. Noting that the Czech Republic was not joining 'Europe' (because they had always been there), he stated: 'We are joining the European Union and our task is thus much more prosaic: we must learn how to live in the Brussels structures and the complicated supranational entity those structures have created' (*Radio Free Europe/Radio Liberty* 29 April–1 May 2004).

*Table 5.8: Support for a larger and more powerful Union (%)*

|  | More members – more security | More members – more influence in the world |
|---|---|---|
| Cyprus | 84 | 85 |
| Bulgaria | 76 | 79 |
| Romania | 74 | 72 |
| Slovakia | 72 | 75 |
| Malta | 71 | 81 |
| Hungary | 70 | 72 |
| Poland | 69 | 69 |
| Czech Republic | 67 | 69 |
| Slovenia | 67 | 73 |
| Estonia | 64 | 72 |
| Latvia | 61 | 71 |
| Lithuania | 59 | 62 |
| Turkey | 53 | 56 |
| 2004 members | 68 | 66 |

Source: *Candidate Countries Eurobarometer* 2004.1.

There is one more question in the CCEB survey that may be used to assess the levels of public support for further enlargements. In the spring of 2004, respondents in the candidate countries were asked to evaluate the consequences of further enlargements of the EU. In Table 5.8, we have chosen to highlight the reactions towards two statements, on regional security ('The more countries there will be in the EU, the more peace and security will be guaranteed in Europe') and on the global role of the EU ('The more member countries within the Union, the more important it will be in the world').

Citizens in the new member states are generally in favour of including new members into the EU: 68 per cent agree that more members equals more security in Europe, and 66 per cent feel that more members will make the EU a more influential actor in the world. Turkey and the three Baltic countries are the most sceptical countries in the sample, but even in these countries, around 53–64 per cent of the respondents acknowledge the advantages of an enlarged Union (Table 5.8).

In all, attitudes towards further enlargements are clearly more positive in the new than in the old member states, with the original six save Italy expressing the most sceptical views. It seems obvious that this large share of enlargement sceptics does not speed up any further expansions of the EU; the old member states are, after all, in the majority within the Union.

**Diffuse Support through Common Foreign Policy?**

The above analyses have clearly shown that an overwhelming majority of citizens both in the old and new member states support an important role for the EU in what could be called high politics, that is, in foreign policy, defence and security. We have seen that a majority of citizens in EU25 clearly support the idea of a single voice in world politics: eight out of ten EU citizens agree that an international crisis justifies a common EU position; 63 per cent agree that the EU should have its own Foreign Minister; approximately 64 per cent tend to agree that the EU should have its own seat in the United Nations Security Council; and 71 per cent support the idea of a common rapid military reaction force. It should also be noted that when asked about whether individual governments, NATO or the EU should make policy decisions on European defence, the Union turned out to be the most trusted actor. Furthermore, the relatively approving attitudes towards a European foreign policy among European citizens can be found at the elite level as well. It has been noted that European leaders consult each other almost automatically before they act in international affairs (Manners and Whitman 2001, 249–52; Bale 2005, 260).

As for transatlantic relations, EU citizens remain unimpressed with the role of the US in world politics, especially as regards such issues as the environment and world peace. The US as a military power is acknowledged by the respondents, but in a negative sense – as a potential threat on par with Israel, Iran and North Korea. This clearly implies that most Europeans feel that whatever the desired role of the EU might be, it should be *different* from that of the United States today.

The public opinion surveys utilised in this chapter indicate that the very idea of enlargement of the EU is not popular at the moment. The May 2004 enlargement was accepted, but a majority of citizens in the old member states now oppose the idea of future enlargements. The notion of a 'united Europe' or 'wider Europe' obviously has its limitations. Not surprisingly, citizens in the new member states are decidedly more in favour of further enlargements. It remains to be seen whether the former outsiders will turn more narrow-minded once inside the Union themselves (cf. Ágh 2004). In other words, when it comes to *wider* cooperation people are sceptical, whereas *deeper* cooperation appears significantly easier to accept. The balancing power of the Union *vis-à-vis* the United States is a matter of major significance in this context; there is a risk that ever larger Union is ever less capable of speaking with one voice in the world.

Throughout the chapter, we have found substantial cross-national variation in public support for deeper political integration. Baltic respondents are clearly less protective of the classical prerogatives of the nation-state than Scandinavians and Britons. But even the latter are not completely against. Sweden, the uncontested leader of the Eurosceptic camp, actually features a slight majority favouring a common EU foreign policy and a rather solid majority supporting the notion of a common European defence and security policy.

How, then, are we to interpret these results in more analytical terms? One possibility is to return to the various dimensions of political support that we introduced in the previous chapter. Most fundamentally, support for a political system may be broken down into two categories: instrumental or specific versus diffuse support (Easton 1965a; 1965b). The former is given on a *quid pro quo* basis in exchange for favours and palpable benefits. The latter is the kind of support that makes everything run smoothly also in times of adversity when the system fails to provide its members with the gratifications to which they feel entitled. Diffuse support builds up over time and takes the form of emotional attachments to and identification with – in this case – the European Union. The distinction between these two categories is obviously not very clear; they form a continuum where specific support gradually turns into diffuse support.

It is obvious that in this chapter we have primarily been dealing with specific support; the US war on terrorism and the Iraq crisis have provided a context that is very specific indeed. But the analyses are also revealing in terms of diffuse support for the EU. In fact, we are inclined to argue that the call for the EU to take over foreign policy, defence and security may very well be seen as a sign of diffuse support for the Union. Or more precisely, the data strongly suggests that there is a large reservoir of support for the European Union as a cohesive political actor in the world stage. Above all, this is evident both within the old guard as well as among recent arrivals to the Union. As noted by George and Bache (2001, 403), a common European Foreign and Security Policy 'is an area where the potential for progress is considerable, and the indications are that effective progress will increase the legitimacy of the EU'.

Another important dimension that we have alluded to on several occasions is that of pragmatism versus 'sensitivity'; in many respects it is a variation on the theme specific versus diffuse. There is certain fluidity, certain vagueness and certain randomness to the visions of Europe that may be gauged from the data. Respondents are not always consistent when prodded for their opinions on social and political issues. Not knowing, not being interested or not being sufficiently well informed is frequently perceived as embarrassing, and respondents may be inclined to answer whatever springs into their minds just to get off the hook.

But be that as it may, one should not underestimate the importance of national interests. The EU member states with global interests of their own, particularly France and the UK, can 'use' the CFSP and the ESDP to pursue their own interests in the world, without being accused of neo-colonial behaviour. EU members with a more limited focus in the world may support a European foreign policy in order to become far more influential in world politics than they would if they acted alone (Bale 2005, 260–61). Despite public support for the CFSP and the ESDP, then, national interests are not expected to disappear any time soon. It is thus likely that, in the foreseeable future, big decisions in high politics will be national, not European. Consequently, as noted by Bale (2005, 258), there is still precious little evidence of Europeanisation when it comes to the impact of the EU on the member states' defence policies.

## NOTES

1. The standard *Eurobarometer* surveys – conducted on behalf of the European Commission and published twice a year since 1973 – encompass representative samples of the population aged 15 years and over in the EU member states. The sample sizes amount to approximately 1 000 respondents per country except in Luxembourg (600) and in the UK (1 000 in Great Britain and 300 in Northern Ireland). In order to monitor the integration of the five new *Länder* into unified Germany and the EU, 2 000 persons have been sampled in Germany since autumn 1990 (1 000 in Eastern Germany and 1 000 in Western Germany). All interviews are carried out face-to-face in the respondents' homes. The *Eurobarometer* machine-readable data files used in this chapter were kindly provided by the Norwegian Social Science Data Services (NSD), Bergen, Norway.

The first wave of the *Candidate Countries Eurobarometer* (CCEB) was carried out in October 2001 in all the 13 countries applying for membership of the EU. Its methodology is almost identical to that of the standard *Eurobarometer*. The CCEB replaced the *Central and Eastern Eurobarometer* (CEEB), which was conducted in post-communist Europe in 1990–1997 (CEEB 1– 8). The ten new member states have subsequently been included in the standard *Eurobarometer*, from autumn 2004 (EB 62) and onwards.

2. Common aid programmes for Africa were in fact initiated already in 1963 (Peterson and Smith 2003, 196). The very origins of the Union's development policy could be traced even further back, to 1957, with the association of some overseas European colonies (Holland 2002).

3. Just days before 1 May 2004, EU–Russian negotiations were still going on. According to EU commission spokesman Diego de Ojeda, the policy of the EU was that both Estonia and Latvia fulfilled the 'entry criteria' on democracy and human rights. De Ojeda also underlined the need for speeding up the integration of the Russian-speaking non-citizens into the societies of Latvia and Estonia, but at the same time also admitted that citizenship legislation was primarily a national issue. De Ojeda noted that the EU 'would like to see the integration of the Russian minorities [sic!] accelerated', and that the EU believes 'that the accession to the European Union will [...] improve the situation of the Russian minorities' (*Radio Free Europe/Radio Liberty* 22 April 2004). In other words, the EU apparently chose to sweep the whole delicate issue under the carpet, for the time being. On 27 April 2004, the EU and Russia finally signed an agreement, which entailed an extension of the already existing Partnership and Cooperation Agreement (PCA). The deal addresses trade and the transit of goods to and from Kaliningrad, while references to the protection of national minorities were only included in general terms (*Radio Free Europe/Radio Liberty* 27 April 2004). The Russian demand, that the phrase 'social integration' should be explicitly included

in the joint statement was successfully prevented by Estonia and Latvia. In the end, no precise country or minority was specified.

4. The *Flash Eurobarometers* are ad hoc telephone interviews conducted at the request of any service of the European Commission, by the EOS Gallup Europe institutes in the EU member states. These surveys are designed to get a snapshot of public attitudes on various topical issues rather than to monitor public opinion over time. The *Flash Eurobarometer* 151 surveys used here were conducted in October 2003, interviewing a total of 7 515 citizens in the 15 old EU member states (approximately 500 respondents per country). Each national sample is representative of the population of 15 years and above.

# REFERENCES

Ágh, Attila (2004), 'Smaller and Bigger States in the EU25: The Eastern Enlargement and Decision-Making in the EU', in Algimantas Jankauskas et al., eds, *Central Europe beyond Double Enlargement*, Institute of International Relations and Political Science, Vilnius University and Konrad Adenauer Foundation.
Bale, Tim (2005), *European Politics: A Comparative Introduction*, Basingstoke, Palgrave Macmillan.
Berglund, Sten, Joakim Ekman and Frank H. Aarebrot, eds (2004), *The Handbook of Political Change in Eastern Europe, Second Edition*, Cheltenham, UK and Northampton, MA, USA, Edward Elgar.
Bomberg, Elizabeth and Alexander Stubb, eds (2003), *The European Union: How Does it Work?*, Oxford, Oxford University Press.
Bretherton, Charlotte and John Vogler (1999), *The European Union as a Global Actor*, London and New York, Routledge.
*Candidate Countries Eurobarometer* 2004.1, publication, Brussels, European Commission.
Christiansen, Thomas and Ben Tonra, eds (2004), *Rethinking EU Foreign Policy: Beyond the Common Foreign and Security Policy*, Manchester, Manchester University Press.
Craig, Paul and Gráinne de Búrca (2003), *EU Law*, Oxford, Oxford University Press.
Dalton, Russel J. (1988), *Citizen Politics in Western Democracies*, Chatham, New Jersey, Chatham House Publishers.
Dalton, Russel J. (2002), *Citizen Politics. Public Opinion and Political Parties in Advanced Industrial Democracies*, New York and London, Chatham House Publishers.
Duchesne, Sophie and André-Paul Frognier (1995), 'Is There a European Identity?', in Oskar Niedermayer and Richard Sinnott, eds, *Public Opinion and Internationalized Governance*, Oxford and New York, Oxford University Press.
Easton, David (1965a), *A Framework for Political Analysis*, New York, Prentice-Hall.
Easton David (1965b), *A Systems Analysis of Political Life*, New York, London and Sydney, John Wiley & Sons.
*Eurobarometer* 59 (spring 2003), 61 (spring 2004), and 62 (autumn 2004), Machine-readable data files and publications, Brussels, European Commission.
Fawn, Rick, ed. (2003), 'Ideology and National Identity in Post-communist Foreign Policies', Special issue of the *Journal of Communist Studies and Transition Politics* Vol. 19, No. 3.
*Flash Eurobarometer* 151 (2003a), 'Iraq and Peace in the World', Brussels, European Commission, Directorate-General 'Press and Communication'.
*Flash Eurobarometer* 151 (2003b), 'Globalisation', Brussels, European Commission, Directorate-General 'Press and Communication'.
Fulbrook, Mary (1999), *German National Identity after the Holocaust*, Cambridge, Polity Press.
George, Stephen and Ian Bache (2001), *Politics in the European Union*, Oxford, Oxford University Press.
Habermas, Jürgen (2004), *Der gespaltene Westen*, Cologne, Edition Suhrkamp.
Hansen, Peo (2000), *Europeans Only? Essays on Identity Politics and the European Union*, Department of Political Science, Umeå University.

Heilbrunn, Jacob (1996), 'Germany's New Right', *Foreign Affairs*, Vol. 75, No. 6, November/December 1996, 80–98.
Hettlage, Robert (1999), 'European Identity – Between Inclusion and Exclusion', in Hanspeter Kriesi, Klaus Armingeon, Hannes Siegrist and Andreas Wimmer, eds, *Nation and National Identity. The European Experience in Perspective*, Zürich, Verlag Rüegger.
Hill, Christopher, ed. (1996), *The Actors in Europe's Foreign Policy*, London, Routledge.
Hill, Christopher (1998), 'Convergence, Divergence and Dialectics: National Foreign Policies and the CFSP', in Jan Zielonka, ed., *Paradoxes of European Foreign Policy*, London, Kluwer.
Holland, Martin (2002), *The European Union and the Third World*, Basingstoke, Palgrave Macmillan.
Holland, Martin (2004), 'When is Foreign Policy not Foreign Policy? Cotonou, CFSP and External Relations with the Developing World', in Martin Holland, ed., *Common Foreign and Security Policy: The First Ten Years*, London, Continuum.
Howorth, Joylan and John T.S. Keeler, eds, (2003), *Defending Europe, NATO and the Quest for European Autonomy*, Basingstoke, Palgrave Macmillan.
Janning, Josef (1999), 'Europäische Integration', in Werner Weidenfeld and Karl-Rudolf Korte, eds., *Handbuch zur deutschen Einheit 1949–1989–1999*, Frankfurt and New York, Campus.
Kohli, Martin (2000), 'The Battlegrounds of European Identity', *European Societies* Vol. 2, No. 2, June 2000, 113–37.
Linde, Jonas (2004), *Doubting Democrats? A Comparative Analysis of Support for Democracy in Central and Eastern Europe*, Örebro, Örebro Studies in Political Science 10.
Lundestad, Geir (1998), *No End to Alliance. The United States and Western Europe: Past, Present and Future*, Basingstoke, Palgrave Macmillan.
Lundgren, Åsa (1998), *Europeisk identitetspolitik. EU:s demokratibistånd till Polen och Turkiet*, Uppsala, Acta Universitatis Upsaliensis.
Manigart, Philippe (2001), 'Public Opinion and European Defence', Royal Military Academy, Belgium.
Manners, Ian and Richard G. Whitman, eds (2001), *The Foreign Policies of European Union Member States*, Manchester, Manchester University Press.
Markovits, Andrei (2005), *European Anti-Americanism and Anti-Semitism in a Changing Transatlantic Relationship*, Princeton, Princeton University Press.
McCormick, John (2002), *Understanding the European Union: A Concise Introduction*, Second edition, Houndmills and New York, Palgrave.
Niedermayer, Oskar and Richard Sinnott, eds (1995), *Public Opinion and Internationalized Governance*, Beliefs in Government Vol. 2, New York, Oxford University Press.
Peterson, John and Mark Pollack (2003), *Europe, America, Bush*, London, Routledge.
Peterson, John and Michael E. Smith (2003), 'The EU as Global Actor', in Elizabeth Bomberg and Alexander Stubb, eds, *The European Union: How Does it Work?*, Oxford, Oxford University Press.
*Radio Free Europe/Radio Liberty* homepage (www.rferl.org), Thursday, 22 April 2004, 'EU/Russia: Pre-enlargement deal announced on Kaliningrad'.
*Radio Free Europe/Radio Liberty* homepage (www.rferl.org), Monday, 26 April 2004, 'EU: Will Enlargement Make the Bloc more Pro-American?'
*Radio Free Europe/Radio Liberty* homepage (www.rferl.org), Tuesday, 27 April 2004, 'EU/Russia: Landmark agreement deal signed, but loose ends remain'.
*Radio Free Europe/Radio Liberty* homepage (www.rferl.org), Thursday, 29 April 2004, 'EU: Historical division of Europe overcome, but new problems loom (part 1)'.
*Radio Free Europe/Radio Liberty* homepage (www.rferl.org), Thursday, 29 April 2004, 'Despite queue, further enlargement fading amid "fatigue" (part 2)'.
*Radio Free Europe/Radio Liberty* homepage (www.rferl.org), Thursday, 29 April 2004, 'Analysis: EU welcomes new members, but where is the enthusiasm?'.
*Radio Free Europe/Radio Liberty* homepage (www.rferl.org), Saturday, 1 May 2004, 'EU leaders welcome historical expansion'.
Sinnott, Richard (1995), 'Bringing Public Opinion Back In', in Oskar Niedermayer and Richard Sinnott, eds, *Public Opinion and Internationalised Governance*, Oxford and New York, Oxford University Press.
Silber, Laura and Allan Little (1996), *The Death of Yugoslavia*, Revised edition, London, Penguin.

Smith, Karen E. (1999), *The Making of EU Foreign Policy. The Case of Eastern Europe*, Houndmills and New York, Palgrave.

Smith, Karen E. (2003), *European Union Foreign Policy in a Changing World*, Cambridge, Polity Press.

Smith, Michael E. (2004), 'CFSP and ESDP: From Idea to Institution to Policy', in Martin Holland, ed., *Common Foreign and Security Policy: The First Ten Years*, London, Continuum.

Soetendorp, Ben (1999), *Foreign Policy in the European Union: History, Theory and Practice*, London, Longman.

Stent, Angela and Lilia Shevtsova (2002), 'America, Russia and Europe: A Realignment?, *Survival*, Vol. 44, No. 4, 121–34.

Wallace, Helen and William Wallace, eds (2000), *Policy-Making in the European Union*, Fourth edition, Oxford, Oxford University Press.

Wiatr, Jerzy J. (2004), 'Central Europe and NATO after the Iraqi Crisis', in Algimantas Jankauskas et al., eds, *Central Europe beyond Double Enlargement*, Institute of International Relations and Political Science, Vilnius University and Konrad Adenauer Foundation.

# 6. The Challenge of Euroscepticism and Nationalism

Nationalism – and particularly the extreme versions thereof – is not conducive to intergovernmental cooperation. The European Union sets out to be more than just a forum for intergovernmental cooperation and may be adversely affected even by moderate forms of nationalism. Open conflicts along this dimension could very well bring the complex decision-making machinery of the Union to a temporary halt, raising the spectre of a complete deadlock. The successful unfolding of the European project of integration is in fact contingent upon the gradual erosion of national constraints on European political elites as well as the people they represent (cf. Chapter 3). Brussels and Strasbourg are far away places for many Europeans, who are therefore reluctant to transfer more power to the Union.

In some countries Brussels seems particularly far removed. Norwegian voters have twice advised against EU-membership (1972 and 1994); Swiss voters have even rejected the notion of a loose affiliation with the EU within the framework of the European Economic Space (EES); and as we have seen in the preciding chapters, within the EU, the UK, Denmark and Sweden have established themselves as outspoken EU-sceptics. But the differences within the Union should perhaps not be exaggerated. The decision by almost all the original 15 EU members – on the eve of the eastward enlargement of the Union on 1 May 2004 – to introduce temporary restrictions on the free movement of labour from the new member countries in Central and Eastern Europe is telling in this respect. As enlargement day moved closer, more and more EU countries, including those originally committed to an open-door policy *vis-à-vis* the enlargement countries, opted for 'transitional arrangements' designed to restrict the free movement of labour to the original 15 EU members in Western Europe from the eight East European enlargement countries.

The public debate accompanying this decision-making process in Western Europe was not without nationalistic overtones. Protectionist sentiments were in fact so widespread that leading politicians with solid democratic credentials could not afford to neglect them. German Chancellor Gerhard Schröder thus branded suggestions by German industrial leaders to move industrial facilities eastwards as 'unpatriotic' (*Radio Free Europe/Radio Liberty* 29 April–1 May 2004). Fellow Social Democrat Göran Persson, Swedish Prime Minister, used a slightly different strategy, as he rallied to the cause of Central and East European workers by calling for 'transitional arrangements' protecting them from exploitation by Swedish employers. Indeed, political elites are generally in favour of European integration, but they still operate under rather strongly pronounced national constraints.

The aims of this chapter are twofold. On the one hand, we seek to explore to what extent nationalism, the continuing primacy of national values in the minds of European citizens, generates scepticism towards the continent's integration process. On the other hand, we set out to examine in what ways this Euroscepticism may serve as an obstacle to that very process.

We start off with a short conceptual discussion about the relationship between nationalism and Euroscepticism. We then make an attempt to put Euroscepticism into a historical perspective by confronting it with Stein Rokkan's conceptual map of Europe (see Chapter 2). The following section on party-based Euroscepticism represents a move from the systemic to the sub-systemic level. The final section on resistance to multiculturalism with its emphasis on European citizens represents yet another shift of perspective, aimed at providing a more comprehensive picture of the multi-dimensional phenomenon under scrutiny.

## Nationalism and Euroscepticism

There is no doubt that a substantial part of what we will here refer to as 'Euroscepticism' is based on the primary importance of national interests, and can therefore be classified as 'nationalism'. In fact, the strength of populist and nationalist right-wing parties in several recent European elections can at least to a certain extent be seen as a counterreaction to European integration.[1] There are, however, also those who oppose the Union from a more global perspective, especially in Green parties. Finally, it is obvious that the agricultural sector has encountered particularly serious problems because of EU integration, which helps explain why many parties with close ties with that sector have been leaning towards Euroscepticism. Some of these parties – with agrarian roots – have traditionally been 'nationalistic' as well. Thus, before analysing the prospects for serious 'nationalist' (or Eurosceptic) constraints on the European integration project, we are well advised to be a little more specific about the concept of nationalism in the context of the EU, as well as about the concept of

Euroscepticism. It is easy to get the impression that these phenomena are two sides of the same coin. It is not necessarily so.

We start with an elaboration on different kinds of 'nationalisms' and their respective impact on sentiments for or against the EU. In a recent article in *Perspectives on Politics* (March 2004), Zsuzsa Csergo and James M. Goldgeier suggest a typology for analysing nationalism in the specific context of the European Union (Table 6.1). The merit of this typology is that it distinguishes between different kinds of nationalisms, thus alerting us to this phenomenon in various forms and degrees, throughout contemporary Europe. Nationalism – or the national principle – will be understood here as the idea that social and political organisation should centre on nation-building and national sovereignty (Csergo and Goldgeier 2004, 21).

*Table 6.1: A typology of nationalism in the EU*

| Type of nationalism | Main objective | Perception of the EU |
| --- | --- | --- |
| Traditional | Ensure congruence of political and cultural boundaries (nation-state) | Alliance of states |
| Sub-state | Strengthen political representation for homeland *vis-à-vis* state | Alliance of nations |
| Trans-sovereign | Create institutions to link nations across state boundaries | Alliance of nations |
| Protectionist | Preserve national culture in face of immigration/social change | Alliance of states |

*Source*: Csergo and Goldgeier (2004, 21).

Thus, however broadly defined, the national principle or idea represents something distinctly different from alternative social and political organising principles, for example regionalism, pan-Europeanism and universalism. The typology also puts us in a better position to evaluate the potential danger of nationalism in the EU, both as a threat to liberal democracy and as an obstacle to effective decision-making within the Union. For example, the nationalist challenge may come in the form of anti-EU sentiments coupled with xenophobia, or in the form of pro-EU sentiments combined with a strong emphasis on national sovereignty. While the latter entails a mere constraint on deepening integration, the former may be seen as a challenge to democracy and the whole project of European integration. The point here is simply that there are *varieties* of 'the nationalist challenge' in the new Europe, and Brussels may thus have to address different kinds of nationalist challenges in different parts of the

Union. There is in fact even a strong case to be made for casting the nationalist challenges as structurally determined or built into the European integration project.

In terms of the typology above, we may describe the European Union as an alliance of nations with strongly pronounced elements of trans-sovereignty. But there is more to the EU than just that; the common political institutions – the European Commission, the Council of Ministers, the European Parliament and the European Court of Justice – do represent the all-Union or federal level in a state and nation building project without parallels since the days of the Holy Roman Empire (Axtmann 2001). This is sufficient to trigger all-out rejection of the EU by extreme nationalists, and the spectre of a federal European super-state may occasionally be enough to mobilise even moderate nationalists against any transfer of power from the national to the federal level.

The European Union has successfully coped with nationalist challenges of varying intensity from the very beginning. Charles de Gaulle's verbal attacks against the technocrats and bureaucrats of the European Commission and his vision of Europe as a continent of nations (in French: *une Europe des nations*) in the mid-1960s would clearly qualify as Euroscepticism, perhaps even of the hard variety (see below), in the contemporary discourse on Europe and the European Union.

Enlargement has not tilted the balance between supporters and opponents of the European Union, but it has made everything even more complex and unpredictable than before. Constitutional amendments, further enlargements and other crucial changes must now have the approval of 25, as opposed to 15, member states, ten of whom have limited experiences of EU bargaining processes. The combination of these factors – the increasing number of actors who are yet to be socialised into standard EU negotiating and decision-making practices – may possibly result in a deadlock bringing the entire organisation to a halt, reminiscent of the kind of decision-making paralysis that spelled the end of the Third and Fourth French Republics and the German Weimar Republic (Sartori 1976). We will return to this and other developmental scenarios in the concluding chapter.

**Mapping Euroscepticism**

In Chapter 4 we have already discussed reasons for Euroscepticism by using a simple method of categorisation in terms of accession waves and geography. Here we want to take a step further by drawing attention to Stein Rokkan's conceptual map of Europe that we introduced in Chapter 2 (Table 2.1). For the following analysis, we use the figures from Figure 4.5 on the generalised opposition to EU membership among the old member states (1991–2004) and the new member states and candidate countries (2001–04);

the information is based on pooled data from the standard *Eurobarometers* and *Candidate Countries Eurobarometers*, respectively. In Figure 4.5, we saw a fairly sharp distinction between the Eurofriendly and Eurosceptical countries, both among the established EU members and the countries outside the EU as the surveys were conducted.

Relative latecomers to the Union dominate the Eurosceptic camp in the EU15. Austria, Sweden and Finland became members in 1995. Denmark and the UK have admittedly been members for a longer period of time, since 1973. In recent years, however, Denmark and the UK have, alongside Sweden, established themselves as outspoken EU-sceptics. The Danes caused some alarm in June 1992, when 50.7 per cent of the voters rejected the Maastricht Treaty. The Treaty had to be modified to accommodate Danish special interests in order to secure a majority (56.8 per cent) in the follow-up referendum in May 1993. British voters too have articulated opposition. In the June 2004 elections to the European Parliament, the distinctly EU-critical UK Independence Party (UKIP) took no less than 12 seats in the Strasbourg parliament, almost half the number of seats won by the Conservatives (27 seats). In Sweden, the Eurosceptical (albeit not anti-EU) 'June Movement' gained three seats. A year previous to that, on 14 September 2003, Swedes had voted against the introduction of the euro in a popular referendum. Norway, finally, is not even a EU member, but has been included here as a point of reference. Attitudinally, the country fits neatly into the sceptical, non-continental European camp. As already noted, the Norwegian voters have repeatedly voted against EC membership. Generally speaking, Euroscepticism thus seems to be – at least partly – related to lack of long-term experience with European integration. Conversely, it is no coincidence that the pro-EU camp includes the six founding members of the European Communities: West Germany, France, Italy, and the Benelux countries (cf. Wallace and Wallace 2000).

The *Candidate Countries Eurobarometer* surveys conducted in recent years have shown that, as a rule, citizens in the 2004 member states tend to be rather supportive towards the EU, as a whole (cf. Chapters 4 and 5). The most Eurosceptical voices are found in Malta, Estonia and Latvia, and more recently and to a lesser extent, in Poland and the Czech Republic (*Candidate Countries Eurobarometer* 2004.1). In the remaining countries, articulate opposition is not particularly strong, not even in Turkey. In the 'soon-to-be' member states of Romania and Bulgaria, an average of only 2–4 per cent find the prospect of a future EU membership a bad idea. It is worth bearing in mind, however, that the low turnout in the June 2004 European Parliament elections can be seen as an indication of pervasive Euroscepticism in contemporary Central and Eastern Europe.

In a recent article in the *European Journal of Political Research*, Tobias

Theiler (2004) suggests a number of possible predictors of opposition to European integration. Noting that no single one of these variables is a reliable predictor by itself, Theiler nevertheless identifies a range of criteria that may explain why some countries or populations are more reluctant than others to participate in the European integration process. Here, we will see if these explanations are empirically grounded.

*Table 6.2: Euroscepticism on the conceptual map of Europe*

| Religious heritage | Late, devolved states from western seaward empires | Early states formed in western seaward empires | City-belt Europe | States based on former core nations of Central European empire states | Late, devolved states from Central European empires | Late, devolved states from eastern empires |
|---|---|---|---|---|---|---|
| Protestant countries | **Norway** | **Denmark England** | | **Sweden** | **Finland** | **Estonia Latvia** |
| Mixed countries, substantially secularised countries or national orthodox countries | Ulster | France | Netherlands | Germany | Czech Republic | |
| Counter-reformation countries and non-secularised Orthodox countries | Eire **Malta** Cyprus | Spain Portugal | Belgium Luxemburg Italy | **Austria** Hungary | Poland Slovakia Slovenia | Lithuania Romania Bulgaria Greece |

*Source:* Data from Figure 4.5. In countries marked in bold, more than 15 per cent of respondents believe that their country's EU membership is 'a bad thing' (as opposed to 'a good thing').

Theiler's first predictor is geographical location and cultural background. Focusing on the origins of Euroscepticism in German-speaking Switzerland, Theiler uses Western Europe as a point of reference. The suggestion is that whether a given population belongs to 'northern' or 'southern' part of the EU matters for public opposition to European integration (Theiler 2004, 639). It remains a bit unclear what 'northern' and 'southern' Europe precisely signifies here; Theiler mentions the Anglo-Saxon or Germanic heritage versus the Latin cultural background as well as the Catholic/Protestant difference. These dimensions are obviously overlapping, but not entirely. As demonstrated by Table 6.2, we use a slightly different conceptualisation with religious heritage and distance from the city belt as key variables.

The outcome is very clear indeed. Most Eurosceptical countries have a common denominator, namely Protestantism: Norway, Denmark, England,

Sweden, Finland, Estonia and Latvia (Table 6.2). Malta and Austria, by contrast, do not fit into this pattern. Some problems remain, however. For one thing, it is hardly self-evident *why* the Catholic/Protestant difference should matter. For another thing, the religious heritage dimension is closely related to geographical location, that is, distance from the city belt.

Another way of analysing Euroscepticism is to focus on the enlargement waves as a predictor (Table 6.3).

*Table 6.3: Euroscepticism by accession waves and proximity to city-belt Europe*

| Accession waves | Late, devolved states from western seaward empires | Early states formed in western seaward empires | City-belt Europe | States based on former core nations of Central European empire states | Late, devolved states from Central European empires | Late, devolved states from eastern empires |
|---|---|---|---|---|---|---|
| Original six | | France | Belgium Luxemburg Italy Netherlands | Germany (west) | | |
| 1970–80s | Ireland (Northern Ireland) | **Denmark** **England** Spain Portugal | | | | Greece |
| 1990s | | | | Germany (east) **Austria** **Sweden** | **Finland** | |
| 2004 | **Malta** Cyprus | | | Hungary | Czech Republic Poland Slovakia Slovenia | **Estonia** **Latvia** Lithuania |
| 2007 | | | | | | Romania Bulgaria |

*Source:* Data from Figure 4.5. In countries marked in bold, more than 15 per cent of respondents believe that their country's EU membership is 'a bad thing' (as opposed to 'a good thing').

The underlying hypothesis would be that Euroscepticism is related to lack of actual experience with European integration, long-term or short-term. The geographical pattern would thus mirror the enlargement waves: the old member states would harbour little Euroscepticism, while in the more recent member states we would find larger numbers of sceptical citizens. This would be our guess, when it comes to Western Europe anyway.

The ten May 2004 members, however, should arguably be treated differently. In Central and Eastern Europe, public support for future membership of the European Union has remained rather impressive throughout the post-communist period. For sure, more recent opinion surveys have modified the picture somewhat, but we would nevertheless expect most post-communist citizens to be supportive of EU membership (see Chapter 4).

At the same time, if we assume that long-term experience with some sort of European integration matters as well, the countries of Central and Eastern Europe have a somewhat mixed record. The countries of Central Europe – including Slovenia, the Czech Republic, Hungary, Poland, and Slovakia – were once wholly or mainly subsumed in the great multi-national Prussian-German and Habsburg empires and, consequently, they are profoundly anchored in the Western tradition, which entails Western Christianity, at least a measure of experience of the rule of law, the separation of powers, constitutional government and civil society (cf. Berglund et al. 2004). The three Baltic states, Estonia, Latvia and Lithuania, share a common history of Soviet occupation in the 20th century. In a longer historical perspective, however, these countries have been all but unaffected by Western thought, located as they are at the crossroads between Russia, Germany and Scandinavia. Although the pattern is not perfect, these historical legacies nevertheless work towards setting the Central European and Baltic countries apart from the countries of South Eastern and Eastern Europe, with their traditions of Eastern Christianity or Islam, clientelism and Ottoman rule. Romania and Bulgaria thus make up a third category, as Balkan countries.

We should thus expect variation in support for European integration, between the old and the new member states and, also, *among* the new member states and the candidate countries.

As it turns out, our assumptions are only somewhat to the point. Certainly, in the founding members of the European integration project, no serious levels of Euroscepticism are manifest. With the exception of Denmark and the UK, the countries that joined the EC in the 1970s and 1980s are relatively EU-friendly as well. And, as expected, the latecomers, Sweden, Finland and Austria stand out as Eurosceptical countries. However, Table 6.3 does not display a clear-cut pattern for the rest of the member states. Among the ten new members, we find Eurofriendly as well as Eurosceptical countries at both ends of the city-belt dimension. Estonia, Latvia and Malta stand out as more or less Eurosceptic recent arrivals to the EU. In opinion polls from 2001 to 2004, more than 15 per cent of the respondents in these countries have been what we define as Eurosceptics (Figure 4.5, Table 6.3).

Turning once more to Theiler (2004), he suggests 'political history' as another possible predictor of public opposition to European integration.[2] In the case of Western Europe this is an issue of obvious relevance. Consider for example the longstanding and secure levels of support for the European integration project in the post-war Federal Republic of Germany. Nazi rule, the Second World War and the Holocaust left no room for even the most modest forms of German nationalism; instead, a firm commitment to democracy and European cooperation became the hallmark of West Germany (cf. Fulbrook 1999; Ekman 2001).

In the case of Central and Eastern Europe, the two Eurosceptical countries in our sample, Estonia and Latvia, have one obvious thing in common, namely being political entities that (re-)emerged out of the Cold War as states in their own right. In the 1990s, these countries have faced two simultaneous processes of identity transformation – a process that involves state- and nation-building at home, and a parallel process that involves Europeanisation. Latvians and Estonians are inclined to summarise their predicament as 'trading one union for another'. This goes a long way towards accounting for their mixed feelings about the European Union. But it does *not* help account for the all-out Eurofriendly posture of neighbouring Lithuania, caught up in the same processes of identity transformation. It is tempting here to come up with an *ad hoc* explanation, by drawing attention again to the common Polish–Lithuanian history and reclassifying Lithuania as an 'old state' – that is a state with a long pre-history and a self-sufficient national identity – by virtue of this experience.

The empirical observations of this section thus indicate that *no single predictor* can explain the presence of Euroscepticism in *all* countries in our sample. Instead, what we have is a set of *overlapping* explanations. We have seen that accession waves matter (Table 6.3), but this predictor overlaps to some extent with the geographical and cultural dimension in the old member states (Table 6.2). As for the new member states, it is very likely that the post-Soviet citizens in Estonia and Latvia are especially hesitant to get involved in a new supra-national project, having experienced only 15 years of national independence. At the same time, the presence of Euroscepticism in Malta reveals that there are other possible explanations that matter as well.

Finally, returning to the four different types of nationalism introduced in Table 6.1, we can probably conclude that in Eurosceptical countries, Euroscepticism remains anchored in traditional and/or protectionist nationalism. Conversely, countries – and citizens – more favourably disposed towards the European integration project are presumably more likely to embrace nationalisms with implicit or explicit federal connotations, referred to as 'sub-state' and 'trans-sovereign' nationalism in Table 6.1. We do not have survey data matching the categories in this particular table, but we know enough about the role of the state as a determinant of support for the Union to exclude the presence of traditional and protectionist nationalism among Eurofriendly countries and citizens (see multivariate analysis in Chapter 4). Eurofriendliness is probably more fragile than it looks given the almost overwhelming support for the Union, and, though not always numerically strong, Euroscepticism tends to be a well-organised enemy. This will be the topic of the following section.

**Party-based Euroscepticism and Possible Threats to Democracy**

Drawing on Paul Taggart and Aleks Szczerbiak (2002, 7), we may distinguish between two types of Euroscepticism; soft and hard (Table 6.4).

*Table 6.4: Types and indicators of party-based Euroscepticism*

|  | Working definition | Indicators |
| --- | --- | --- |
| Hard Euroscepticism | This kind of Euroscepticism appears in countries where there is a principled opposition to the EU and European integration. It may be seen in parties who think that their countries should withdraw from membership, or whose policies towards the EU are tantamount to being opposed to the whole project of European integration as it is currently conceived. | Single-issue anti-EU parties. Hard anti-EU rhetoric based on party ideology. If expressed as conditional support for EU membership, conditions are *de facto* unattainable. |
| Soft Euroscepticism | This brand of Euroscepticism appears in countries where there is *not* a principled objection to European integration or EU membership but where concerns on one (or a number) of policy areas lead to the expression of qualified opposition to the EU, or where there is a sense that 'national interest' is currently at odds with the EU's trajectory. | Anti-EU rhetoric as part of the party's political repertoire. |

The two categories in the dichotomy clearly do not meet the textbook requirement of being exhaustive and mutually exclusive. As is frequently the case, we are up against partially overlapping categories. The border between 'hard' and 'soft' Euroscepticism is blurred, and some parties may indeed defy classification. Modern mass parties have complex organisations and speak with many voices. Similar comments apply to the electoral cartels that contest elections under a common party label. Officially pro-EU parties may have strong Eurosceptic factions of varying shades, and the other way around. Most parties are not single-issue parties, and most issues are not equally salient all the time. European integration and the European Union are not always on the domestic political agendas of the member countries. The position attributed to a political party on the Euroscepticism scale may vary over time, and snapshots purporting to represent the positions of the respective political parties right there and then may very well produce an impression quite different than the full sequence of pictures over time.

Crude as it might be, Table 6.5 provides an overview of Eurosceptic parties and movements in the EU, including current candidate countries. The data for Western Europe are based on those of Taggart and Szczerbiak (2002, 7); the data for Eastern Europe were gauged from the second edition of the *Handbook of Political Change in Eastern Europe* (Berglund et al. 2004) and the *Elections Around the World* website (www.electionworld.org, accessed in January 2005). Eurosceptic parties make themselves felt throughout Europe. With the exception of Spain and Malta, the current 25 EU member countries all feature some form of Euroscepticism. On the average, the post-enlargement countries have somewhat fewer Eurosceptic parties than the original fifteen West European members of the union.[3] But the difference between East and West is not only marginal, it is also likely to vanish the more deeply the countries of Eastern Europe are drawn into the EU.

The left-hand column of the table lists parties rejecting European integration in general and the European Union in particular. They represent what we refer to as hard Euroscepticism. Many of them have also gained notoriety as parties of the right-wing extreme with a strongly nationalistic rhetoric, bordering on xenophobia, frequently at odds with the principles of liberal democracy. The Flemish Bloc, now known as the National Front, in Belgium, the Danish People's Party and the Progress Party, in Denmark, the National Front (le Pen) and the National Movement (Mégret), in France, and the Republicans in Germany and the Czech Republic are all part of a well documented right-wing backlash against the European Union. But there is also evidence of left-wing opposition by extremist parties with questionable democratic credentials, in France, the Czech Republic and Hungary.

The combination of political extremism and all-out rejection of the European Union constitutes a dual threat to the EU. Parties, thrust into power on such an electoral platform, will do their best to pull their respective countries out of the Union; and, as if this were not enough, they may end up subverting the very foundation of democracy at home. Fearing such a development in the aftermath of the parliamentary elections in 1999, the EU exposed Austria to sanctions after the formation of a conservative coalition government, including (at the time) Jörg Haider's Freedom Party (FPÖ). Two years later, Jean Marie le Pen, charismatic leader of the National Front, seemed to have the French presidency within reach. A coalition covering the entire political spectrum but the extreme right thwarted le Pen's ambitions and secured Chirac's re-election, thus protecting the European Union from a possibly debilitating conflict with one of its founding members.

Mainstream and single-issue parties, representing the hard version of Euroscepticism, cannot be dismissed as a threat to democracy but will remain a potential threat to the European Union for as long as they hold on to the hard version of Euroscepticism. The parties representing the soft brand of Euroscepticism prefer to slow down the process of integration, to remove certain policy sectors and issues from the sphere of competence of the Union, or to introduce a moratorium on measures leading up towards a further deepening of the process of integration. They may even be supportive of the EU as long as it complies with their respective visions of the Union.

*Table 6.5: Party-based Euroscepticism*

| EU15 | Hard Euroscepticism | Soft Euroscepticism |
|---|---|---|
| Austria | | Freedom Party (FPÖ) |
| Belgium | Flemish Bloc (VB)<br>National Front (FN) | |
| Denmark | Danish People's Party (DF)<br>Progress Party (FRP)<br>Unity List (EL) | Socialist People's Party (SF) |
| Finland | Communist Party of Finland (SKP) | True Finns (*Perussuomalaiset*)<br>Christian League (KL) |
| France | Communist Party (PCF)<br>*Lutte Ouvrière* (LO)<br>Revolutionary Communist League (LCR)<br>National Front (FN) [le Pen]<br>National Republican Movement (MNR) [Mégret] | Republican Citizens Movement (MRC)<br>Movement for France (MPF)<br>Rally for France and Independence of Europe (RPF) |
| Germany | Republicans (REP)<br>Germans People's Union (DVU)<br>German National Democratic Party (NPD) | Party of Democratic Socialists (PDS) |
| Greece | Communist Party (KKE) | Democratic Social Movement (DIKKI)<br>Political Spring (POLAN) |
| Ireland | | Green Party (GP)<br>Socialist Party (SP)<br>Sinn Fein (SF) |
| Italy | | Northern League (LN) |
| Luxembourg | | Action Committee for Democracy and Pensions Justice (ADR)<br>The Left (DL) |
| Netherlands | | Green Party (GL)<br>Socialist Party (SP)<br>Political Reformed Party (SGP)<br>List Pim Fortuyn (LPF) |
| Portugal | | Communist Party (PCP)<br>Greens (OV) |
| Spain | | |
| Sweden | Green Party (mp)<br>Left Party (v) | Centre Party (C) |
| United Kingdom | UK Independence Party (UKIP)<br>Greens | Conservative Party (cons)<br>Democratic Unionist Party (DUP) |

*Table 6.5 (continued)*

| New member states | Hard Euroscepticism | Soft Euroscepticism |
|---|---|---|
| Cyprus | | Progressive Party of the Working People (AKEL) |
| Czech Republic | Communist Party of Bohemia and Moravia (KSČM) | Civic Democratic Party (ODS) Association for the Republic-Republican Party of Czechoslovakia (SPR-RSČ) |
| Estonia | | Centre Party (*Keskerakond*) Estonian Rural People's Party (*Rahvaliit*) |
| Hungary | Hungarian Justice and Life Party (MIÉP) Hungarian Workers' Party (MP) | Fidesz-Hungarian Civic Party (FIDESZ-MPP) Independent Smallholders' Party (FKGP) |
| Latvia | | Latvian Social Democratic Alliance (LSDP/LSDSP) Conservative Union for Fatherland and Freedom (LNNK) |
| Lithuania | | Centre Union of Lithuania (LCS) Lithuanian Peasant Party (LVP) |
| Malta | | |
| Poland | Self Defence (*Samoobrona*) League of Polish Families (LPR) | Law and Justice Party (PiS) Polish Peasant Party (PSL) National Christian Alliance (ZChN) |
| Slovakia | | Movement for a Democratic Slovakia (HZDS) Slovak National Party (SNS) Christian Democratic Movement (KDH) |
| Slovenia | New Slovenia Christian People's Party (NSI) | Slovenian National Party (SNS) |
| Candidate countries | | |
| Bulgaria | | |
| Romania | | Greater Romania Party (RM) 'Romania Mare' Party (PRM) |
| Croatia | Croatian Right's Party (HSP) | |

*Sources*: Taggart and Szczerbiak (2002); Berglund et al. (2004); data from the *Elections Around the World* website (www.electionworld.org, January 2005).

With a total of eight Eurosceptic parties, including five parties of the right- and left-wing extremes rejecting the EU out of principle, France stands out as the very centre of Euroscepticism, well ahead of Poland, Denmark, Germany, Hungary, and the UK with 4–5 entries, of which at least two represent all-out rejection of the EU. With no parties at all questioning the European Union, Spain and Malta are located at the other end of the continuum along with Bulgaria, one of two candidate countries slated for membership in 2007. Austria, Ireland, Italy, Luxembourg, the

Netherlands, Portugal, Cyprus, Estonia, Latvia, Lithuania and Slovakia do feature Eurosceptic movements but only of the soft variety. We would therefore be inclined to classify them as part of the pro-EU camp along with Romania, the other candidate country scheduled for membership in 2007.

*Table 6.6: Eurosceptical parties: electoral and parliamentary support (%)*

| EU 15 | | Hard Eurosceptic parties | | Soft Eurosceptic parties | |
|---|---|---|---|---|---|
| | | Share of votes | Mandates | Share of votes | Mandates |
| Austria | 2002 | | | 10.0 | 9.8 |
| Belgium | 2003 | 13.6 | 13.5 | | |
| Denmark | 2001 | 15.0 | 14.5 | 6.4 | 6.7 |
| Finland | 2003 | | | 6.9 | 5.0 |
| France | 2002 | 19.7 | 0 | 1.2 | 0.4 |
| Germany | 2002 | | | 4.3 | 0.3 |
| Greece | 2004 | 5.9 | 4.0 | 1.8 | 0 |
| Ireland | 2002 | | | 11.6 | 7.2 |
| Italy | 2001 | | | 3.9 | 4.8 |
| Luxembourg | 2004 | | | 11.6 | 7.2 |
| Netherlands | 2003 | | | 18.7 | 17.9 |
| Portugal | 2000 | | | 7.0 | 5.2 |
| Spain | | | | | |
| Sweden | 2002 | 12.9 | 13.5 | 6.1 | 6.3 |
| UK | 2001 | 2.1 | 0 | 32.4 | 5.9 |
| New member states | | | | | |
| Cyprus | 2001 | | | 34.7 | 33.9 |
| Czech Rep. | 2002 | 18.5 | 20.5 | 24.5 | 29.0 |
| Estonia | 2003 | | | 38.4 | 41.0 |
| Hungary | 2002 | 7.2 | 0 | 41.9 | 42.5 |
| Latvia | 2002 | | | 9.4 | 7.0 |
| Lithuania | 2004 | | | 12.4 | 16.3 |
| Malta | 2003 | | | | |
| Poland | 2001 | 18.1 | 19.8 | 18.5 | 18.7 |
| Slovakia | 2002 | | | 31.1 | 34.0 |
| Slovenia | 2004 | | | 6.3 | 8.6 |
| Candidate countries | | | | | |
| Bulgaria | 2001 | | | | |
| Romania | 2000 | | | 19.5 | 24.3 |
| Croatia | 2003 | 6.4 | 5.3 | | |

*Note:* Table 6.6 is based on data from the most recently held nationwide, parliamentary elections (in the case of bicameralism: only the Lower House is taken into account) in the 25 member states and three candidate countries. The timing of the elections varies from one country to another; the election year is reported after each country label. The numbers in the two following columns represent the electoral and parliamentary weight of hard versus soft Eurosceptic parties, expressed in terms of percentages. The Eurosceptic parties of relevance are listed in Table 6.5. In the event that a country has several hard or soft Eurosceptic parties, the percentages quoted here stand for the aggregate performance by the relevant parties.

*Sources:* Taggart and Szczerbiak (2002); Berglund et al. (2004); data from *Elections Around the World* website (www.electionworld.org, January 2005).

The pattern that emerges when we look at the diffusion of Euroscepticism as presented in Table 6.6 confirms some, but only some, previous findings. We would, for instance, have expected Sweden rather than France or Germany to land squarely within the Eurosceptic camp. In the final analysis though, it is not the number of parties that counts but their relative strength or weight. In the German case, the three right-wing and strongly anti-EU parties, listed in Table 6.6, turn out to be without electoral and parliamentary significance at the federal level.[4] The reformed East German communist party, the Party of Democratic Socialism (PDS), which was classified as a representative of the soft brand of Euroscepticism, did make it into the *Bundestag*, but just barely so.[5]

When approached in the light of such background data, Germany clearly qualifies among the pro-EU countries with little or no room for organised Euroscepticism. Even France may possibly qualify. Political extremism appeals to one French voter out of five, but most of the extremist votes are actually wasted and do not result in parliamentary representation (Table 6.6). Such is the logic of the French plurality system with two rounds of election whenever the first round does not result in an absolute electoral majority (50 per cent or more) for any of the candidates. The standard British plurality system also goes towards reducing the importance of Eurosceptic parties.

A preliminary screening of all the 25 countries based on Table 6.6 would put Belgium, the Czech Republic, Denmark, Poland and Sweden rather close to the Eurosceptic end of the continuum. These five EU members all have to cope with parties strongly opposed to the European Union with an electoral and parliamentary backing of 12 per cent or more. Czech and Polish parties with fundamental objections against the EU actually enjoy the support of almost 20 per cent of the voters and proportional representation provides them with a parliamentary base commensurate with their electoral strength. Advocates of what we refer to as soft Euroscepticism also seem to have a much more stable platform in the Czech Republic and Poland than in Belgium, Denmark and Sweden. With two of the East European enlargement countries at the negative end of the continuum, the table may be seen as an indication that the integration of the new members is not likely to be entirely smooth. Brussels may, on the other hand, interpret the presence of Spain, Greece and Portugal, three countries with a political history reminiscent of that of the Central and East European enlargement countries, either at or very close to the opposite pro-EU extreme as a sign that there is light at the other end of the tunnel. But seasoned political analysts would be well advised to issue a word of caution. Table 6.6 provides us with a snapshot of the current alignments for or against the EU in the 25 member countries and the four candidate countries. It gives us a highly informative picture, but like most snapshots it does not capture all the relevant details. The focus is exclusively on parties. Single-issue movements that reappear whenever the EU dominates the domestic agenda as in Denmark and more recently in Sweden, have therefore been left out in spite of their impressive mobilising potential in popular referenda. The emphasis has explicitly been on the current state of affairs and not on long-term trends. We should thus be prepared for sudden re-alignments. A dramatic shift in one of the member countries – for example, a return in France to proportional representation or a decisive electoral breakthrough by *Samoobrona* or the League of Polish Families – may in fact be sufficient to tilt the delicate balance.

*

There is not always a perfect match between party ideological positions and voter preferences. European political elites have a solid reputation as more Eurofriendly, and more open to foreign influences than the citizens they represent. Indeed, the formation of Eurosceptic parties is often cast as deliberate attempts by political entrepreneurs to correct for and take advantage of this democratic deficit. This scenario, in turn, makes it virtually impossible for mainstream parties to pursue a Eurofriendly course, as though the fears and prejudices of their respective constituents did not matter. In democracies, voter preferences always matter, and all parties are somehow constrained by public opinion.

This is why we now turn to the crucial link in a democratic political system, the voters and their relative openness to the outside world. We have touched upon this theme now and then in previous chapters and dwelled upon at some length in Chapter 3, which is cast in terms of exclusion and inclusion in national legislation. But we have not yet examined people's attitudes towards other people representing other backgrounds, values and norms. We make this a primary objective in this section of obvious relevance for the current debate throughout Europe.

**Resistance to Multiculturalism**

Citizens of the European Union are theoretically free to go, seek gainful employment and settle wherever they wish within the European Union. In the long run – so the economists tell us – migration will have a positive impact on the standard of living throughout the EU. In the short run, however, migration might have a destabilising impact on the delicate social and economic equilibrium of the country at the receiving end. If the guest workers remain unemployed, they will eventually increase the burden on the social security system. If, on the other hand, they do get gainful employment, but only at the expense of other workers who lose their jobs because of the increasing competition, the guest workers will be indirectly responsible for the growing financial burden on the social security system and, more importantly still, they will be thoroughly disliked by their fellow workers.

This is what prompted Swedish Prime Minister Göran Persson and other leading EU politicians to go back on previous commitments to the new member states and call for restrictions on the free movement of labour from Eastern Europe. A proposal to that effect was presented to and rejected by the Swedish *Riksdag* a few weeks prior to Enlargement Day, on 1 May 2004. Sweden therefore became one of the few West European EU countries to welcome the new East European member states without imposing discriminatory restrictions on them. One single year admittedly does not provide the most solid basis for generalisations, but the data at hand strongly suggests that Prime Minister Persson's fears were grossly exaggerated. Migration from Eastern Europe to Sweden has so far been more limited than anticipated and of little or no significance for the Swedish social security system.

With its peculiar mixture of high taxes and low salaries, Sweden may not be the most attractive target for East European migrants, and other countries more at risk. Whatever the case might be, migration remains a hot issue throughout continental Europe. Denmark has received notoriety for its hard-nosed approach towards immigration and asylum seekers. Turkey's uphill battle for membership of the European Union will not be over with the approval of the European Commission. As required by standard procedure, it will have to be ratified by all member states, at least one of which – France – will defer the decision to a referendum, a roundabout but very efficient and democratically correct way of keeping Turkey – a country with cultural roots removed from those of Western Europe – out of the Union. But there is also a great deal of concern about 'salary dumping' from within the Union as evidenced by the repeated references to the 'Polish plumber' in the French electoral campaign on the Draft Consitution. There is – so it would seem – a growing resistance against foreign influences in Western Europe. This trend may be less pervasive in Eastern Europe, but it does make its presence felt. The struggle against foreign takeovers and domination is already a recurrent theme in countries like Poland and Bulgaria. It is a phenomenon well worth dwelling upon at some length.

Students of comparative politics frequently complain that the secondary data at hand fall short of their specific needs. There may be too many empty cells or missing data in the data matrix and the indicators that are in the public domain may be less than ideal. In this case, however, there is no cause for such complaints. We are in fact in the privileged position of having an official report on a theme and with indicators almost tailor-made to our specific needs as a starting point. We are referring to the summary report, published on 15 March 2005 by the European Monitoring Centre on Racism and Xenophobia (EUMC). It addresses itself to the following theme: *Majorities' Attitudes towards Minorities: Key Findings from the Eurobarometer and the European Social Survey.*

*Figure 6.1: Resistance to a multicultural society (%)*

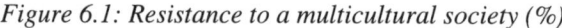

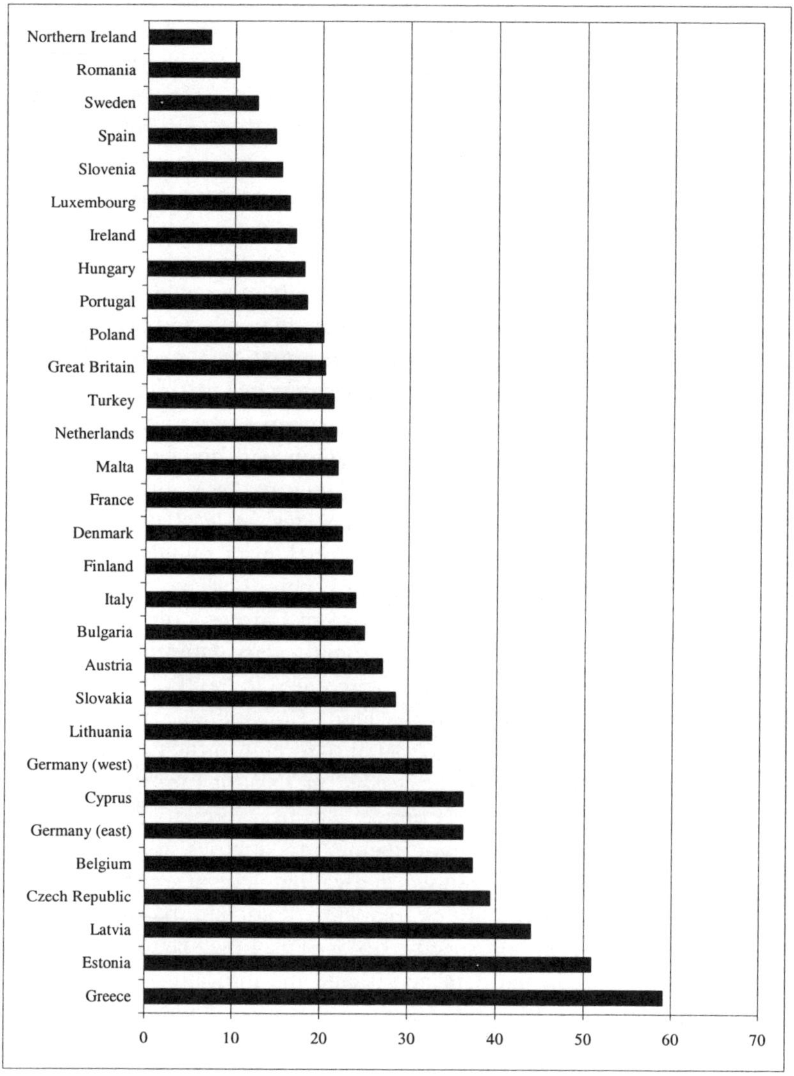

Source: European Monitoring Centre on Racism and Xenophobia, March 2005.

*Figure 6.2: Limits to a multicultural society (%)*

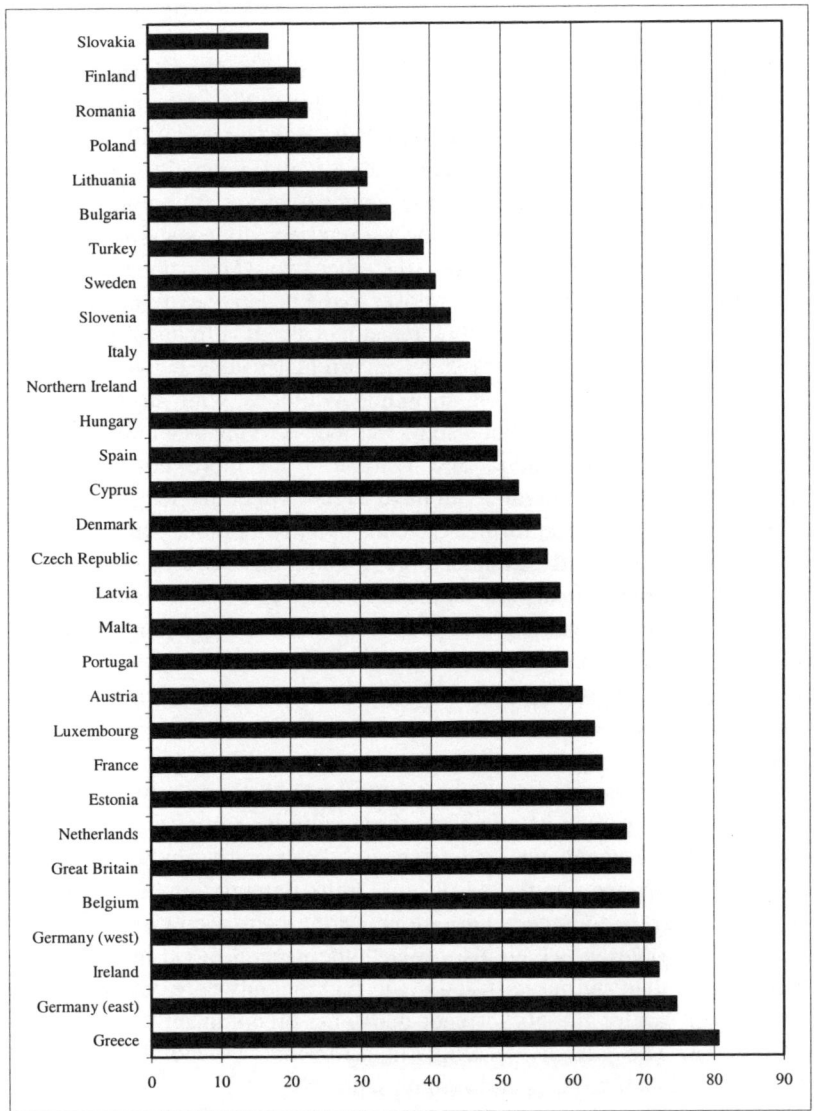

Source: *European Monitoring Centre on Racism and Xenophobia*, March 2005.

The report examines to what extent European publics vary in their support for ethnic inclusion. In the *Eurobarometer* surveys, attitudes were assessed according to the extent to which respondents agreed or not with certain statements. In Figure 6.1, we have used the following statement: 'It is a good thing for any society to be made up of people from different races, religions or cultures'. Those who disagree to this statement have been classified as resisting multiculturalism.

The outcome is quite fascinating. The aggregate scores vary from less than or slightly above 10 per cent – Northern Ireland, Romania and Sweden – to 40 per cent or more for Estonia, Latvia and Greece. With almost six citizens out of ten rejecting multiculturalism, Greece actually stands out as outright xenophobic. Long-term EU membership may possibly reduce resistance to multiculturalism. Of the original six, four stand out as quite open to ethnic and cultural diversity, the other two – Germany and Belgium – position themselves considerably closer to the negative extreme.

Belgium is in fact a particularly interesting case. It is frequently cited as a consociational democracy, rocked by recurrent tensions between Flemish speaking Flanders and French speaking Walloons with Brussels – the capital not only of Belgium but also of Europe – serving as a unifying force. The Czech Republic, Latvia and Estonia – all more hostile towards multiculturalism than Belgium – all have a record of ethnic tensions, Czechs versus Slovaks within the former Czechoslovak federation, ethnic Russians versus the Latvian and Estonian core populations. Greece, at the very bottom of the graph, finally has ethnically-related grievances with respect to Cyprus and more recently with respect to the Former Yugoslav Republic of Macedonia (FYROM). The countries at the other end of the scale – Sweden, Luxembourg, and nowadays also Poland – tend to be quite homogeneous.

Figure 6.2 adds another dimension. It is based on the following survey question: 'There is a limit to how many people of other races, religions or cultures a society can accept. (Our country) has reached its limits; if there were to be more people belonging to these minority groups we would have problems.' Once again, we find Greece at the negative extreme. A very solid majority indeed – eight out of ten – think immigration has reached its saturation level. But Greece is not alone. More than seven Germans out of ten share this opinion, which also reflects the general mood in Britain and France (more than six out ten). Italy is in fact the only core country to land on the other side of the 50 per cent mark, i.e. predominantly in favour of immigration. The citizens of Bulgaria, Lithuania, Poland, Romania and Slovakia are much more open to immigration than Italian voters. Estonians and Latvians, on the other hand, make common cause with anti-immigration sentiments in Germany, France and the UK, presumably yet another by-product of the ethnic cleavage in these Baltic countries.

**Conclusions**

The first two conclusions to be drawn from this inquiry into the challenge of Euroscepticism and nationalism are trivial in the sense that they are likely to be dismissed as established truths. Most observers would probably agree that the relationship between Euroscepticism and nationalism is indeed complex. We would also expect the conclusion that it is difficult, perhaps impossible, to specify the EU orientation of political regimes in terms of categories that meet the textbook requirement of being exhaustive and mutually exclusive.

On a somewhat lower level of analysis, we have introduced a number of alternative ways of tapping Euroscepticism and demonstrated that they do not always overlap. We have one set of indicators based on *Eurobarometer* surveys tapping attitudes towards the EU in general, and more specifically, towards multiculturalism and immigration. The validity of the last two items as indicators of EU orientation may not be intuitively obvious, and it is in fact tempting to discard them as measures of tolerance/intolerance or inclusiveness/exclusiveness. But then, on the other hand, it is hard to imagine a borderless labour market in Europe without at least a minimum of tolerance for ethnic and cultural diversity. We finally have another set of indicators revolving around political parties. The basic dichotomy is that between pro-European and Eurosceptical parties; the latter are then divided into hard- and soft-liners as suggested by Taggart and Szczerbiak (2002, 7), which makes it possible for us to calculate electoral as well as parliamentary support for different shades of Euroscepticism. This is excellent, but we must keep in mind that the European dimension is not equally important for all voters. Eurosceptical parties may very well attract pro-European voters or the other way around. We must also bear in mind that electoral arithmatics affects the outcome. Other things being equal, proportional representation (PR) opens up parliamentary prospects for a variety of minor parties like most contemporary Eurosceptical parties; electoral systems with strong majoritarian elements like the British and French systems do not favour Euroscepticism unless espoused by one of the two major parties or blocs of parties (Table 6.6).

The summary table conveys a somewhat diffuse impression (Table 6.7). In the first column we have the combined electoral strength of hard and soft Euroscepticism. Anything below 10 per cent electoral backing is considered low, anything above 10 per cent high. Three countries – Spain, Bulgaria and Malta – do not have any Eurosceptics in parliament. The two former stand out as distinctly EU friendly on all three attitudinal dimensions displayed in the following columns, Malta only on one.

Germany and Latvia, on the other hand, have a Eurosceptical profile on all dimensions but the first. The remaining countries in this group – Greece, Portugal, Finland, Slovenia and Italy – share the fate of Malta and come up on the Eurosceptical side on at least one of the attitudinal items, usually including the item tapping attitudes towards immigrants with its strongly negative overtones (Table 6.7).

*Table 6.7: Party-based Euroscepticism, public opinion and xenophobia (a summary)*

|  | Party-based Euroscepticism (hard and soft) Based on Table 6.6 | Public Euroscepticism Shaded: above 10 % Eurosceptics Based on Figure 4.5 | Resistance to multiculturalism Shaded: above EU25 mean Based on Figure 6.1 | Negative or hostile attitudes towards immigrants Based on Figure 6.2 |
|---|---|---|---|---|
| Hungary | 49.1 | 9 | 17.9 | 48.5 |
| Czech Rep. | 43.0 | 13 | 39.3 | 56.4 |
| Estonia | 38.4 | 16 | 50.8 | 64.3 |
| Poland | 36.6 | 11 | 20.1 | 30.1 |
| Cyprus | 34.7 | 12 | 36.2 | 52.3 |
| UK | 34.5 | GB: 23 Norther Ireland: 9 | GB: 20.3 Northern Ireland: 7.1 | GB: 68.1 Northern Ireland: 48.4 |
| Slovakia | 31.1 | 6 | 28.5 | 17.1 |
| Denmark | 21.4 | 21 | 22.3 | 55.4 |
| France | 20.3 | 14 | 22.2 | 64.1 |
| Romania | 19.5 | 2 | 10.3 | 22.6 |
| Sweden | 19.0 | 33 | 12.5 | 40.7 |
| Netherlands | 18.7 | 6 | 21.6 | 67.5 |
| Belgium | 13.6 | 9 | 37.3 | 69.2 |
| Lithuania | 12.4 | 10 | 32.6 | 31.1 |
| Luxembourg | 11.6 | 5 | 16.2 | 63.0 |
| Ireland | 11.6 | 5 | 16.9 | 72.1 |
| Austria | 10.0 | 21 | 27.0 | 61.3 |
| Latvia | 9.4 | 18 | 43.9 | 58.2 |
| Greece | 7.7 | 8 | 59.0 | 80.6 |
| Portugal | 7.0 | 8 | 18.2 | 59.2 |
| Finland | 6.9 | 21 | 23.5 | 21.6 |
| Croatia | 6.4 | Data missing | Data missing | Data missing |
| Slovenia | 6.3 | 10 | 15.3 | 42.8 |
| Germany | 4.3 | East: 10 West: 12 | East: 36.2 West: 32.6 | East: 74.6 West: 71.5 |
| Italy | 3.9 | 7 | 23.9 | 45.5 |
| Spain | 0 | 9 | 14.6 | 49.3 |
| Bulgaria | 0 | 4 | 24.9 | 34.4 |
| Malta | 0 | 21 | 21.8 | 58.9 |
| Norway | Data missing | 32 | Data missing | Data missing |
| Turkey | Data missing | 11 | 21.3 | 39.0 |

Turning to the other end of the spectrum, we find only three countries – the Czech Republic, Estonia and Cyprus – with a pronounced Eurosceptical profile across the board. Denmark and Romania come out as Eurosceptical only on the first dimension, while the remaining countries in the group have

Eurosceptical scores on at least one of the three attitudinal dimensions, usually including the item on immigrants with its skewed distribution in favour of the negative evaluations (Table 6.7).

This leads us to the conclusion that Euroscepticism is indeed a multifaceted concept, including behavioural and attitudinal dimensions. These two dimensions are not independent; they overlap to some extent as is readily apparent from Table 6.7. We finally have indications that we may be well advised to reconsider the survey-related indicators, particularly the item tapping negative or hostile attitudes towards immigrants. We still maintain that the item is theoretically relevant as an indicator of EU orientation, albeit in an oblique way. The problem is that it is not discriminatory enough. Anti-immigrant sentiments are in fact so widespread throughout the Union and among the applicant and candidate countries that this item does not discriminate between countries as well as the two other items.

## NOTES

1. Sweden may be a deviant case. In this country, the parties of the radical left have positioned themselves on a strongly anti-EU platform with a rhetoric resembling that of the radical right of other West European countries, albeit without the xenophobic overtones of the elect orally insignificant actors of the far right in Swedish party politics.
2. Theiler suggests some further possible predictors of Euroscepticism in his article, like wealth and ethnical/cultural diversity. These, however, will not be considered in our analysis.
3. EU15 has an average score of 2.8 as opposed to 2.4 for the ten new member states.
4. Though insignificant at the federal level, the German extreme right has carved out a niche for itself in regional and local politics. In Saxony and Brandenburg, two of the new *Bundesländer*, the parties of the radical right have gained parliamentary representation; and two of the three parties (NPD and DVU) are cooperating so as to maximise their odds in the competition for the small segment of the German electorate with semi-fascist leanings.
5. The PDS gained representation in the Bundestag only by virtue of its uncontested strongholds in the capital of the former German Democratic Republic (GDR).

## REFERENCES

Axtmann, Roland (2001), 'State-Formation, Multi-Level Governance and Supranationalism in Europe: The Case of the Holy Roman Empire of German Nation', ECPR General Conference, Canterbury.
Berglund, Sten, Joakim Ekman and Frank H. Aarebrot, eds (2004), *The Handbook of Political Change in Eastern Europe. Second Edition*, Cheltenham, UK and Northampton, MA, USA, Edward Elgar.
*Candidate Countries Eurobarometer* 2001, 2002, 2003.2, 2003.4, 2004.1, Machine-readable data files and codebooks, Brussels, European Commission.
Csergo, Zsuzsa and James M. Goldgeier (2004), 'Nationalist Strategies and European Integration', *Perspectives on Politics*, Vol. 2, No. 1, March 2004.

Ekman, Joakim (2001), *National Identity in Divided and Unified Germany: Continuity and Change*, Örebro, Örebro Studies in Political Science.
*Elections Around the World* website (www.electionworld.org), January 2005.
*Eurobarometer* 36 (autumn 1991) to 61 (spring 2004), Machine-readable data files and codebooks, Brussels, European Commission.
*European Monitoring Centre on Racism and Xenophobia* (2005), 'Majorities' Attitudes towards Minorities: Key Findings from the Eurobarometer and the European Social Survey', EUMC website (http://eumc.eu.int).
Fulbrook, Mary (1999), *German National Identity after the Holocaust*, Cambridge, Polity Press.
*Radio Free Europe/Radio Liberty* homepage (www.rferl.org), Thursday, 29 April 2004, 'EU: Historical division of Europe overcome, but new problems loom (part 1)'.
*Radio Free Europe/Radio Liberty* homepage (www.rferl.org), Thursday, 29 April 2004, 'Despite queue, further enlargement fading amid "fatigue" (part 2)'.
*Radio Free Europe/Radio Liberty* homepage (www.rferl.org), Thursday, 29 April 2004, 'Analysis: EU welcomes new members, but where is the enthusiasm?'.
*Radio Free Europe/Radio Liberty* homepage (www.rferl.org), Saturday, 1 May 2004, 'EU leaders welcome historical expansion'.
Sartori, Giovanni (1976), *Parties and Party Systems: A Framework for Analysis*, Cambridge, Cambridge University Press.
Taggart, Paul and Aleks Szczerbiak (2002), 'The Party Politics of Euroscepticism in EU Member and Candidate States', SEI Working Paper No. 51/Opposing Europe Research Network Working Paper No. 6, Sussex European Institute, University of Sussex.
Theiler, Tobias (2004), 'The Origins of Euroscepticism in German-speaking Switzerland', *European Journal of Political Research*, Vol. 43, Issue 4, June 2004.
Wallace, Helen and William Wallace, eds (2000), *Policy-Making in the European Union*, Fourth edition, Oxford, Oxford University Press.

# 7. *Politikverdrossenheit*, Globalisation and Individualism

In the preceding chapters, we have studied a number of crucial determinants of Europe's future integration. We have examined the nature of public support for the EU, and found out that there is indeed a great deal of support, but it is essentially dependent on the overall development of democracy, both nationally and continentally. We have also concluded that the majority of Europeans believe that increased collaboration in the fields of foreign and defence policy is generally beneficial for Europe and the world, and that this may grant further integration a significant dose of legitimacy. But we have also noted that in spite of the general support for integration, there are still strong nationalist and/or Eurosceptic tendencies across the continent that can potentially hamper continental cooperation – for good or bad.

There are, however, factors that may prove even more important in the long run, factors that exist above, below and beyond the ones that we have discussed so far. These create, as it were, the overall conditions within which the European integration is, and will be, bound to operate. Above all, the European Union must be able to cope with the global markets – while simultaneously being part of those markets itself – and with the challenges posed by people's changing values and identities. The present chapter seeks to shed some light on these challenges by way of an exploration of people's perceptions of these issues. The aim is thus to review, in a preliminary manner, what the relationship between 'the overall conditions', citizens' attitudes to them, and European integration is or might be. This may help us understand the general imperatives of European cooperation in the future.

We have chosen three factors that in our view primarily shape these overall conditions. The first of these is people's relationship with politics, and particularly the way they have turned away from it, both at national and European levels. This is of course crucial: people may continuously display positive EU attitudes, but if these attitudes do not materialise as political activity – voting is the minimum level – *the* main problem of integration, its democratic deficit, cannot be solved; the new institutional or constitutional solutions for the Union are then also in vain. In the absence of a good English term, we use the German word *Politikverdrossenheit* to describe these feelings of alienation from politics. It is noteworthy that the term has a double connotation: it not only alludes to a passive estrangement from politics but also to an active, reflective attitude towards it; it is a self-conscious form of alienation.

The other two factors of our exploration, 'globalisation' and 'individualism', are even more complex and multidimensional – to the extent that we will not even try to define them in any precise manner, but treat them as some sort of 'empty signifiers' (Laclau 1996, Ch. 3). Two points need to be made, however. First, these two phenomena are mutually linked in a great number of ways. Individualism, for example, can be seen as the mental spirit of globalisation, as its basic source of energy. In recent social theory, this linkage has been widely discussed, in many different terms. The dominant idea has been that globalisation necessarily produces counterreactions at the local or individual level; Roland Robertson's (1992; cf. Bauman 1998) by now widely known term glocalisation well captures this idea. Post-modern or post-materialist ideas, such as floating and multiple identities or 'the small is beautiful', can also be seen as counterweights to an ever more 'global' world. Secondly, globalisation and individualism are among the most important reasons for *Politikverdrossenheit*. People may have become too individualistic so that they no longer care about the conduct of common affairs. Or they may feel that the global market forces are so all-powerful that politics has no chance to control them any longer. These complex relationships inform our analyses to some degree – a fact that the reader should bear in mind.

In spite of the complexity of the notion, it is certainly justified to assume that most Europeans have some sort of general understanding of what globalisation actually stands for, what its implications, risks and promises are. They often have mixed feelings about it; they feel that in a non-governed form globalisation is something negative, but if it is managed well, it can be turned into a positive force. In relation to the EU, this assumption gives us two alternative hypotheses. (1) Due to globalisation, people tend to be more positive towards the European Union than they would otherwise be. They believe that the Union can protect them from the faceless effects of globalisation, and even turn globalisation into a positive phenomenon. (2) Alternatively, people resist European integration because it seems to be committed to the current neo-liberal policies and therefore only assists the advancement of globalisation. Among other things, the European Union contributes to the disappearance of jobs to cheaper countries.

The meanings of individualism vary a great deal, from freedom from any external pressure, to personal development and pure hedonism (Vogt 2005, 185). We cannot go into the details of these different meanings here. Suffice it to note that we again resort to what we believe is people's common-sense understanding of the notion: although individualism carries strong positive connotations, those of freedom and adventurous experiences, there is easily a negative connotation involved as well – that of selfish pleasure-seeking, indifference towards other people. The hypotheses are thus fairly similar to those formulated in respect of globalisation. (1) Individualism makes people uninterested in the European Union. They are only interested in maximising their own life chances, and common affairs are therefore seen as waste of time. (2) Alternatively, the EU is perceived as an institution conducive to individualism, for example by creating new possibilities for business and pleasure. Its liberal values are the best guarantee of individualism.

It is relatively easy to draw a causal link between 'public support for the EU' and the future of integration. It is much more difficult to see what it actually means for integration if people increasingly seek the fulfilment of their individual aspirations rather than work for the common cause of humanity. The arrows in Figure 7.1, visualising the structure and 'causalities' of the present chapter, should therefore not be understood too literally.

*Figure 7.1: Contextualising the future of the EU*

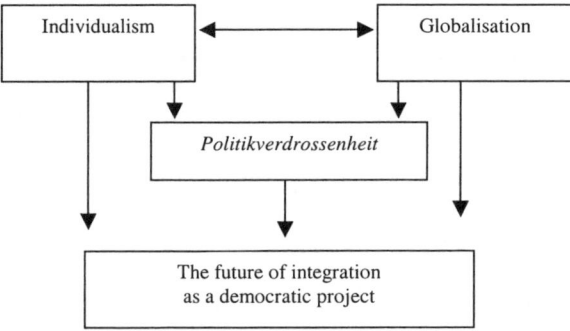

We will start with the first mentioned factor, people's relationship with politics in the EU context, then proceed to analysing globalisation, and finally turn to the peculiarities of individualism. In the conclusion a number of somewhat more philosophical points about the circumstances within which the EU needs to operate in the future will be discussed, and an analogy between the historical evolution (Chapter 2) and the potential future development of integration drawn. Unlike in the previous chapters, with the nation-state as the primary unit of analysis, the emphasis here is on an all-European discussion, although a few cross-national comparisons are also made. Since the themes are so multifaceted, it is obvious that the empirical evidence is bound to remain somewhat fragmentary.

## *Politikverdrossenheit*

Alarm bells have been ringing for at least twenty years now, as people's enthusiasm for politics, and particularly political parties, has (presumably) been declining. The discussion may no longer be quite as lively as it was in the 1990s, however, simply because it has become increasingly apparent that political activity can find new channels; new political phenomena such as the alter-globalisation movement have entered the stage with force. The question thus seems to be of an increasingly complex relationship: rather than simply turning away from politics, many people still have a reflexive attitude to it, follow it closely, and then decide *not* to get engaged; it is a matter of distance rather than disinterest. The notion of *Politikverdrossenheit* can capture this attitude well, although the principal connotation of the term is negative.[1]

A great number of theories can explain this increasingly complex public relationship with politics, and particularly the need to hold a distance to it. It may be a sign of people's overall disillusionment, of their deeply pessimistic attitudes to the way society functions and, above all, how it is governed. This is the attitude that has traditionally caused concerns among the advocates of participatory democracy, and among those worried about the EU's democratic deficit. But it may also be a sign of helplessness on the face of the problems of today; people may sense that politics is not able to change the course of their lives anyway – or, for that matter, of the world; the problems are simply too complex for politicians to solve ('so let technocrats and bureaucrats solve them!'). This is the argument that is, by definition, most closely related to globalisation. Third, it may also be a sign of well being. Things are, after all, so well that there is indeed no need to become politically engaged. Finally, it may be a sign of scepticism, of a realisation that life goes on as it has always done; no true revolution is possible anyway. This is the *Švejkian* spirit, historically a crucial element of European mentality; it may close down some horizons of possibility, but those that remain open are truly realistic. (The notion of 'Euroscepticism' that we discussed in Chapter 6 could be understood from this perspective, too.)

How do these potential explanations then survive in light of empirical evidence? Let us begin our exploration with brute facts, as opposed to survey-based approximations. Election turnouts are generally regarded as the most concrete indication of people's relations with politics. With turnout data we can also create a historical overview of the development of these relations, seldom possible with survey data. Table 7.1 shows the turnouts in the elections to the European Parliament (EP) since 1979 when general elections were held at the European level for the first time. The overall trend is very clear: turnouts have been declining throughout the Union. (The continuously high percentages of Luxemburg and Belgium depend on the fact that EP elections are organised simultaneously with national parliamentary elections, in which voting is mandatory.) Well under 50 per cent of all EU citizens used their right to vote in the last (2004) EP elections. It is noteworthy, however, that in the first EP elections of the 'old' member states, the turnouts were often (un)reasonably high; the factor of initial excitement of EU membership was definitely there. As Union membership has become an everyday, acceptable reality, there is no particular need to participate in its political procedures. Politics as usual prevails.

*Table 7.1: Turnouts in the elections to the European Parliament (%)*

| Member states | 1979 | 1984 | 1989 | 1994 | 1999 | 2004 | Last–first |
|---|---|---|---|---|---|---|---|
| Germany | 65.7 | 56.8 | 62.3 | 60 | 45.2 | 43.0 | −22.7 |
| France | 60.7 | 56.7 | 48.7 | 52.7 | 46.8 | 42.8 | −17.9 |
| Belgium | 91.4 | 92.2 | 90.7 | 90.7 | 91.0 | 90.8 | −0.6 |
| Italy | 84.9 | 83.4 | 81.5 | 74.8 | 70.8 | 73.1 | −11.8 |
| Luxemburg | 88.9 | 88.8 | 87.4 | 88.5 | 87.3 | 89.0 | +0.1 |
| Netherlands | 57.8 | 50.6 | 47.2 | 35.6 | 30.0 | 39.3 | −18.5 |
| United Kingdom | 32.2 | 32.6 | 36.2 | 36.4 | 24.0 | 38.8 | +6.6 |
| Ireland | 63.6 | 47.6 | 68.3 | 44.0 | 50.2 | 58.8 | −4.8 |
| Denmark | 47.8 | 52.4 | 46.2 | 52.9 | 50.5 | 47.9 | +0.1 |
| Greece | | 77.2 | 79.9 | 71.2 | 75.3 | 63.2 | −14.0 |
| Spain | | 68.9[a] | 54.6 | 59.1 | 63.0 | 45.1 | −23.8 |
| Portugal | | 72.4[a] | 51.2 | 35.5 | 40.0 | 38.6 | −33.8 |
| Sweden | | | | 41.6[b] | 38.8 | 37.8 | −4.8 |
| Austria | | | | 67.7[c] | 49.4 | 42.4 | −25.3 |
| Finland | | | | 60.3[c] | 31.4 | 39.4 | −20.9 |
| Czech Republic | | | | | | 28.3 | |
| Estonia | | | | | | 26.8 | |
| Cyprus | | | | | | 71.2 | |
| Latvia | | | | | | 41.3 | |
| Lihuania | | | | | | 48.4 | |
| Hungary | | | | | | 38.5 | |
| Malta | | | | | | 82.4 | |
| Poland | | | | | | 20.9 | |
| Slovenia | | | | | | 28.3 | |
| Slovakia | | | | | | 17.0 | |
| EU | 63.0 | 61.0 | 58.5 | 56.8 | 49.8 | 45.7 | −17.3 |

Sources: European Parliament. Mattila and Raunio (2005). [a]1987, [b]1995, [c]1996

In the eastern new member states, the turnouts in the 2004 EP elections were so low that they in fact undermined the legitimacy of the electoral process. There definitely was no reaction of initial enthusiasm – which is not that surprising given the modest participation in these states' EU membership referenda in 2003. The turnouts were much lower than in the corresponding referenda in the Nordic countries in the 1970s and 1990s, albeit the percentages of yes-voters were much higher (Szcerbiak and Taggart 2004). This clearly reflects the generally hostile mood against politics and, above all, politicians in the former communist countries. After the euphoria of early post-communist transformation, a significant part of the countries' citizens rapidly grew disillusioned as the new circumstances proved in many ways more demanding than the old ones and the politics of the new era appeared far too similar to that of the past – different from what people had expected during their glorious revolutions. Moreover, many former communists boldly transformed their political power into economic power, becoming, in many ordinary people's view illegally, the *nouveaux riches* (Vogt 2005, Ch. 4). These attitudes have continued to prevail, even though political life in most of these countries has stabilised.

It is thus evident that a clear *majority* of Europeans do not consider the European Parliament sufficiently important to make them vote. As Table 7.2 shows, the situation is clearly different at the national level. Many countries still have reasonably high election turnouts in national parliamentary (NP) elections, although the decline is clearly visible here, too. In 16 of the 25 EU member states the turnouts of the early 2000s NP elections were over 20 per cent higher than in the EP elections of 2004. Lithuania seems to be the only major exception in this respect, but this does not depend on the popularity of the EP elections but rather on the low turnout in national elections. Moreover, at least according to *Eurobarometer* 61 from 2004, people's anticipated willingness to participate in national elections is on a clearly higher level than in EP elections. In the former case, this willingness is also less dependent on the individual's future expectations and general satisfaction with life than in the latter case.

The conclusion thus appears evident. People are still primarily attached to their national polities, and the European level plays only a secondary role – even for those who actually cast their vote in the EP elections. This is well in line with what we have earlier noted about the primary identity of EU citizens: the national identity is still far more important than the European identity (Table 4.2). It is also closely related to one of the main arguments of Chapter 3: the mechanisms of the recreation of national cultures and polities are still far superior to those that exist for the creation and recreation of the European polity. However, the May–June 2004 French and Dutch referenda about the European Constitution may have dimmed this picture to some degree. What was important was that the elections were very thoroughly debated throughout Europe, much more thoroughly than any other EU elections before. Maybe they created, paradoxically, a truly European polity for the first time, a polity that is able to challenge the national level. This indicates that the reconstruction of the institutional structures of the Union might indeed result in a truly meaningful European-level polity.

Table 7.2: Comparison between turnouts in the national parliament (NP) and the European Parliament (EP) elections (%)

| Member states | NP mid 1970s | ca. 1990 | NP early 2000s | EP 2004 | NP 2000s –70s/90 | EP 2004 –NP 2000s |
|---|---|---|---|---|---|---|
| Germany | 90.7[1] | 77.8 | 79.1 | 43.0 | –11.6 | –26.1 |
| France | 81.3 | 66.2 | 60.3 | 42.8 | –21.0 | –17.5 |
| Belgium | 90.3 | 92.7 | 91.6 | 90.8 | +0.5 | –0.8 |
| Italy | 93.4 | 87.4 | 81.4 | 73.1 | –12.0 | –8.3 |
| Luxemburg | 90.1 | 87.4 | 89.0[2] | 89.0 | –1.1 | 0.0 |
| Netherlands | 88.0 | 80.3 | 80.0 | 39.3 | 8.0 | –40.7 |
| United Kingdom | 78.9 | 77.8 | 59.4 | 38.8 | –19.5 | –20.6 |
| Ireland | 76.3 | 68.5 | 62.2 | 58.8 | –14.1 | –3.4 |
| Denmark | 88.2 | 82.8 | 87.1 | 47.9 | –1.1 | –39.2 |
| Greece | 79.6 | 84.6 | 75.0 | 63.2 | –4.6 | –11.8 |
| Spain | 77.0 | 70.0 | 77.2 | 45.1 | +0.2 | –22.1 |
| Portugal | 91.7 | 68.2 | 62.3 | 38.6 | –29.4 | –23.7 |
| Sweden | 91.8 | 86.7 | 80.1 | 37.8 | –11.7 | –42.3 |
| Austria | 92.9 | 86.1 | 84.3 | 42.4 | –8.6 | –41.9 |
| Finland | 73.8 | 68.4 | 69.7 | 39.4 | –4.1 | –30.3 |
| Czech Republic | | 96.8 | 58.0 | 28.3 | –38.8 | –29.7 |
| Estonia | | 66.8 | 58.2 | 26.8 | –8.6 | –31.6 |
| Cyprus | 85.3 | 94.3 | 91.8 | 71.2 | –6.5 | –20.6 |
| Latvia | | 89.9 | 71.5 | 41.3 | –18.4 | –30.2 |
| Lithuania | | 75.3 | 43.2[3] | 48.4 | –32.1 | +5.2 |
| Hungary | | 65.1 | 70.5[4] | 38.5 | +5.4 | –32.0 |
| Malta | 95.0 | 96.0 | 95.7 | 82.4 | +0.7 | –13.3 |
| Poland | | 43.2 | 46.3 | 20.9 | +3.1 | –15.4 |
| Slovenia | | 83.3 | 60.5 | 28.3 | –22.8 | –32.3 |
| Slovakia | | 98.9 | 70.1 | 17.0 | –28.8 | –53.1 |

Notes: (1) West Germany; (2) Organised in conjunction with the European Parliament elections; (3) Average of 1st and 2nd rounds; (4) 1st round.

Sources: European Parliament; International Institute for Democracy and Electoral Assistance (www.idea.int); Berglund et al. (2004).

Election turnouts provide us with one picture of people's political activity, polls can provide a different one. There is an abundance of questions explicitly related to people's interest in politics and political participation in various European-wide surveys; the problem is that no survey alone is particularly thorough or systematic in this respect. The European Social Survey of 2002–03 (ESS), however, includes a set of questions that serves our purposes well, in spite of the fact that the country coverage of ESS is not as good as that of the *Eurobarometer* (including the *Candidate Countries Barometer*). As we can see in Table 7.3, approximately half of the Europeans proved to be at least somewhat interested in politics in the early 2000s; in several countries the percentage is well over 60, which is in fact a fairly high figure. The clear geographical pattern in the table is of particular interest. The eight states where interest in politics is lowest, all belong either to Catholic Southern Europe – the percentage in Spain, 21, is remarkably low – or are former communist countries. By contrast, all the countries that score high on this scale save Austria belong to the Protestant and North Western Europe.

*Table 7.3: Interest in politics in a number of European countries (%)*

|  | Very or quite interested in politics[1] | Active role in politics – definitely not[2] | Active role in politics – probably or definitely | Politics too complicated – seldom or never[3] | Politics too complicated – regularly or frequently |
|---|---|---|---|---|---|
| Netherlands | 66 | 42 | 20 | 32 | 32 |
| Germany | 63 | 28 | 28 | 33 | 26 |
| Denmark | 63 | 21 | 53 | 33 | 29 |
| Switzerland | 61 | 34 | 25 | 30 | 29 |
| Austria | 59 | 45 | 16 | 36 | 30 |
| Sweden | 58 | 24 | 33 | 34 | 27 |
| UK | 52 | 39 | 27 | 23 | 41 |
| Norway | 50 | 21 | 30 | 29 | 23 |
| Ireland | 46 | 44 | 21 | 31 | 36 |
| Finland | 46 | 34 | 19 | 20 | 49 |
| Hungary | 46 | 63 | 13 | 29 | 38 |
| Belgium | 45 | 49 | 16 | 29 | 36 |
| Luxemburg | 43 | 60 | 22 | 31 | 34 |
| Slovenia | 42 | 44 | 17 | 27 | 36 |
| Poland | 40 | 47 | 19 | 23 | 45 |
| France | 40 | 58 | 15 | 22 | 44 |
| Portugal | 36 | 54 | 15 | 24 | 41 |
| Italy | 33 | 49 | 15 | 26 | 40 |
| Czech R. | 32 | 51 | 14 | 23 | 33 |
| Greece | 32 | 20 | 40 | 18 | 63 |
| Spain | 21 | 58 | 10 | 24 | 42 |
| Total | *46* | *42* | *21* | *27* | *37* |

*Notes*: (1) The full question reads: 'How interested would you say you are in politics – are you very, quite, hardly, or not at all interested'. (2) The full question reads: 'Do you think that you could take an active role in a group involved with political issues? Definitely not, probably not, not sure either way, probably, definitely.' Below average shaded. (3) The full question reads: How often does politics seem so complicated that you can't really understand what is goin on? Never, seldom, occasionally, regularly, frequently.' Below average shaded.

*Source*: European Social Survey (2002–03).

In the case of the other two items displayed in the table, the situation looks somewhat less clear geographically, although the same pattern is there. Perhaps the most significant observation concerning the second item is that over 40 per cent of all respondents were sure that they would *not* take an active role in any group involved in political affairs (this was the 'lowest' reply option out of five) – despite the fact that the survey was conducted during the inevitable, controversial march towards the Iraq war. In most countries less than one in four could consider active participation in the activities of a political group. The high figure in the case of the Netherlands, and the low one in Greece, seem somewhat odd.[2] They may be interpreted as yet another indication that interest in politics is not the same thing as active political participation.

The third question included in the table dealt with the sense of complexity of politics. Over one third of all respondents regarded politics as too complicated, whereas less than one third did not normally find it difficult to follow what was going on in politics. Only five countries, Germany, Denmark, Switzerland, Austria and Sweden, have a majority of citizens self-confident enough to rate politics as understandable rather than too complicated. In Finland, the share of respondents belonging to the latter group, 49 per cent, appears surprising, but it may possibly be attributed to the traditionally strong belief in authority in that country. In conclusion, it is very clear indeed that the perceived complexity of politics is one significant determinant of people's (dis)interest in politics. As many as 74 per cent of all those respondents who said that they found politics complicated regularly or frequently were hardly or not at all interested in politics. But whether these figures depend on the fact that politics in the era of globalisation truly *is* complicated, or whether the respondents simply have ceased trying to find out what is going on in politics, is impossible to judge on the basis of these data.

Table 7.4 already anticipates the analyses of the two ensuing sections. It provides us with one possible, though not particularly surprising, explanation for why people, at least in the old member states, are not interested in politics: those who are pessimistic about their personal life in general also tend to have problems in trusting various political bodies. What is interesting, however, is that the difference between the optimists and the pessimists is particularly visible with respect to the representative political bodies, whereas in the case of such institutions as the army and the police, the difference is much smaller in relative terms. Even among the pessimists, a clear majority trust them. It is also interesting to see, on the one hand, that the European Union is generally trusted *more* than the national representative bodies. On the other hand, the Union seems to be a particularly divisive issue between the pessimists and the optimists; there is a bigger difference in percentages than in the case of all the other alternatives.

In the new member states, the main patterns seem fairly similar, but the levels of trust are, without exceptions, clearly lower. The number of those who trust political parties, 7 per cent, is of course very low, giving evidence to what was said above about disillusionment in there countries, and to the fact that the party systems have not the same traditions as in the western part of the continent. The systems have been unstable, and many leading politicians have made themselves guilty for questionable deeds.

*Table 7.4: Trust in societal institutions and personal future expectations in EU15 and trust in societal institutions in the new member states (%)*

| | Total EU15 'tend to trust' | Total EU15 'tend not to trust' | Next 5 years, personal situation improve, 'trust', EU15 | Next 5 years, personal situation worse, 'trust', EU15 | Total NMS – tend to trust | Total NMS – tend not to trust |
|---|---|---|---|---|---|---|
| **Political parties** | 16 | 76 | 17 | 10 | 7 | 82 |
| Big companies | 26 | 61 | 31 | 16 | 23 | 56 |
| **The national government** | 30 | 61 | 33 | 16 | 17 | 74 |
| **The national parliament** | 35 | 54 | 39 | 23 | 16 | 76 |
| Trade unions | 36 | 50 | 39 | 29 | 22 | 52 |
| The religious institutions | 41 | 46 | 38 | 36 | 45 | 41 |
| **The European Union** | 41 | 42 | 48 | 26 | 40 | 37 |
| The press | 46 | 47 | 48 | 40 | 49 | 41 |
| Justice/national legal system | 48 | 44 | 49 | 40 | 27 | 62 |
| The United Nations | 49 | 35 | 53 | 37 | 50 | 27 |
| Television | 54 | 40 | 53 | 48 | 57 | 35 |
| Charitable/voluntary org. | 61 | 28 | 65 | 52 | 51 | 30 |
| Radio | 63 | 28 | 67 | 54 | 60 | 30 |
| The army | 63 | 26 | 64 | 57 | 58 | 26 |
| The police | 65 | 29 | 63 | 58 | 42 | 48 |

Sources: *Eurobarometer* 61 (2004); *Candidate Countries Eurobarometer* 2004.1. Data weighted by population size (without weighting the levels of trust are clearly higher, i.e. in smaller countries people have more trust in institutions). Those who believed that their personal situation would improve within the next five years outnumbered those who believed that it would get worse by a factor of three to one.

Two general conclusions need to be drawn on the basis of the data above. First, a very significant number of Europeans are still interested in politics. They may not trust their political leaders but nonetheless believe that they can cope with them. Perhaps they are even thankful for those who are still willing to get involved in the dirty business of politics. Indeed, most Europeans believe that political participation would be good and necessary in itself. In *Special Eurobarometer* 60.1 (2003), for example, 77 per cent of the respondents believed that 'citizens should participate more actively in politics in our country'. This is yet another piece of evidence of the high levels of diffuse support (see earlier chapters) for the democratic political systems in Europe; the trust in such institutions as the army, the police and the free media, can also be interpreted from this perspective. The party system, possibly the most important determinant of 'specific support', is now perceived as the main problem. It seems outdated and unable to connect the national polities and the European level – which would be crucially important, particularly for those who support integration. If only the appropriate linkages between the national and European levels were in place, *Politikverdrossenheit* would lose much of its potential to challenge European integration.

This leads us to the second conclusion. A large number of the citizens, maybe one third, are deeply estranged from politics – and maybe from life – and the European Union simply represents one despised element thereof. Moreover, the EU may in fact help generate this estrangement: the Union creates a new political entity in parallel with the national one, and thus makes it more difficult to know where political decisions are made and by whom. Politics simply becomes more complex and blurred – and the identity of the Union itself remains unclear. This may also explain the big difference between optimists and pessimists regarding their trust in the Union.

So far we have only talked about one explanation for this estrangement, people's overall satisfaction with life, their optimism or pessimism in relation to their future. But as we indicated at the outset, there may be other reasons. We will now turn to one, and possibly the most significant, of them, namely globalisation.

**Globalisation**

The linkage between European regional integration and various globalisation processes has raised a number of conflicting views in recent years. There is no disagreement at the most general level, however: the linkage is very close. Colin Hay and Nicola J. Smith's (2005, 12) depiction of 'twin processes' is certainly justified. For the steadfast proponents of the current form of globalisation, the Union needs to be geared towards guaranteeing Europe's success in the globalising world markets without challenging the basic principles of these markets; the Union thus ought to support the (neo-)liberal economic policies full-heartedly. Others emphasise that regional cooperation is imperative if the power of the global economic actors, above all multinational companies and pension funds, is to be controlled at least to some degree; the argument is that globalisation is expensive for Europe, but 'no globalisation' would be even more expensive (interestingly, the same argument was used to justify the most recent enlargement of the Union). Environmental problems have also been important in this context: in EU-positive 'green thinking' one of the central arguments has been that these problems require global solutions – or at least regional ones.

In the context of this book we cannot pause to contemplate what the true nature of this linkage is. Instead, we will try to understand how the citizens of Europe see the relationship between globalisation and European integration. Two issues are particularly important: namely their attitudes in general, that is, whether globalisation is interpreted negatively or positively and whether globalisation can possibly be controlled, and by whom.

Table 7.5: Attitudes to globalisation and support for EU membership in EU15 and attitudes to globalisation in the new member states (%)

| (For EU15:) Generally speaking, do you think that our country's EU membership is… | ...a good thing | | ...a bad thing | | ...neither good nor bad | | New member states | |
|---|---|---|---|---|---|---|---|---|
| Positive consequences of globalisation: | tend to agree | tend to dis-agree | tend to agree | tend to dis-agree | tend to agree | tend to dis-agree | tend to agree | tend to dis-agree |
| Overall, globalisation is a good thing for our country | 49 | 34 | 28 | 55 | 32 | 42 | 31 | 35 |
| Overall, globalisation is a good thing for me | 38 | 39 | 20 | 59 | 23 | 48 | 23 | 38 |
| Globalisation represents a good opportunity for my country's companies | 53 | 27 | 36 | 43 | 40 | 32 | 27 | 37 |
| Globalisation increases the variety of products for sale in our country | 65 | 19 | 56 | 25 | 56 | 22 | 52 | 17 |
| Globalisation cuts the prices of products and services through increased competition. | 51 | 31 | 36 | 44 | 40 | 36 | 41 | 24 |
| Potential threats of globalisation: | | | | | | | | |
| Globalisation leads to power being concentrated in large companies, at the exp of others | 68 | 17 | 64 | 19 | 63 | 16 | 55 | 14 |
| Globalisation increases global environmental problems | 55 | 25 | 61 | 19 | 56 | 19 | 48 | 18 |
| Globalisation represents a threat to employment in our country | 55 | 28 | 64 | 19 | 60 | 19 | 39 | 25 |
| Globalisation makes it more difficult to control the quality of food products sold in our country | 57 | 25 | 64 | 17 | 58 | 20 | 42 | 23 |
| Globalisation leads to a duller and more uniform world. | 39 | 40 | 43 | 33 | 38 | 33 | 33 | 28 |

Sources: *Eurobarometer* 61 (2004). Data weighted by population sizes; *Candidate Countries Eurobarometer* 2004.1. The data of the latter had not been released by the end of July 2005, when this book was finished.

When asked in general terms it seems that the majority of Europeans are in favour of the current mode of globalisation. For example, in the *Flash*

*Eurobarometer* 151b from 2003, 63 per cent of the respondents in the old member states were in favour of 'the development of globalisation'.[3] The percentage varied a lot, though, from 47 per cent in Greece to 78 per cent in the Netherlands. Table 7.5 provides us with a more nuanced picture of people's general attitudes to globalisation. We have divided the ten statements on globalisation included in *Eurobarometer* 61 and *Candidate Countries Eurobarometer* 2004.1 (early 2004) into two groups, so that the upper group represents positive aspects of globalisation and the lower its potential threats. In the old member states, we cross-tabled these statements with the item on the support for EU membership, and the outcome proved unquestionable: those who support their country's EU membership also hold reasonably positive attitudes to globalisation, and vice versa. The difference is particularly striking when the influence of globalisation on one's personal life was assessed; compared with EU opponents, twice as many EU supporters thought that the influence was positive (38 vs. 20 per cent, respectively). It is noteworthy, however, that EU supporters by no means pay tribute to all aspects of globalisation but often deem it to be *both* a negative and a positive phenomenon. They attach, in other words, a number of promises to globalisation but are equally aware of its inherent risks – but more often than other respondents they believe that these risks can be lived with. EU opponents generally see more threats in globalisation than others.[4]

Another significant observation is that the respondents are clearly less optimistic about their own chances to benefit from globalisation than those of their country (the first and second statements in the table). There are certainly a number of good explanations to this, but one possibility is that the respondents find it difficult to believe in the most common globalisation-favouring argument, namely 'in the long run everyone will benefit from globalisation'. They have come to the conclusion that this trickle-down effect does not necessarily concern them, the individuals, even though it might reach the collective level; globalisation then appears as an existential threat rather than an essentially benevolent phenomenon. Moreover, it becomes apparent that globalisation is primarily related to the sphere of the economy; almost two thirds of the respondents in the old member states agreed that the phenomenon leads to power concentration.

The citizens of new member states attach positive meanings to globalisation clearly less often than those of the old member states. What is more interesting, however, is that relatively many of them have no precise views of the various processes of globalisation at all. Also with respect to the critical aspects of globalisation, they disagree much less often than the long-time EU citizens.[5] One good explanation for this is that the post-communist economic and political transformation has determined societal life to a much greater degree than globalisation in these countries. The transformation has been so profound that whatever globalisation brings about pales in comparison anyway. Besides it is impossible to know whether, say, the disappearance of one's job depends on globalisation or transformation. Globalisation is thus not regarded as an all-powerful threat in these countries but it does not represent a distinct opportunity either.

In what ways do the attitudes to globalisation vary in the old member states, then? To answer this question, we constructed a crude index of globalisation support on the basis of the replies to the first five statements of Table 7.5. If the respondent agreed with all of these statements, he/she got 5 points; 16.6 per cent of all respondents did so. And if the respondent did not agree with any of the statements, he/she got zero points; 21.9 per cent of the respondents belonged to this group. Then we further divided the respondents into three groups: those with 4 or 5 points belong to what we call 'globalisation optimists'; those with 0 or 1 point are 'globalisation pessimists'; and those with 2 or 3 points 'globalisation hesitators' (they are not displayed in the table).

It is obvious that the index is only very indicative but, as Table 7.6 shows, the outcome is so clear that we are inclined to believe that it truly reveals something essential of how globalisation is perceived in different countries. It may be noted that citizens of the most sceptical EU members, the Nordic countries of Sweden, Denmark and Finland, seem to have a clearly more positive understanding of globalisation than others. They are followed by another group of three countries, from the Northwestern corner of the Union. South European countries, then, are much less optimistic about their chances to succeed in the global era. As already shown (Table 7.5), globalisation optimism is much more widespread among the supporters of the European Union than among its opponents, even though a substantial part of the EU *opponents* of the Northwestern cluster see globalisation as beneficial.[6] It is also worth noting that, if we had used the statements on potential threats of globalisation, that is, the latter five statements of Table 7.5, the differences between countries would have been clearly smaller. However, on average the respondents from the original six member states saw clearly more threats in the process of globalisation than other old members.

Why do the EU-sceptical Nordic countries appear so positive in relation to globalisation? The first and best explanation is no doubt that these countries have survived economically reasonably well in the age of globalisation. It is therefore difficult for their citizens to see globalisation as merely a threat. Secondly, it turns out that the percentage of those who think that globalisation is a promise *and* EU membership a good thing is very high indeed, well over 50 per cent and up to 74 per cent in Sweden. In contrast, for example in Spain where the image of the EU has tended to be on a high level (see e.g. Figure 4.3), the connection between 'globalisation optimism' and 'support for the EU' is not pronounced at all; maybe three quarters of those who support Spain's EU membership do *not* judge globalisation in optimistic terms. This, and for example the fact that in Sweden over half of those who are against their country's EU membership are optimistic with regard to globalisation, shows that the linkage between globalisation and support for the European Union is by no means a linear or one-dimensional issue.

Table 7.6: *Attitudes to globalisation in the old EU member states (%)*

|  | Globalisation optimists, total | Globalisation pessimists, total | Optimists among EU supporters* | Optimists among EU opponents |
|---|---|---|---|---|
| Sweden | 56 | 15 | 74 | 52 |
| Denmark | 45 | 24 | 59 | 26 |
| Finland | 40 | 23 | 53 | 26 |
| Netherlands | 38 | 28 | 46 | 17 |
| Ireland | 37 | 40 | 43 | 27 |
| UK | 34 | 28 | 47 | 28 |
| Portugal | 29 | 44 | 38 | 12 |
| Luxemburg | 26 | 38 | 29 | 27 |
| Italy | 25 | 46 | 32 | 16 |
| Germany | 25 | 40 | 37 | 9 |
| Greece | 23 | 42 | 27 | 12 |
| Austria | 23 | 37 | 44 | 5 |
| Belgium | 21 | 46 | 29 | 5 |
| Spain | 19 | 57 | 23 | 9 |
| France | 18 | 47 | 30 | 4 |

* EU supporters are those who reply to the question 'Generally speaking, do you think that our country's membership of the European is...' that it is 'a good thing'. See also Table 7.5.

Source: *Eurobarometer* 61 (2004).

Whether people believe that globalisation, or some aspects of it, can be controlled somehow and by someone, is apparently a very important issue from the point of the European Union: if people believed in the capacity of the Union in this respect, this would certainly guarantee the Union a great deal of legitimacy in the future. Table 7.7, based again on *Eurobarometer* 61, indicates that the EU can indeed claim some credit in this field. Over one fourth of all respondents see the Union as a potential regulator of globalisation, which is the highest percentage of the institutions and organisations of which the respondents had to choose. Consumer rights associations obtained the second highest percentage. This may appear somewhat surprising, but it may simply testify to the fact that people think of globalisation as an economic phenomenon and that they through consumption can possibly have an influence on it – if at all.

Particularly striking is that those bodies that have been specifically created for global governance come far behind the European Union. The percentage gained by the United Nations, 13 per cent, is definitely not flattering. Some 9 per cent of the respondents, in turn, believed that no one could control globalisation, which is in fact surprisingly few.

Those who support their country's EU membership are *generally* much more optimistic about the possibilities for controlling globalisation than the EU opponents. The differences between these two groups are, however, not particularly great, except in the case of the European Union itself (39 versus 11 per cent). This naturally suggests that one reason for EU support is the Union's assumed potential to harness globalisation (basically, it would be possible to include this factor in the multivariate analysis of Chapter 4, but since there are questions about globalisation in only a very limited number of Eurobarometers this was not possible). It is also noteworthy that EU opponents prove highly sceptical towards all organisational efforts to control globalisation; some 16 per cent of them believe that 'no one' can control globalisation, whereas the corresponding figure for EU supporters is just over 5 per cent.

*Table 7.7: Who can control globalisation? Data on EU15 and new member states (%)*

|  | Total | Membership: a good thing | Membership: a bad thing | Sweden | Portugal | France | UK | Men | NMS |
|---|---|---|---|---|---|---|---|---|---|
| Political parties | 7 | 9 | 5 | 10 | 4 | 5 | 5 | 7 | 11 |
| National government | 19 | 22 | 16 | 25 | 24 | 20 | 20 | 19 | 13 |
| EU | 27 | 39 | 11 | 40 | 31 | 21 | 17 | 30 | 27 |
| Green/ecol. groups | 16 | 18 | 14 | 22 | 7 | 19 | 18 | 16 | 22 |
| Trade unions | 9 | 9 | 8 | 8 | 6 | 11 | 9 | 9 | 7 |
| Consumer rights associations | 26 | 28 | 24 | 18 | 14 | 33 | 17 | 26 | 24 |
| Multinational companies | 5 | 5 | 4 | 18 | 2 | 3 | 4 | 5 | 7 |
| WTO | 17 | 21 | 15 | 36 | 5 | 12 | 21 | 19 | 15 |
| UN | 13 | 16 | 11 | 28 | 11 | 7 | 17 | 15 | 18 |
| World Bank/IMF | 10 | 12 | 8 | 30 | 3 | 6 | 8 | 12 | 11 |
| US government | 3 | 3 | 3 | 12 | 0.6 | 1 | 3 | 3 | 5 |
| Anti-globalisation movements | 13 | 15 | 13 | 10 | 5 | 21 | 8 | 13 | 15 |
| NGOs | 13 | 15 | 12 | 5 | 4 | 21 | 11 | 14 | 10 |
| Citizens themselves | 23 | 23 | 25 | 26 | 15 | 31 | 21 | 25 | 25 |
| No one | 9 | 5 | 16 | 3 | 9 | 13 | 6 | 9 | 8 |

*Note:* Multiple replies are possible.

*Sources: Eurobarometer* 61 (2004); *Eurobarometer* 2004.1. Data weighted by population size. The percentage of those who answered 'don't know' was 13.6.

We also selected four individual countries with different geographies and integration histories to illustrate the differences across the continent. The first observation is that the differences between countries are indeed significant. For example, in Sweden 40 per cent trust the EU to serve as a regulator of globalisation, as opposed to a meagre 17 per cent in the equivalent British study. In France, 30 per cent place their hope in citizens themselves, but in Portugal only 15 per cent do. The most important aspect, though, is that the small countries in the North display the greatest amount of optimism when it comes to the possibilities for controling globalisation. Above all, they are more optimistic than the rest that multilateral organisations can bring about significant changes in the world. This may also reflect the fact that most of these countries have always strongly emphasised the role of the UN system in global governance in their foreign policy. In Southern Europe, in contrast, the multilateral institutions were very sparingly trusted. The differences between Sweden and Portugal illustrate this well.

Men appear somewhat more optimistic than women when it comes to controlling globalisation. In the case of the EU the difference is particularly great, which corresponds well with the fact that men have generally been more positive to the Union than women. The other socio-demographic background factors (age, education, rural versus urban), in contrast, did not seem to generate any significant differences.

All in all, Europe seems profoundly divided in respect of people's attitudes to globalisation, both between and within countries. The most significant division line is that between the North-West and the South-East. In North-Western Europe, the majority of people clearly believe that globalisation can benefit them and their country, and that it is possible to control the phenomenon by multilateral means. In Southern Europe people who think along these lines are equally clearly in minority. In the new member states, globalisation is still perceived in much more vague terms, and determined by the overall transition. There is, however, reason to believe that at least some of these countries – Estonia and Latvia are the most obvious candidates – will fairly soon join the North-Western cluster of globalisation optimists. Within countries the cleavage is equally profound. Attitudes to globalisation truly divide European societies, very much in the same manner as attitudes to the EU do, although most people do not seem to think of the phenomenon in black-and-white terms.

What is important is that a large share of Europeans perceive the European Union as a factor that can bring some sort of balance and justice to globalisation; it is very difficult to assess how big this share is, but it is in any case significantly bigger than the share of those who believe that the Union simply promotes the most ruthless aspects of this all-encompassing phenomenon. However, in the opinion of South Europeans, it seems that the

Union should provide protection from globalisation; by contrast, North Europeans would prefer the EU to regulate and further the most positive aspects of globalisation. This fairly positive image in relation to globalisation is, we believe, clearly something that the Union could try to 'exploit' more. If more and more people were to believe that globalisation could indeed be harnessed by way of regional cooperation, this might help bring about a functional European political sphere. At the moment, however, a very significant percentage of those who believe that globalisation is a threat, also see the European Union in negative terms. In their view, if someone can control globalisation in the first place, it is definitely not the EU.

**Individualism**

As is well known, much of modern sociology and social theory deals with individualism. It figures as *the* central consequence of industrialisation and modernisation, and dominates the discussion on changing values in the world. By way of example, the shift towards post-materialist values in Western industrialised societies, observed and predicted by Roland Inglehart and his disciples since the 1970s, is based on the idea of increasing individualism, on the individual's ability to find the meaning of life where others may not find it.[7] Value changes on the axis between hedonism and normativeness have generated another significant debate; the question is of how the individual copes with the lurking conflict between her own wishes and the norms of society – norms that seem to be increasingly flexible and unstable. More recent theoretical innovations, such as the notions of risk society and reflexive modernity, emphasise people's improving ability to independently assess the nature of the world – and thus they also promote the thesis of increasing individualism. Of the sociological sub-disciplines, the sociology of consumption is inherently interested in the ways in which the individual defines himself via consumption in the age of mature capitalism – and thereby in fact becomes an individual. (See e.g. Simmel 1959; Inglehart 1997; Klages 1985; Beck et al. 1994; Lehtonen 1999).

Robert Putnam (2000) in his bestseller on how Americans have started to 'bowl alone' provides a somewhat different perspective in stark contrast to the theoretical ideas with development-inspired undertones. Instead of participating actively in civic organisations and activities Americans increasingly spend time at home with activities without face-to-face contacts with others. In Europe too, various time consumption studies have shown that people indeed use less and less time for group or civic activities. The changes are, however, piecemeal and it may be too early to draw any conclusions on the basis of them. But be that as it may, from this perspective, the notion of individualism is closely related to the nature of civil society and human loneliness. In other words, what seemed to be a promise of individualism easily turns into alienation and atomisation – and a weak civil society.

In the East European context the debate on individualism has had a very specific connotation over the past 15 years. The post-communist transformation has meant a move from a collectively organised society where the individual was carefully guided from cradle to grave to a society where the individual is bound to make decisions for and by himself, to take initiative, to rely on himself. This requirement of individualism, of self-direction, has in fact created a new cleavage in these societies: it has been much easier for the young and well educated and urban to cope with it than for older generations. Indeed, there is some evidence that the young generations have been moving towards more individualistic value patterns. What has been rather conspicuous, however, is that this new individualism has often turned into a widely despised phenomenon, into hedonism that in many people's view threatens the very foundations of society (Lauristin and Vihalemm 1997; Vogt 2005).

We cannot go into the details of these fascinating debates here. Instead, let us simply define our starting points. First, individualism – understood as freedom and capacity and need to fulfil one's own particular hopes and desires, if necessary at the expense of others – is increasingly a factor to be reckoned with in today's Europe. It is a natural result of the ever more multicultural and fragmented nature of European societies, of the rising number of cultural habits, tastes, norms and possibilities available for everyone. Secondly, individualism can be both positive and negative from the society's overall perspective. As the Eastern European case above shows, these two 'forms' or embodiments of individualism are very close to each other; the difference between them is often reminiscent of a line drawn on water.

We concentrate on two aspects of individualism, essential both in general terms and from the point of view of future European integration. One aspect (the latter in our analysis) is that of freedom. An individualistic individual must have the possibility to do things without being restricted by anyone or anything. From this perspective, for the process of integration to flourish in the long run, the European Union would need to create such spaces of freedom within which this becomes possible. The other aspect is people's relationship with each other; the way they *trust* each other; their respect for each other; even their willingness to work together with each other towards a common cause. It is, of course, an immensely difficult question to know what the nature of these interpersonal relations should be like so that they would be conducive to 'individualism'.[8] We assume, however, that for 'positive' individualism to develop, these relations need to be good. Individual initiative has much better chances if people can in one way or the other anticipate other people's reactions. Only under the conditions of trust is it possible to create individual spaces of freedom; and the more people trust each other, the more space there is for freedom.

Table 7.8, based on the *European Social Survey* 2002–03, provides us with an overview of the extent to which people claim to trust each other in today's Europe (see also Table 7.4 and Figures 4.7 and 4.8 on institutional trust). The first significant observation is that the differences between individual countries are indeed remarkable (maybe even so remarkable that one starts wondering whether respondents in different countries have understood the question in the same way). Of the Danes, only a tiny minority do not generally trust people, and half of them believe that people can be expected to act helpfully. By contrast, it seems to be a widely accepted norm in Greece that people are not to be trusted and that they ultimately only seek benefits for themselves.

*Table 7.8: Indicators of social trust (%)*

|  | People can not be trusted[1] | People can be trusted | People look out for themselves[2] | People try to be helpful |
|---|---|---|---|---|
| Denmark | 6 | 67 | 11 | 47 |
| Norway | 8 | 61 | 12 | 45 |
| Finland | 8 | 59 | 16 | 39 |
| Sweden | 15 | 52 | 14 | 47 |
| Netherlands | 15 | 42 | 19 | 30 |
| Switzerland | 17 | 41 | 19 | 30 |
| Luxemburg | 21 | 29 | 33 | 22 |
| Ireland | 23 | 39 | 16 | 46 |
| UK | 23 | 28 | 18 | 33 |
| Austria | 25 | 32 | 24 | 31 |
| Belgium | 28 | 28 | 36 | 21 |
| Spain | 29 | 27 | 37 | 19 |
| Germany | 31 | 24 | 26 | 23 |
| France | 31 | 19 | 37 | 19 |
| Italy | 33 | 21 | 40 | 14 |
| Czech Rep. | 39 | 20 | 47 | 15 |
| Hungary | 40 | 16 | 41 | 17 |
| Portugal | 41 | 16 | 47 | 13 |
| Slovenia | 44 | 18 | 41 | 21 |
| Poland | 48 | 12 | 62 | 10 |
| Greece | 5 | 15 | 63 | 9 |
| Total | 27 | 32 | 31 | 26 |
| Total N | 11 509 | 13 515 | 13 047 | 11 072 |

*Notes*: (1) The respondents were given a scale from 0 through 10, where 0 was 'you can't be too careful' and 10 'most people can be trusted'. The scale has been recoded so that the first column represents the values from 0 through 3, and the second 7 through 10. Total N in the remaining group = 17 052. (2) The same scale and system of recoding used. The wordings were the same as in the column headings. Total N in the remaining group = 17 931.

*Source*: European Social Survey 2002–03.

It is also notable how clear the geographical pattern is, once again. The Nordic countries are the only countries where more than half of the respondents are able to trust their fellow citizens, and they also score well in regard of people's helpfulness. The Benelux countries, Switzerland and the British Isles follow suit. Southern Europe and the former communist countries display a much grimmer picture; at least two-fifths of the citizens of these countries think about other people in rather negative terms. Although the conclusion may be too bold, these differences indicate that when it comes to human interaction, no distinctively European pattern exists – not yet, at least.

We reasoned above that the more trust there is, the better chances positive individualism ought to have. But how does this positive individualism relate to people's willingness to participate in the conduct of common affairs, to show their individuality and capacity to autonomous decision-making through the world of politics – and possibly to get involved in European affairs in the long run? The question is obviously linked tightly to what we said about people's relationship to politics in the first part of this chapter.

*Table 7.9: Social trust and interest in politics. Row percentages*

|  | People can't be trusted | People can be trusted | People look out for themselves | People try to be helpful |
|---|---|---|---|---|
| Interested in politics | 38 | 56 | 40 | 50 |
| Not at all interested in politics | 27 | 13 | 24 | 16 |
| Politics too complicated to understand – never or seldom | 24 | 31 | 26 | 27 |
| Politics too complicated to understand – regularly or frequently | 46 | 31 | 44 | 35 |
| Could take an active role in a political group – yes | 18 | 27 | 19 | 22 |
| Could take an active role in a political group – no | 71 | 60 | 69 | 67 |

Source: ESS 2002/3. Data weighted by population size. For coding, see the legends of Tables 7.8 and 7.3.

In Table 7.9 we have simply cross-tabled the respondents' interest in politics with their propensity to trust their fellow citizens.[9] The method may be unsophisticated, but the outcome could hardly be clearer. In the case of all our 'relationship with politics' items, those who trusted each other and/or believed that people are helpful, are significantly more interested in politics, and find it complicated less often. Consequently, in those countries, where the level of interpersonal trust is high, interest in politics is common. It thus appears safe to argue that the more trust, and positive individualism, there is in society, the better chances politics has, at least in the long run. But of course, the question is then by no means of revolutionary politics, but of dull, everyday, piecemeal conduct of common affairs. We also believe that the attitudes towards politics are significant for the overall development of civil society, and thus agree with the observation that several scholars have made earlier: the welfare state model, particularly as it is known in the Nordic States, creates favourable conditions for civil society rather than curbs them (Bartkowski and Jasińska-Kania 2004).[10]

*Table 7.10: The meanings of the European Union in EU15, the new member states, Bulgaria and Romania (% of respondents mentioning the issue; multiple answers possible)*[1]

|  | Freedom to travel, study and work[2] | Euro | Peace | Stronger say in the world | Cultural diversity | Economic prosperity | Democracy | Loss of our cultural identity | Social protection |
|---|---|---|---|---|---|---|---|---|---|
| Belgium | 43 | 67 | 27 | 26 | 22 | 18 | 21 | 8 | 8 |
| Denmark | 54 | 35 | 40 | 30 | 28 | 28 | 26 | 15 | 15 |
| Germany (west) | 52 | 58 | 44 | 32 | 36 | 16 | 33 | 13 | 11 |
| Germany (east) | 47 | 54 | 46 | 27 | 31 | 10 | 20 | 13 | 9 |
| Greece | 42 | 49 | 45 | 34 | 21 | 27 | 28 | 14 | 21 |
| Italy | 60 | 48 | 29 | 29 | 26 | 18 | 23 | 9 | 12 |
| Spain | 51 | 50 | 19 | 29 | 29 | 32 | 24 | 5 | 14 |
| France | 51 | 58 | 35 | 31 | 38 | 21 | 20 | 16 | 9 |
| Ireland | 45 | 51 | 20 | 22 | 15 | 32 | 10 | 12 | 10 |
| Luxemburg | 58 | 61 | 43 | 30 | 31 | 28 | 27 | 14 | 19 |
| Netherlands | 54 | 56 | 28 | 37 | 18 | 24 | 24 | 18 | 10 |
| Portugal | 35 | 46 | 14 | 21 | 16 | 16 | 13 | 6 | 8 |
| UK | 45 | 28 | 18 | 21 | 19 | 16 | 13 | 30 | 11 |
| Finland | 69 | 65 | 28 | 18 | 30 | 14 | 10 | 14 | 6 |
| Sweden | 64 | 31 | 42 | 32 | 32 | 11 | 18 | 13 | 5 |
| Austria | 38 | 53 | 23 | 21 | 20 | 12 | 11 | 16 | 13 |
| NMS | 62 | 45 | 37 | 26 | 30 | 30 | 31 | 12 | 23 |
| Rom/Bulg | 54 | 30 | 44 | 30 | 38 | 55 | 43 | 16 | 48 |
| EU15[3] | 51 | 50 | 31 | 28 | 28 | 19 | 22 | 14 | 11 |

*Notes*: (1) The full question reads: 'What does the European Union mean to you personally?' In addition to the ones in the table, the respondents were also given the following options: Unemployment (mentioned by 19 per cent of the respondents); bureaucracy (25 per cent); waste of money (26 per cent); more crime (19 per cent); not enough control at external frontiers (23 per cent). (2) In the *Candidate Countries Barometer*, the formulation was: 'Freedom of movement within the EU'. (3) Weighted by population size.

*Sources*: *Eurobarometer* 61 (2004); *Candidate Countries Eurobarometer* 2004.1.

Let us now turn to our other main element of individualism, 'freedom', or to be more precise freedom *for* something. One of the defining features of modern (western) societies is that people have and must have possibilities to do a great many things, to try various career patterns, to create their own cultural tastes. The existence of such protection mechanisms as comprehensive health care and social security systems is no longer deemed to be sufficient. This 'freedom for' has been a particularly significant aspect of the transformation in Eastern Europe, for during communism the ideal of 'freedom from' conditioned these societies; it has even been an aspect that has prevented disappointments encountered in the new era from determining the entire process of democratisation.

The 'freedom for' is, as most concepts of this chapter, so multifaceted a notion that we can only shed light on it very imperfectly.[11] Moreover, it is not easy to find (quantitative) data that could well illustrate the extent to which individuals appreciate freedom in their life; the need for freedom tends to materialise only when non-freedom becomes a real option. Let us therefore right away link our analysis of freedom to the process of Europe's integration. Table 7.10 shows what kind of meanings people attach to the EU. What is important here is that, in most old member states, 'the freedom of movement' – clearly a 'freedom for' – is one of the primary images of the Union, and when the whole of the EU is considered, it is the most common one. There are in fact a few remarkably high values. In Finland and Sweden well over 60 per cent of the respondents associate the Union with the freedom to study, work and travel abroad. The other issue that could be regarded as closely related to individualism, namely 'cultural diversity', also succeeds well.[12] What is notable is that in comparison with the contrary meaning, 'loss of cultural identity', almost twice as many respondents, 28 per cent, believed that the Union promotes cultural diversity in the continent.

It is also remarkable how seldom the Union is now associated with its original *raisons d'être*, namely those of preserving peace and democracy in Europe. There are big differences between countries, however. In Germany, Greece and Sweden integration as a peace process is still acknowledged by more than 40 per cent of the respondents, whereas in the UK, Ireland and Portugal peace and democracy appeal to hardly one fifth of them.

Surprisingly few associate the Union with economic prosperity, but it is particularly alarming that 'social protection' is clearly something that does not spring to people's mind when the Union is mentioned. This is also significant from the point of view of globalisation: as we have noted above, social protection against globalisation is something that people particularly in Southern Europe expect the EU to offer. If the Union succeeded in this, their views about globalisation would certainly be more positive than they are today. In this respect there certainly is a correlation between integration and globalisation.[13] Finally, as the legend of the table mentions, the number of those respondents for whom the Union primarily means 'bureaucracy' or waste of money is also significant, 25 per cent. For these people apparently, the Union definitely is not an institution that promotes the individual's freedom, but one that seeks to limit it unnecessarily and stupidly. We have had access to raw data only from the old EU member states, but as the two last rows of the table show, the outcome might have been fairly similar in the new member states as well.

In the case of the old member states, we also analysed these views in light of a few socio-demographic factors and the respondents' support for EU membership (Table 7.11). The fact that women are generally more EU-sceptical is clearly visible; they attach positive meanings to the Union more seldom than men – and negative somewhat more often. The difference was, however, minimal in the case of the two individualistic issues, freedom of movement and cultural diversity.

Table 7.11: The meanings of the European Union in EU15 (% of respondents mentioning the issue; multiple answers possible)

|  | Freedom to travel, study and work | Euro | Peace | Stronger say in the world | Cultural diversity | Economic prosperity | Democracy | Loss of our cultural identity | Social protection |
|---|---|---|---|---|---|---|---|---|---|
| Total | 51 | 50 | 31 | 28 | 28 | 19.3 | 21.9 | 14 | 11 |
| Men | 52 | 49 | 33 | 31 | 29 | 22 | 24 | 14 | 12 |
| Women | 51 | 50 | 28 | 26 | 27 | 16 | 20 | 15 | 10 |
| 15–24 | 60 | 54 | 31 | 29 | 32 | 23 | 23 | 11 | 13 |
| 25–39 | 53 | 52 | 27 | 29 | 31 | 20 | 21 | 15 | 10 |
| 40–54 | 50 | 48 | 30 | 30 | 29 | 17 | 23 | 15 | 11 |
| 55+ | 46 | 47 | 34 | 27 | 23 | 18 | 21 | 16 | 11 |
| Rural | 47 | 50 | 30 | 26 | 25 | 18 | 18 | 14 | 10 |
| Urban | 53 | 49 | 31 | 30 | 30 | 20 | 24 | 15 | 12 |
| Left[1] | 57 | 51 | 33 | 33 | 33 | 21 | 25 | 12 | 13 |
| Centre | 53 | 49 | 32 | 29 | 28 | 20 | 22 | 15 | 11 |
| Right | 51 | 51 | 33 | 28 | 29 | 22 | 24 | 19 | 11 |
| Membership: a good thing | 63 | 55 | 43 | 43 | 38 | 33 | 34 | 6 | 17 |
| Bad thing[2] | 31 | 40 | 13 | 9 | 14 | 4 | 7 | 36 | 5 |
| Neither + – | 48 | 49 | 24 | 20 | 23 | 9 | 14 | 16 | 7 |

Notes: (1) 20 per cent of the respondents did not reveal their political preferences on a left-centre-right scale. Right-wing respondents mentioned all those issues not specified in the table clearly more often than the left-wingers. (2) Of those who think that their country's EU membership is 'a bad thing', the Union represents 'unemployment' for 33 per cent ('a good thing' respondents 11 per cent); bureaucracy 37 per cent (17 per cent); waste of money 56 per cent (12 per cent) more crime 33 per cent (12 per cent); and 'not enough control at external borders' 36 per cent (16 per cent).

Source: Eurobarometer 61 (2004). Data weighted by population size.

It comes as no surprise that the young respondents associate the Union with freedom of movement and cultural diversity more often than the older respondents (the same is true for urban population). For many of these young people the Union primarily materialises in the form of student exchange programmes and job opportunities abroad after their studies; this is something that has been possible only over the past 15 years or so. For those over 55 years of age the traditional justification of integration and peace still seems important in relative terms. They are also somewhat more often afraid of the loss of their cultural identity than others. If the views now held by young respondents were to become increasingly popular, they would clearly strengthen the image of the EU as an organisation promoting individualism. Political preferences affect the meanings of the EU less than age. However, those with leftist sympathies are more prone to think of the EU in terms of freedom of movement and cultural diversity, whereas the right-leaning respondents attach negative attributes to the Union somewhat more often.

Finally, the extent to which people support Union membership very clearly determines the meanings of the Union. Indeed, it seems that those who support their country's EU membership without difficulty associate the Union with a number of positive things, including the individualistic ones. This might imply that these people do think about the Union in terms of their personal freedom, as an element that expands the scope of choices in their personal life, a guarantor of good life. In contrast, for those who resist Union membership, a number of negative images spring to mind when the Union is mentioned. Some 56 per cent of them believe, for example, that the EU is equivalent to a 'waste of money'. It is also obvious that for many of these people the EU is a significant risk for their cultural – and collective – identity.

Before concluding this part of the chapter, we still need to draw attention to a few pieces of empirical evidence that can also be seen as illustrations of European individualism – or the lack of it. The *Special Eurobarometer* 60.1 from the autumn of 2003 on European values tells us, within the same set of questions, the following things. (1) EU citizens generally seem to hold environmentally friendly views. 70 per cent of the respondents believed that 'protecting the environment should be a priority for our country even if it affects the economic growth'. (2) Simultaneously, these same Europeans proved somewhat intolerant: 83 per cent of them agreed with the statement that 'criminals should be punished more severely'. (3) Furthermore, these respondents apparently did not want the state to have a strong role in society, because 64 per cent of them agreed with the contention 'The state intervenes too much in our lives'; 30 per cent disagreed. (4) At the same time, however, their views were highly egalitarian. Sixty per cent agreed and 32 per cent disagreed with the statement 'we need more equality even if this means less freedom for the individual'. Needless to say, these figures contradict each other in a profound manner. Even though we cannot analyse them thoroughly here, the message conveyed by them is obvious: Europeans seem to hold both individualistic and communitarian, both materialistic and post-materialistic values, and, most importantly, often simultaneously.

So can we draw any general conclusions about the nature of individualism, and its relationship with the EU, on the basis of the evidence provided above? The general impression is no doubt that of confusion. It seems that no European pattern of individualism exists. The great differences in terms of interpersonal trust that we have observed clearly suggest this, and so do the pieces of information presented in the paragraph above. The impression becomes even stronger if we also begin to think about recent political developments in Europe, say, the emergence of minority rights, or the popularity of national populist parties; they rather seem to attest to increasing communitarianism than individualism. From this perspective it is in fact unjustified to talk about, as the official EU discourses so often do, 'our common values'.

The other main conclusion is that the European Union is now clearly and positively associated with freedom of movement and cultural diversity, especially among the young, much more often than with a 'peace process' or promoter of democracy. At least two noteworthy points follow from this. First, it may be seen as a minor confirmation of the common hypothesis of increasing individualism. The European Union, and the meanings people attach to it, simply changes along with the *Zeitgeist*. Second, it seems obvious that marketing the European Union as an entity of peace and democracy less and less guarantees the legitimacy of the Union. Instead, it should probably concentrate even more on creating spaces of freedom for ordinary Europeans, also rhetorically. But this should not be done at the expense of those who do not trust their fellow citizens, who still hold traditional collective values dear, or who are generally so dissatisfied with their life that they remain utterly alienated from politics – in other words, those who are not yet individualists in the positive sense of the word. Individualism should not undermine the mechanisms of social protection.

**Conclusions**

Let us return to the question that has informed the analyses of this chapter. To what extent do and can globalisation and individualism make possible or constrain, as such and through *Politikverdrossenheit*, the process of European integration? We have of course not been able to provide anything like comprehensive answers – it would have been unrealistic to expect that – but a few important points and suggestions, important from the point of view of future integration and its democratic nature, have nevertheless come to the fore.

First of all, globalisation does pose a significant challenge to the European Union, but it is a challenge that, at the end of the day, in most people's view includes both promises and threats; at least in the Northwestern part of the continent, the majority sees more promises than threats. What is particularly important is that, as we have seen, there is already now a significant percentage of Europeans, maybe as many as 30 per cent, who believe that one of the EU's *primary* justifications is its potential role as a central actor in various processes of globalisation, and this percentage is likely to increase. In other words, if the integration is to continue under a bright sky, this is a role that the Union should be ever more aware of and propagate more. There is, however, one major problem here: there are clearly two competing or even conflicting views about globalisation in Europe. Roughly, for the people of Southern Europe, the role of the Union ought to be that of a shelter against globalisation, whereas in the North, the primary task is to see to it that globalisation proceeds smoothly, though without exploiting the society's weakest individuals.

These two competing views mean, however, that it is precisely through its global position, its global policies, that the European Union can and ought to become a meaningful polity. It is an essentially political question whether the EU wants to seriously slow down globalisation or whether it only wants to become its soft regulator. This would also mean that the Union, along with other regional organisations and in the absence of a functioning global polity, would become a central nexus of global politics and global civil society, very much in the same way as the state has traditionally been for the national civil society. This is also highly important if globalisation is to have a proper political dimension in the long run, mechanisms of political control and moral consciousness. We thus agree with Kees van Kersbergen and others – and with Hegel:

> Global society, one might say, looks from a certain point of view like a *civil society* which is able to operate largely outside of the control of the nation state or any equivalent of it. From this point of view, global society is the realization of the nightmare about which Hegel wrote in his *Philosophy of Right*. In the absence of a 'state in the proper sense', he argues, society would be nothing more than 'soulless community', in which every 'substantial link' between the members is lacking – to put the point in Hegel's own terminology. Such a society would lack any *Sittlichkeit*, that is ethical life proper to itself (Van Kersbergen et al. 1999, 203).

Secondly, the European Union should cultivate its image as an institution that is geared towards increasing peoples' chances of having an individualistic lifestyle, without compromising the needs for social protection. The institutions of integrated Europe should, in other words, be able to promote freedom and trust across the continent. This is, of course, a very tall order indeed, although at least in one respect the conditions should be there. What is known as the common European values are inherently individualistic; the idea of a common European identity that European leaders have sought to keep on the agenda has not been able to change this fact. The promotion of, say, transparency and accountability can essentially lead to increasing levels of trust, and thereby positive individualism. On the other hand, it seems to us that, although we have mentioned this only in passing, for a significant number of people, the Union still represents loathed bureaucracy, inefficiency and waste of money; for these people, the Union definitely does not represent a haven of freedom and it cannot contribute to increasing levels of interpersonal trust.

Closely related to this, the current nature of integration includes a specific problem, a project with ever more all-encompassing aspirations as it has become. By trying to get involved in new areas of life, to regulate them, the EU easily comes to limit the scope and possibilities of the individual's freedom. In the worst case, the logic is not that different from that of the former communist systems that sought to impose their values and practices on all spheres of life. This means that rather than seeking to cover ever new aspects of life with ever more detailed policies and regulations, the Union should concentrate on a limited number of fields, and make these fields truly political, that is, give space for a profound political debate on what should be done and when and by whom. At the very least, the Union should avoid the currently so typical discourse of 'the train and the track', of one possible direction for integration ('forward!'). This kind of thinking is inherently deterministic, and does not promote the individual's individuality, her democratic, political freedom.

Thirdly, we believe that to the extent that the EU can cope with the challenges posed by globalisation, the majority of people are almost bound to remain or become political also at the European level, or at least observe European politics from a *reflexive* distance. Globalisation significantly reduces the power of nation-states or, more precisely, nation-states only remain meaningful as parts of larger frameworks; the national polity can regain its legitimacy through the European level.[14] The risk, then, is basically the same as with individualism: politics will not have a role if the process of integration appears predetermined, a one-truth project, if it engages in fields where the individual should be the master. Integration must have a genuine political dimension. If it does not, we will have to start talking about *Europaverdrossenheit*.

We also need to bear in mind, however, that the existence of *Politikverdrossenheit* can be interpreted positively. One of the essential freedoms that we, human beings, citizens, have is freedom from politics; freedom from participation in political affairs; freedom not to be part of what is usually and liberal-romantically called civil society. From this perspective, what we have in this chapter described as indifference towards politics is only an expression of an essential human need of individuality.

Finally, in Chapter 2 we introduced a simple formula of two parallel historical processes of European integration, namely the political top-down integration, with origins in the age-old ideas of a unified Europe, and economic, bottom-up integration based on the economic needs to create common standards and rules across the continent and make trade easier. The figure that we can draw on the basis of our discussions above is analogous to this formula. What is remarkable, however, is that as economic practices and principles historically emerged from below, in the age of globalisation, they are increasingly determined from above, although it is not always clear who the real actors are (often, of course, the main actors include at least the WTO, the World Bank and IMF). By contrast, as political projects and values were imposed from above in the course of history, in the age of individualism they increasingly emerge from below.

*Figure 7.2: Two parallel current and future determinants of European integration*

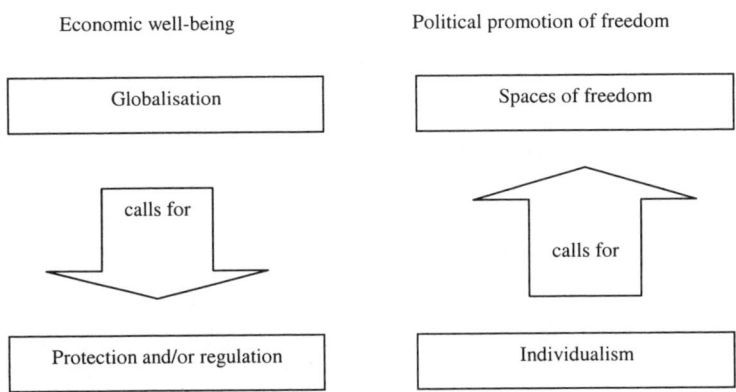

Be that as it may, Europe needs to find a balance between these phenomena, a balance between economic globalisation and political individualism. It needs to provide people with opportunities for self-fulfilment and self-organisation – this is the bottom-up perspective – but it also needs to consciously create, from above, a collective called Europe that is capable of balancing the powers of globalisation. It is naturally very difficult to cope with these competing and conflicting factors, with factors that are also internally highly conflict-laden. The European Union must be able to do the splits, and to do them in several different directions simultaneously. But it is precisely this, the political conflicts that the metaphor of the splits implies, that can make the European polity a meaningful entity in the long run, and make people forget about their lurking *Europaverdrossenheit*.

# NOTES

1. Various new theories of democracy, deliberative democracy in particular, as well as such notions as reflexive politics and sub-politics, have naturally also helped bring about this increasingly nuanced understanding of contemporary politics. See for example Beck et al. (1994); Dryzek (2000).
2. Regarding the Greek case, in a *Special Eurobarometer* of autumn 2003, *Citizenship and Sense of Belonging*, there was a question tapping respondents' interest in *both* politics *and* economics. With a level of interest of 89 per cent, Greece came out at the very top within EU15. The lowest interest rate was recorded for Belgium, 47 per cent, which should be compared with the EU15 average of 62 per cent.
3. Only 13 per cent were 'totally in favour', but even less, 8 per cent, were totally against. Before the question was asked, the respondents (N = approximately 500 in each country) were given a definition of globalisation: 'Globalisation is the general opening-up of all economies, which leads to the creation of a truly world-wide market'. The word 'development' thus refers to this definition.
4. The writers of the report *Globalisation*, based on the *Flash Eurobarometer* 151b of October 2003, remark that as many as 40 per cent in France and 42 per cent in Belgium of those who initially supported globalisation see it as a threat.
5. In the *Flash Eurobarometer* of October 2003, *Globalisation*, 23 per cent of the respondents claim they have not heard of globalisation. If this is true, it raises the question to what extent the data presented in this chapter are reliable in the first place.
6. We also tried to measure the correlation between EU support and globalisation optimism. In addition to the globalisation index, we decided to construct a somewhat more complex item of EU support than the one used in Tables 7.5 and 7.6. It is based on two questions. The first question pertains to support for EU membership [of respondent's own country]; the second question sets out to assess the general image of the European Union. The question reads as follows: 'Does the EU conjure up for you a positive, neutral or negative image'. Positive answers on both questions yield a score of 6 (37.1 per cent did); negative answers on both counts yield a score of 2 (12.0 per cent did). It turned out that there was a significant correlation (at the 0.01 level) between the indices of globalisation optimism and EU support in all countries under scrutiny. The value of Spearman's rho varied between 0.140 in Greece and 0.365 in Austria, the overall value being 0.204 (data not weighted). However, we could not find any significant clusters among the countries in this respect. In the Nordic countries the correlations were fairly high, but somewhat lower than in Austria and France.
7. Inglehart's post-materialism thesis has, of course, been widely discussed and often challenged. Empirical research also seems to imply that no significant increase in people's post-materialism has taken place in recent years. For example, Wil Arts and Loek Halman (2004) argue that country-specific, historical factors often play a more significant role that the broad scheme of modernisation–post-materialism–individualism. See Thome (2003) for a brilliant critic of Inglehart's post-materialism thesis.
8. An alternative notion here is social capital.
9. We also tried to measure whether we could find a correlation between interpersonal trust and interest in politics. We indeed could: Pearson's $r$ between the first columns of Table 7.3 and 7.8 is –0.605 (significant at the 0.01 level). In other words, it is fairly likely that in a society with high levels of interpersonal trust, the level of people's interest in politics is also on a high level.
10. Of course, the question that this argument raises is 'What conditions have created the Nordic welfare states?' In the context of this book, it is not possible to give any thorough answers to this.
11. It is, for example, closely related to people's general satisfaction with life; perhaps the existence of freedom is even the most important element of it. From this perspective, given that the levels of satisfaction have not increased in the Western world in any significant manner over the past decades, we can of course wonder whether the sense of individuality has actually increased.
12. We could of course regard 'euro' as an individualistic element, too, but the logic of it is somewhat different, which is why it is not discussed in the text.
13. In *Special Eurobarometer* 60.1, from the autumn of 2003, the picture was somewhat different when the respondents were asked to rank the values that best represent the EU. 'Peace' was the most important one (38 per cent), followed by human rights and democracy (36 per cent and 30 per cent). Individual freedom was mentioned only by 13 per cent of the respondents. However, when

the respondents were asked to rank the values from their own personal perspective, the order was clearly different. Peace was still the most important value (60 per cent), followed with respect for human life, human rights and individual freedom (46 per cent, 37 per cent, 30 per cent). Equality came far behind with 16 per cent. The individuals' own values were thus clearly liberal-individualistic.

14. In a sense, the phenomenon that has determined Italy's relationship with Europe should happen elsewhere in the continent as well. In Italy people have always been sceptical about the nation-state, but been highly supportive of EU institutions. The problems of national politics have made Italians look for better functioning political practices from the European level (Tossutti 2002).

## REFERENCES

Arts, Wil and Loek Halman (2004), 'European Value Changes in the Second Age of Modernity', in Wil Arts and Loek Halman, eds, *European Values at the Turn of the Millennium*, Leiden and Boston, Brill.
Bartkowski, Jerzy and Aleksandre Jasińska-Kania (2004), 'Voluntary organizations and the development of civil society', in Wil Arts and Loek Halman, eds, *European Values at the Turn of the Millennium*, Leiden and Boston, Brill.
Bauman, Zygmunt (1998), *Globalization. The Human Consequences*, Cambridge, Polity Press.
Beck, Ulrich, Anthony Giddens and Scott Lash (1994), *Reflexive Modernization. Politics, Tradition and Aesthetics in the Modern Social Order*, Cambridge, Polity Press.
Dryzek, John. S. (2000), *Deliberative Democracy and Beyond. Liberals, Critics, Contestations*, Oxford and New York, Oxford University Press.
Hay, Colin and Nicola J. Smith (2005), 'Horses for Courses? The Political Discourse of Globalisation and European Integration in the UK and Ireland', *West European Politics*, vol. 28, No. 1.
Inglehart, Ronald (1997), *Modernization and Postmodernization. Cultural, Economic and Political Change in 43 Societies*, Princeton, Princeton University Press.
Kersbergen, Kees van, Robert H. Lieshout and Grahame Lock (1999), 'Conclusion: Developing the Research Agenda', in Kees van Kersbergen, Robert H. Lieshout and Grahame Lock, eds, *Expansion and Fragmentation. Internationalization, Political Change and the Transformation of the Nation State*, Amsterdam, Amsterdam University Press.
Klages, Helmut (1985), *Wertorientierungen im Wandel. Rückblick, Gegenwartsanalyse, Prognosen*, Frankfurt and New York, Campus Verlag.
Laclau, Ernesto (1996), *Emancipation(s)*, London and New York, Verso.
Lauristin, Marju and Triin Vihalemm (1997), 'Changing Value Systems: Civilizational Shift and Local Differences', in Marju Lauristin and Peeter Vihalemm, eds, *Return to the Western World. Cultural and Political Perspectives on the Estonian Post-Communist Transformation*, Tartu, Tartu University Press.
Lehtonen, Turo-Kimmo (1999), *Rahan vallassa: ostoksilla käyminen ja markkinatalouden arki*, Helsinki, Tutkijaliitto.
Mattila, Mikko and Tapio Raunio (2005), 'Kuka edustaan EU:n vastustajia? Euroopan parlamentin vaalit 2004', *Politiikka*, Vol. 47, No. 1.
Putnam, Robert, D. (2000), *Bowling alone: the collapse and revival of American community*, New York, Simon and Schuster.
Robertson, Roland (1992), *Globalization. Social Theory and Global Culture*, London, Sage.
Simmel, Georg (1959), *Das Individuum und die Freiheit*, Berlin, Verlag Klaus Wagenbach.
Szczerbiak, Aleks and Paul Taggart (2004), 'The Politics of Euroepan Referendum Outcomes and Turnout: Two Models', *West European Politics*, Vol. 27, No. 4.
Thome, Helmut (2003), 'Soziologische Wertforschung. Ein von Niklas Luhmann inspirierter Vorschlag für die engere Verknüpfung von Theorie und Empirie', *Zeitschrift für Soziologie*, Jahrgang 32, Heft 1.
Tossutti, Liviana S. (2002), 'Between Globalism and Localism, Italian Style', *West European Politics*, Vol. 25, No. 3.

Vogt, Henri (2005), *Between Utopia and Disillusionment. A Narrative of the Political Transformation in Eastern Europe*, New York and Oxford, Berghahn Books.

# 8. Conclusions: The Future of the European Union

The future is not only uncertain but strictly speaking indeterminate. When addressing the future, we at best make educated guesses about what the future may have in store for us. Short-term predictions are generally much safer than long-term scenarios. A year ago, in the summer of 2004, few analysts would have expected the French and Dutch voters to reject the Draft Constitution in the referendums held on 29 May and 1 June 2005, respectively. Most observers of European politics expected the UK, Denmark or possibly Sweden to bring the process of ratification to a halt. Tony Blair's decision to call a referendum on the Draft Constitution made eminent sense given his priorities and those of the ruling Labour Party on the eve of the parliamentary elections of 2004, but it did not serve the interest of a smooth ratification process. Blair could possibly mobilise a parliamentary majority for the Draft Constitution, but even his considerable rhetorical skills would not have been sufficient to persuade a majority of Britain's profoundly Eurosceptical voters to vote yes to the Draft Constitution.

The possibility of failure was thus there from the very beginning, but vetoes spoken by the UK, Denmark and Sweden somehow hurt less than rejection by core countries like France and the Netherlands, two of the original co-signatories of the Treaty of Rome in 1957 and active promoters of European integration. There is even a standard operating procedure, revolving around catchwords like consultations, negotiations and exemption clauses, for how to cope with member countries reluctant to implement certain EU policies all the way through. Britain, Denmark and Sweden have thus gained acceptance for not joining the monetary union, the two former through formal negotiations and the latter informally, by tacit agreement.

Opinion polls gave advance warning of the pending debacle weeks ahead of the French and Dutch referendums. But, when the results were in, the European Commission nevertheless seemed to be taken by surprise. The appeal to the member states to continue the ratification process, issued by José Manuel Barroso, President of the European Commission, did little to dispel fears that the Union was heading for its worst crisis ever. The climate of crisis was compounded by an open rift between France and the UK on the EU budget. The common European currency took a beating on the international money markets, as friends of the Italian lira, the French franc and the German DM called for a swift return to the old familiar national currencies.

It did not come to dissolution of the monetary union or of the EU, and nor is it likely to happen any time soon. Reporting from the Netherlands in the aftermath of the referendum, CNN dismissed the notion of an imminent breakdown of the monetary union by claiming that European leaders had invested too much prestige in the monetary union to give it up lightly. It was a crude statement, cast in somewhat negative terms, but nevertheless to the point. With the benefit of hindsight, the rejection of the Draft Constitution first by France and then by the Netherlands is currently being deprived of most of the drama initially attached to it. We now hear that the French and the Dutch did not reject the Draft Constitution; the former dissociated themselves from an increasingly unpopular president thought to be to keen on implementing the free movement of goods, labour and capital within the EU, the latter from a succession of governments supposedly too lax on immigration. This may very well be the case. Voters, who take part in referendums, sometimes respond to cues only remotely related to the question put to them.

The overwhelming majority of Swedes, who preferred left- to right-hand side driving in a non-mandatory, consultative referendum in 1955, presumably voted 'no' because they were concerned about the safety of elderly relatives in the event of a change from left to right. But they nevertheless voted 'no' and it took the Swedish government more than a decade to forge a parliamentary coalition broad enough to bypass the verdict of the voters. A 'no' is a 'no' whatever the motives or circumstances that brought it about; and the Draft Constitution will be on hold until the European Commission has worked out a strategy of how to deal with the fallout of the referendums in France and the Netherlands. Such a strategy may indeed be in the making, but if so, it has remained a closely guarded secret. And as if this were not enough, the European Commission will have to work out a budgetary compromise acceptable to the UK and France, both reluctant to give up current privileges whether in the form of reduced levies or fees – the so-called British rebates – or overly generous subsidies to French agriculture.

This leads us to the dual conclusion that the current crisis of the European Union may not be as deep as initially assumed in the wake of the French and Dutch referendums, but definitely deep enough to call for a discussion of alternative developmental scenarios. This is the topic of the following section, where we return to the previous chapters for cues about the short-term perspective of the European Union. The data we rely upon in the preceding chapters are mainly of the survey variety, and the perspective we apply tends to have a grass-root bias. In a final section of this short chapter, we will therefore explicitly focus on the elite level.

**Alternative Scenarios**

The empirical evidence collected and the conclusions drawn in the previous chapters pull in different directions, from breakdown and collapse as foreseen by the Titanic scenario to the United States of Europe, the fulfilment of the federalist dream. Between these two extremes we have a number of middle of the road scenarios, also corroborated by the empirical evidence at hand (Algieri et al. 2003). In Table 8.1 below they are subsumed in the category status quo scenarios. It is the widest of the three scenarios; and a certain overlap with either of the two extremes is inevitable. The exact point, where status quo gives way to change, is notoriously hard to determine. As if this were not enough, the term status quo carries a number of connotations. We use it in the most basic sense. Status quo is equivalent to staying the same. If the EU stays the same, it will remain a European organisation for internationalised governance with supranational elements and the emphasis on extension (more and members), not on functional integration (closer and closer ties between those already in the Union). The catchword is widening rather than deepening integration.

The journey towards the United States of Europe begins with the transfer of power from national parliaments to the European Parliament and the election of a European government responsible for the federal level, including defence, security and foreign affairs. Technically, this transition has already been initiated, but – as we see it – it had been put on hold well before the recent referendums on the Draft Constitution. The latter was primarily designed to codify existing agreements and standard operating procedures and to adapt the decision-making structure of the Union to the challenges of consecutive enlargements, from EU15 to EU25, from EU25 to EU27 etc. The slippery slope towards decay and self-destruction begins with growing Euroscepticism, particularly of the hard variety and with links to extreme nationalism, increasing exclusiveness and, last but not least, decision-making paralysis. The rejection by French and Dutch voters of the Draft Constitution, which currently finds itself in a state of limbo, lends itself to interpretations in terms of decision-making paralysis. The current budgetary deadlock will also qualify, if it is not resolved; technically, the Titanic scenario has also been launched. The tricky part is to determine the overall thrust, if any, of the changes over time. Do they pull in this or that direction, or do they possibly cancel each other out?

In Table 8.1, the three alternative scenarios – the Titanic scenario, the status quo option and the United States of Europe – are juxtaposed with a set of statements from each of the six preceding analytical chapters.

*Table 8.1: Findings and conclusions conducive to three alternative scenarios*

| Conclusions, listed by chapter | Titanic scenario | Status quo | United States of Europe |
|---|---|---|---|
| European integration has traditionally been slow, piecemeal and economy-driven, but it is always open to innovations, also of a political variety (Chapter 2) | A very long-term relationship is not likely to have any short-term impact, but a distinctly positive long-term impact on the process of integration | A very long-term relationship not likely to have any short-term impact, but a distinctly positive long-term impact on the process of integration | A very long-term relationship not likely to have any short-term impact, but a distinctly positive long-term impact on the process of integration |
| (i) The EU has gradually become more and more inclusive (ii) Parallel processes towards exclusiveness seem to be gaining momentum (Chapter 3) | Inclusiveness favours integration, exclusiveness does not | Inclusiveness favours integration, exclusiveness does not | Inclusiveness favours integration, exclusiveness does not |
| (i) The EU enjoys little diffuse support (ii) The EU is marked by a distinct North-South divide (iii) Those satisfied with conditions at home, are likely to support the EU (Chapter 4) | A shortage of diffuse support, polarisation between the North and the South and dependence on nation-states for mediated support do not as such spell breakdown of the EU | A shortage of diffuse support, polarisation between the North and the South and dependence on nation-states for mediated support do not threaten the status quo | Polarisation and low levels of diffuse support are generally problematic. All out dependence on nation-states for mediated support could prove fatal for the federal level |
| There is widespread support for the EU to play an important role in high politics, but scepticism towards further enlargements (Chapter 5) | Pro-federal feelings are anathema to the foes of the Union and in no way conducive to the Titanic model | The EU has always been large enough to accommodate a wide range of opinions on Europe, including pro-federal feelings | The United States of Europe must have common defence and security policies. A moratorium on further enlargements would promote consolidation of the Union |
| Euroscepticism is a pervasive and multi-facetted phenomenon. When combined with extreme nationalism, it constitutes a threat towards democracy (Chapter 6) | Euroscepticism may indeed destroy the EU. The hard version of Euroscepticism is particularly likely to have a destabilising impact | Euroscepticism may destabilise the status quo even in its moderate form | Euroscepticism has no constructive role to play in a tightly knit federal structure |
| Globalisation is one of many challenges confronting the EU and dividing the member states along the North-South dimension (Chapter 7) | Globalisation could easily undermine the EU, if the EU fails to respond to the call for regulation | Globalisation could also be an asset for the EU, particularly to the extent that it casts itself as co-ordinating actor in a globalised world | Globalisation could also be an asset for the EU, particularly to the extent that it casts itself as co-ordinating actor in a globalised world |

The statements do not do justice to the individual chapters, but they do represent central findings and conclusions and may thus serve as a rough litmus test of the likelihood of the three scenarios. The logic is quite simple and straightforward. We will go through each of the three columns to check to what extent our empirical findings and conclusions lend support to the three alternative scenarios. But before we embark on this expedition, a few comments on the chapters may be in order.

The chapters apply varying perspectives. Chapter 2 focuses explicitly on the origins of the EU from a historical perspective and takes us on a breathtaking journey across the European continent from the 800s until today. The trends and patterns identified in this chapter are highly interesting and referred to in subsequent chapters, as we comment upon the role of the former city-belt states in contemporary Europe (see Chapters 2, 4 and 6). European integration may very well be economy-driven; but if we are applying a really long-term perspective well beyond the life time of any human being living right now, it is of limited practical importance at this point in time. The remaining five chapters have a more manageable time frame, but are at times deliberately vague about the predominant trends. We may possibly have overinterpreted subtle distinctions made in the original text, when phrasing the generalisation in the left-hand column; if so, that is purely unintentional.

With these reservations we are finally ready to take a close look at the three columns. We have at least one full hit for the Titanic scenario; Euroscepticism is unequivocally destructive, particularly when it comes in the hard format in collusion with extreme nationalism and xenophobic rhetoric (Chapter 6). Chapter 3 provides a partial hit. Though not yet the dominant trend, exclusiveness also has a distinctly negative impact on European integration. Turning to the other extreme, we have another obvious hit provided by Chapter 5 on the external dimension. If we are to take the data at hand at face value, Europeans are much more open to common foreign policy and defence initiatives than generally thought. All in all, they would also seem to prefer consolidation to further enlargements. Chapters 3 and 7 possibly provide partial hits to the extent that inclusiveness prevails (Chapter 3) and the EU does indeed succeed in carving out a niche for itself as a co-ordinating force in globalised world politics (Chapter 7). But the status quo option is nevertheless the indisputable winner. It scores, at least partially, on inclusiveness, on globalisation, and gets two full hits almost by default, more specifically by virtue of past performance. Low levels of diffuse support, tensions between North and South, and dependence on the member states for mediated support (Chapter 4) may not be ideal, but the EU has somehow managed to cope just as it has succeeded in accommodating pro-federal sentiments for decades without giving in to them (Chapter 5).

We would therefore be inclined to rule out the Titanic model, to attribute some potential to the United States of Europe but place our bets on what we have – the status quo alternative.

## Do Elites Make a Difference?

The question raised here towards the very end of the book might seem unusually naïve. The EU is after all often perceived as an organisation for and by political elites; and we will certainly not dispute that elites do make a difference, if, but only if, they take initiatives. As we write this, more than two months have passed since the budgetary deadlock and the rejection of the Draft Constitution by French and Dutch voters, and we are not likely to see any new initiatives until later on this autumn after the extraordinary German parliamentary elections on 18 September 2005. The campaign is already in full swing; and if we are to believe the opinion polls, Social Democratic Chancellor Gerhard Schröder will be defeated by the Christian Democrats and replaced by Dr Angela Merkel of the CDU. Sources in Germany say that Merkel is much less interested in cultivating the French connection than Schröder (SPD) and his predecessor Helmut Kohl (CDU). If so, we can rule out the frequently cited two-track solution with a fast track for France, Germany and others with an interest in deepening integration and a slow lane for EU countries satisfied with the current pace of integration.

The EU is in fact much more dependent on the whims and visions of the men and women leading Britain, France and Germany and other key member countries than generally appreciated. Tony Blair is currently chairing the EU, amidst speculations that he would be interested in taking over as President of the European Union after his current term as the UK's Prime Minister. With Merkel in Berlin, Blair in Brussels and Chirac about to be replaced as President of France, the priorities and general direction of the European Union might be quite different ten years from now. But the EU is not only about Britain, France and Germany and other key players. The EU is in fact what might be described as a 'unit veto' system, where one single vote may bring the entire system to a standstill (Kaplan 1975). With 25 to 27 member states or more in the Union, this kind of deadlock becomes more and more likely. In this respect, the EU is in fact not that different from the so-called consociational democracies, where the fragile social peace rests on a crude utilitarian calculus (Lijphart 1969). The various groups and factions will show restraint as long, but only as long, as they have reason to believe there is something in it for them as well. Only experience fosters such beliefs. The eight East European members of the Union as of May 2004 all have a limited record of interaction with the EU. In this light, the eastward enlargement was not only an audacious move on the part of the EU but also a high-risk project.

Political leaders come and go, but bureaucrats normally stay on much longer and exert commensurate influence. The EU is certainly no exception from this rule. Working for an organisation with limited accountability, EU bureaucrats probably have more clout than top-level government officials usually have, as sometimes suggested by concerned citizens and frustrated politicians alike. If so, the bureaucrats in Brussels may in fact be in a position to pave the way for a gradual solution of the current constitutional crisis through piecemeal implementation of the Draft Constitution marketed as organisational reforms needed to keep the EU machinery running smoothly with 25, 27, 29 or whatever the actual number of members will be, say, a couple of years from now. Such bureaucratic intervention could easily be dismissed as a self-serving, face-saving strategy, designed by the very actors that have the most to gain by the survival of the organisation. Bureaucrats have vested interests in the survival of the organisation, private or public, they are have chosen to serve, and may be expected to act accordingly. But that is beside the point. The message we are trying to get across here breaks down into three parts.

We are saying that organisational reform of the kind envisaged by the Draft Constitution is vital for the EU to cope with enlargement as of May 2004 and as foreseen in 2007 and onwards. Rules and regulations that were cumbersome already in EU15 may be outright destructive in a community of 30 members. Without organisational reform, the EU might find itself in the same kind of decision-making paralysis as the Weimar Republic in Germany and the Third and Fourth French republics shortly before they collapsed. System breakdown is not in the interest of the bureaucrats in Brussels; and to the extent that they set out to avert this danger by promoting organisational reform from within, they are acting not only in their own interest but in the best interest of the Union as a political entity. *Deadlock upon deadlock followed by outright decision making paralysis constitute the most serious challenge to the EU right now*; it alone lends credibility to the potential of the Titanic scenario that we rejected in the previous section. The challenge has always been there, but it is much more acute now than ever before by virtue of the growing complexity of the EU (from 15 to almost twice that many member states in a few short years) and the rejection of the organisational reforms foreseen by the Draft Constitution.

Applying a truly long-term perspective, Chapter 2 emphasised the importance of gradual, piecemeal economic integration as a solid foundation for subsequent steps towards political integration. Top-down initiatives to promote political integration play a more important role in the following five chapters, all of them with the time frames defined by the EU and its forerunners in Europe after the Second World War (see Appendix: Chronology of European Integration). The top-level officials serving the European Commission presumably see themselves as guardians of the federal dimension and will keep promoting it, also when fighting an up-hill battle. To the extent that the French and Dutch referendums are thought to represent a retreat in the progression towards ever deepening integration,

Brussels may be expected to bide its time and wait for the right moment to compensate for the previous loss of ground.

\*

All in all, we see no compelling reason to back down from the conclusion in favour of the status quo option presented already in the previous section of this chapter. The challenge represented by deadlock and decision-making paralysis is real enough, but we assume that a combination of vested interests and commitment to the cause amongst the leaders of Europe will hold it at bay for the time being.

Having placed our bets not only on the survival of the Union but also on a continuation of current policies, including the open-ended vision of Europe, and ruled out other scenarios, including the Titanic scenario and the two-track option of European integration, we could stop right here, lean back and see what happens.

We will, indeed, do just that, but not without having drawn attention once again to the many uncertainties involved. We have mentioned the change of guards anticipated in several key countries and possible implications thereof. We have also mentioned that Britain is now chairing the EU, and we have even referred to rumours to the effect that Prime Minister Blair is contemplating a second career within the EU, but we may not have emphasised that the budgetary crisis has thrust Britain and Sweden, two notoriously unwilling and recalcitrant partners in the European integration project, into a pivotal position within the EU. Much obviously depends on how they define their respective visions of Europe in the midst of the ongoing crisis.

The bottom-line is that we might have been well advised not to make any predictions at all; economists, on the other hand, would not have been deterred by such problems. They proceed on the assumption of 'other things being equal', and qualify their findings and conclusions accordingly. There is no reason why we should not use the same escape clause and add a *ceteris paribus* assumption to our findings and conclusions.

# REFERENCES

Algieri, Franco, Janis A. Emmanoullidis and Roman Maruhn (2003), *Die Zukunft Europas: 5 EU-Szenarien*, München, Centrum für angewandte Politikforshung (C A P).
Kaplan, Morton A. (1975), *System and Process in International Politics*, New York, R.E. Krieger.
Lijphart, Arend (1969), 'Consociational Democracy', *World Politics,* Vol. 21, No. 2.

# Appendix: Chronology of European Integration

| Year | Treaties and key events | Member states | Economic integration | Political integration | Crises and setbacks |
|---|---|---|---|---|---|
| 1944 | | Belgium, the Netherlands, Luxembourg | The governments of Belgium, the Netherlands and Luxembourg adopt a customs union (while in exile in London) | | |
| 1945 | 9 May: The end of World War II in Europe | | | | |
| 1946 | 19 September: In a speech at the Zurich University, Winston Churchill claims that 'We must build a kind of United States of Europe' | | | | |
| | December: European Union of Federalists (EUF) is formed | | | | |
| 1947 | The Cold War begins | | | | |
| | March: The Truman doctrine is declared; the US shall maintain an active role in Europe | | | | |
| | 5 June: The European Recovery Programme (ERP) a.k.a. the Marshall Plan is announced | | July: The Committee for European Co-operation (CEEC) is set up to receive and distribute Marshall Aid | Marshall Plan rationale: to set up a bulwark against Communism in Europe | |

| | Treaties and key events | Member states | Economic integration | Political integration | Crises and setbacks |
|---|---|---|---|---|---|
| 1948 | Brussels customs union | Belgium, the Netherlands, Luxembourg | 1 January: The Benelux customs union is extended to an economic union | 17 March: Belgium, the Netherlands, France and the UK meet in Brussels: | |
| | Brussels Treaty | | 16 April: The CEEC is transformed into the Organisation for European Economic Co-operation (OEEC) | The Treaty on Economic, Social, and Cultural Collaboration and Cellective Self-Defence is signed | |
| | 24 June: Beginning of the Berlin blockade by the Soviet Union | | | | |
| 1949 | Washington Treaty (NATO) | Belgium, the Netherlands, Luxembourg, France, Portugal, Norway, Denmark, Iceland, the UK, Canada and the US | | 4 April: The Washington Treaty, i.e. the creation of the North Atlantic Treaty Organisation (NATO) | |
| | April: The Federal Republic of Germany (FRG) is established | | | | |
| | | | | May: The Council of Europe is formed | |
| 1950 | June: The Korean War begins | | 9 May: French Foreign Minister Schuman proposes that France, Germany and others should pool their coal and steel resources | | |
| | | Belgium, France, Luxembourg, Italy, the Netherlands and Germany (FRG) | 3 June: Six European states subscribe to the Schuman Declaration (above). The Council of Europe Assembly approves the Schuman plan on 26–28 August | October: The Plevnen Plan for a European Defence Community (EDC) is launched | |
| 1951 | Treaty of Paris (ECSC) | Belgium, the Netherlands, Luxembourg, France, Italy, West Germany (FRG) | 18 April: The original six sign the Treaty of Paris establishing the European Coal and Steel Community | | |

# Appendix: Chronology of European Integration

|      | Treaties and key events | Member states | Economic integration | Political integration | Crises and setbacks |
|------|---|---|---|---|---|
| 1952 | European Defence Community Treaty | Belgium, the Netherlands, Luxembourg, France, Italy, West Germany (FRG) | | 27 May: The original six sign the European Defence Community (EDC) Treaty in Paris | |
|      | ECSC enters into force | | 23 July: The European Coal and Steel Community (ECSC) enters into force. Jean Monnet is appointed President of the High Authority | Rationale: Peace and prosperity in (Western) Europe | |
| 1953 | | | February: The Common Market for coal and iron in place | March: A draft treaty for a European Political Community is adopted | |
| 1954 | EDC collapses | | | | *Collapse of the EDC*<br><br>20–23 August: The original six meets in Brussels. French statesman Pierre Mendès France does not succeed in his request to attenuate the supranational character of the EDC. On 30 August, the French National Assembly rejects the EDC Treaty |
|      | Modified Brussels Treaty: Western European Union (WEU) | | | 23 October: A modified Brussels Treaty is signed in Paris, establishing the Western European Union (WEU) | 10 November: Jean Monnet, President of the ECSC High Authority, resigns after the EDC failure |
| 1955 | | | 1 June: René Mayer is elected President of the ECSC High Authority | May: Germany and Italy join NATO | |

|  | Treaties and key events | Member states | Economic integration | Political integration | Crises and setbacks |
|---|---|---|---|---|---|
| **1955** |  | 23 October: After a referendum, Saarland rejects in autonomous status and joins Germany (FRG) | 1–2 June: The original six agree on further economic integration | 8 December: The Coucil of Ministers of the Council of Europe adopt the blue flag with 12 golden stars |  |
| **1956** | October: The Soviet Union invades Hungary to put down an anti-communist uprising |  | 7 January: The ECSC High Authority confirms the principle of free circulation within the Community of steel products imported from third countries |  |  |
| **1957** | Treaties of Rome | Belgium, France, Germany (FRG), Italy, Luxembourg, the Netherlands | 25 March: The founding of the European Economic Community (EEC) and the European Atomic Energy Community (Euroatom) |  |  |
| **1958** |  |  | 1 January: The Treaties of Rome enters into force | The Rome Treaties gives the Commission competence for external trade negotiations |  |
|  |  |  | 19 March: Robert Schuman is elected President of the European Parliamentary Assembly, which is to substitute the ECSC Assembly |  |  |
|  |  |  | 3–11 July: The basis of a Common Agricultural Policy (CAP) is outlined at a conference in Stresa, Italy |  |  |
| **1959** |  |  | 7 January: Robert Schuman is re-elected President of the European Parliamentary Assembly |  |  |

Appendix: Chronology of European Integration        207

|      | Treaties and key events | Member states | Economic integration | Political integration | Crises and setbacks |
|------|---|---|---|---|---|
| 1959 | EFTA | Austria, Denmark, Norway, Portugal, Sweden, Switzerland, the UK | 20–21 July: Seven OEEC countries establish the European Free Trade Association (EFTA) | | |
|      |     | 31 July: Turkey applies for association with the EEC | 11 September: Piero Malvestiti is elected President of the ECSC High Authority | | |
| 1960 | The Stockholm Convention (EFTA) | Austria, Denmark, Norway, Portugal, Sweden, Switzerland, the UK | 4 January: The EFTA Convention is signed in Stockholm and enters into force on 3 May | | |
|      |     |     | 14 December: The OEEC is replaced by the Organisation for Economic Co-operation and Development (OECD) | | |
| 1961 |     | Ireland (31 July), the UK (9 August) and Denmark (10 August) apply for membership of the EC | | February: At a Summit in Paris, a committee to review political cooperation is set up, led by Christian Fouchet | |
| 1962 |     | 30 April: Norway applies to join the EC | | | |
|      |     |     | 30 July: The regulation creating a Common Agricultural Policy (CAP) enter into force | 18 July: A European Summit meeting is held in Bonn. The original six voice their wish to set up a political union | |
|      |     | 1 November: The association agreement between Greece and the EC enters into force | | | |

208    *The Making of the European Union*

| | Treaties and key events | Member states | Economic integration | Political integration | Crises and setbacks |
|---|---|---|---|---|---|
| **1963** | de Gaulle veto against the UK | | | | January: de Gaulle vetoes British application for membership in the EC |
| | 4 September: Robert Schuman dies | | 20 July: The Yaoundé Convention is signed between the Community and 18 African states | | |
| **1964** | | | 1 June: The Yaoundé Convention enters into force | | |
| | | | 15 July: Costa/ENEL ruling. European Court of Justice holds that Community law overrules national law | | |
| | | 1 December: The Association Treaty signed by the EEC and Turkey enters into force | | | |
| **1965** | Empty Chair crisis | | April: The Merger Treaty is signed (cf. below, 1 July 1967) | | *Empty Chair crisis* 1 July: France breaks off negotiations on financing the CAP and recalls her permanent representative in the Council |
| **1966** | | | | | 28–29 January: France resumes its place in the Council after seven months (Luxembourg compromise) |
| **1967** | The Merger Treaty | May: UK, Ireland, Denmark and Norway apply again for membership of the EC | 1 July: The Merger Treaty, fusing the executives of the European Communities, enters into force | From now on, the European Communities will have a single Commission and a single Council | |

Appendix: Chronology of European Integration 209

|  | Treaties and key events | Member states | Economic integration | Political integration | Crises and setbacks |
|---|---|---|---|---|---|
| 1967 | de Gaulle blocks the UK again | | | | December: General de Gaulle is still unwilling to accept the UK in the Community and blocks the re-opening of negotiations with all applicants |
| 1968 | | | 1 July: The customs union enters into force, abolishing remaining customs duties in intra-Community trade. The Common Customs Tariff is introduced to replace national customs duties in trade with the rest of the world | | |
| 1969 | Towards enlargement | April: de Gaulle resigns. In July, the UK revives its EC application<br><br>1–2 December: At a Summit meeting in Hague, the EC member states reaffirm their agreement on the principle of the enlargement of the Community | 29 July: Second Yaoundé convention is signed | | |
| 1970 | | 30 June: Negotiations with four prospective member states opens (Denmark, Ireland, Norway and the UK) | October: Luxembourg's Prime Minister Pierre Werner presents a plan for the Economic and Monetary Union (EMU) | 27 October: The Davignon Report is approved. The objective is to get 'Europe' to speak with a single voice on major international problems. The Council agrees to create the European Political Cooperation (EPC) mechanism | |

| | Treaties and key events | Member states | Economic integration | Political integration | Crises and setbacks |
|---|---|---|---|---|---|
| 1970 | | December: Association agreement is signed with Malta | | | |
| 1971 | | | 1 January: The second Yaoundé convention enters into force | | |
| | Werner Plan and EMU | | 22 March: The Werner Plan. The EC member states have from now on to take measures to harmonise their budgetary policies and to reduce the margins of fluctuation between their currencies | | August: Collapse of the first EMU experiment |
| 1972 | | | 24 April: The currency 'snake' is set up. The idea is to limit the margin of fluctuation between the member states' currencies | | |
| | 23 April: In a French referendum, 68.3 per cent are in favour of accepting new EC members | 10 May: In a referendum, 83.1 per cent of Irish voters accept accession to the EC | | | June: British Pound is withdrawn from the 'snake' |
| | | 24–25 September: In a referendum, 53.3 per cent of Norwegian voters turn down accession to the EC | | | |
| | | 2 October: In a referendum, 63.4 per cent of Danish voters accept accession to the EC | | | |

Appendix: Chronology of European Integration 211

| | Treaties and key events | Member states | Economic integration | Political integration | Crises and setbacks |
|---|---|---|---|---|---|
| 1972 | | 16 October: The UK ratifies the acts relating to the accession to the EC | | | |
| | | December: Association agreement is signed with Cyprus | | | |
| 1973 | The first enlargement | 1 January: The UK, Ireland and Denmark become members of the EC | 1 January: The Community Free Trade Agreement with Austria, Switzerland, Portugal and Sweden comes into force | | February: Italian Lire is withdrawn from the 'snake' |
| | | | 1 April: The Community's industrial Free Trade Agreement with Iceland comes into force | 6 November: The nine member states declare their commitment to a peaceful solution of the Middle East crises | October: Following the Middle East War, Arab oil producers raise the price of oil, which sent the international economy into recession |
| | | September: Association agreement is signed with Turkey | 5 October: Finland sign an industrial Free Trade Agreement with the EC | 14–15 December: At a summit conference in Copenhagen, a statement on the European identity is released, drafted as part of political cooperation arrangements | |
| 1974 | July: Turkish invasion of Cyprus | | 1 January: Agreements between the ECSC and Austria, Portugal, Switzerland and Sweden come into force. Finland's industrial Free Trade Agreement come into force | 31 January: The Commission addresses to the Heads of Governments a declaration on the state of the Community, stressing the need for bringing national policies closer into line | |

|  | Treaties and key events | Member states | Economic integration | Political integration | Crises and setbacks |
|---|---|---|---|---|---|
| 1974 | | | 30 November: The agreements between the ECSC and Norway and Finland are ratified by all member states of the Community (come into force on 1 January 1975) | | |
| 1975 | | | 28 February: The Community and 46 African, Caribbean and Pacific countries (ACP) sign the first Lomé Convention | 18 March: The Council sets up the European Regional Development Fund (ERDF) and a Regional Policy Committee | |
| | 20 March: The Florence European University Institute is officially established | | | March: The introduction of the European Council, i.e. regular summit meetings between the EC Heads of State and Governments | (9 April: Vote in the British House of Commons. 369 members vote in favour of the UK staying in the Community with 170 voting against it) |
| | | 12 June: Greece formally applies to join the EC | | | (5 June: In a British referendum, 67.2 per cent of voters are in favour of staying in the Community) |
| | | | | 1 August: The final Act of the Conference on Security and Cooperation in Europe is signed in Helsinki by 35 states | |
| | | | | 1–2 December: European Council meeting in Rome. It decides on the election of the European Parliament by universal suffrage, and on a passport union | |

Appendix: Chronology of European Integration 213

| | Treaties and key events | Member states | Economic integration | Political integration | Crises and setbacks |
|---|---|---|---|---|---|
| 1976 | | 9 February: The Council hesitantly accept Greece's application to join the EC | 1 April: The Lomé Convention enters into force | | |
| | Defrenne ruling | | | 8 April: Defrenne ruling. The European Court of Justice holds that the principle of equal pay for men and women is directly applicable | 14 April: The Commission formally decides to reject the application from the Irish Government for exemption from applying the principle of equal pay for men and women |
| | | | | 12–13 June: The European Council meets in Brussels. It agrees on the number and distribution of seats in the Parliament that is to be elected by direct universal suffrage in 1979 | |
| 1977 | | 28 March: Portugal formally applies to join the EC | | 1 June: The treaty reinforcing the budgetary powers of the Parliament enters into force | |
| | | 28 July: Spain formally applies to join the EC | October: Commission President Jenkins declares his resolution to revive the EMU | | |
| 1978 | | | | 9 March: Simmenthal ruling. The European Court of Justice consolidates the principle of preminence of Community law | |

| | Treaties and key events | Member states | Economic integration | Political integration | Crises and setbacks |
|---|---|---|---|---|---|
| 1978 | EMS and ERM | 6 June: The Council accepts Portugal's application to join the EC and opens negotiations | 6–7 July: A European Council is held in Bremen. An agreement is reached on a common strategy to achieve higher economic growth, reduce unemployment and to set up a European Monetary System (EMS) with the Exchange Rate Mechanism (ERM) as the central instrument<br><br>4–5 December: A European Council is held in Brussels. It establishes the EMS based on a European currency unit (the Ecu) | 7–8 April: A European Council is held in Copenhagen. An agreement is reached on the first direct elections to the European Parliament | |
| 1979 | | 5 February: Spanish accession negotiations formally open | | 6 February: The Council formally adopts the guidelines for the Community regional policy and the amendments to the 1975 Regulation establishing the European Regional Development Fund (ERDF) | |
| | 16 March: Jean Monnet dies<br><br>The EMS | | 13 March: The EMS enters into force | 4 April: The Commission adopts a memorandum on the accession of the EC to the European Convention for the Protection of Human Rights and Fundamental Freedoms | |
| | First elections to the EP by direct universal suffrage | | | 7–10 June: The first elections to the European Parliament | |

Appendix: Chronology of European Integration 215

| | Treaties and key events | Member states | Economic integration | Political integration | Crises and setbacks |
|---|---|---|---|---|---|
| 1979 | December: The Soviet Union invades Afghanistan | 28 June: Greek Parliament ratifies the Treaty of Accession | 31 October: The second Lomé Convention is signed (Lomé II) | 31 July: the Commission transmits to the Council a Directive on the right of member states' nationals to reside permanently in the territory of another member state | November: At a European Council in Dublin, Thatcher jeopardizes further cooperation by demanding a British budgetary rebate |
| 1980 | Eurosceptical Britain | | 7–8 March: The EEC–ASEAN Cooperation Agreement is signed (comes into force on 1 October) | June: The EC member states recognise the right of Palestinians to a homeland (the Venice Declaration) | 27–28 April: A European Council is held in Luxembourg. It discusses problems linked with the British contribution to the Community budget (A compromise is reached on 30 April) |
| 1981 | Mediterranean enlargement I | 1 January: Greece becomes member of the EC | | Mediterranean enlargement rationale: Ensure democratic consolidation | |
| 1982 | | | | | 23 February: In a referendum (consultative), Greenland, which became of member of the EC as part of Denmark, opts for withdrawal from the Community |
| | | | | 30 May: Spain joins NATO | |
| | | | | 3–4 December: A European Council is held in Copenhagen. It confirms its political engagement in favour of the enlargement | |

| | Treaties and key events | Member states | Economic integration | Political integration | Crises and setbacks |
|---|---|---|---|---|---|
| 1983 | Towards a Union | | | 17–19 June: A European Council is held in Stuttgart. A Solemn Declaration on the European Union is signed | |
| | | | | 14 September: A draft Treaty establishing a European Union is presented to the European Parliament | |
| 1984 | UK and the EC budget: new controversy | 12 March: the Council signs an agreement on future relations between Greenland and the EC | | 14 February: The Parliament passes the draft Treaty on the establishment of the European Union | 19–20 March: A European Council is held in Brussels. Disagreements occur on the calculation and the amount of compensation to be granted the UK, to reduce its contribution to the EC budget. The ten member states reach an agreement only at a new European Council in Fontainebleau (25–26 June) |
| | | | | 14 and 17 June: The second direct elections to the European Parliament are held | |
| | | | | June and July: The reductions of border checks within the Community are on the agenda. 13 July: The Franco-German Agreement on the gradual abolition of border checks is signed in Saarbrucken | |
| | | | 8 December: Third Lomé Convention is signed | | |

Appendix: Chronology of European Integration 217

|  | Treaties and key events | Member states | Economic integration | Political integration | Crises and setbacks |
|---|---|---|---|---|---|
| 1985 | 7 January: A new Commission takes office, with Jaques Delors as President | 1 February: Greenland leaves the Community but remains associated with it as an overseas territory | January: Delors declares his aim of developing the EMS by bringing the UK into it, and making the ecu a reserve currency | 1 January: The first European passports are issued in most of the EC member states | |
|  |  | 12 June: Spain and Portugal sign Accession Treaties | | | |
|  | The Schengen Agreement | Belgium, Germany (FRG), France, Luxembourg, and the Netherlands | 14 June: The Schengen Agreement on the elimination of border controls | | |
|  |  |  | 2–4 December: A European Council is held in Luxembourg. The member states agree to amend the Treaty of Rome and to revitalize the process of European integration by drawing up a Single European Act (SEA) | | |
| 1986 | Mediterranean enlargement II | 1 January: Spain and Portugal become members of the EC | | Mediterranean enlargement rationale: Ensure democratic consolidation | |
|  | Single European Act (SEA) | | 17 and 28 February: The Single European Act (SEA) is signed in Luxembourg and the Hague, modifying the Treaty of Rome | | |
|  |  |  | 1 May: The third Lomé Convention comes into force | 29 May: The European flag is officially taken into use | |

| | Treaties and key events | Member states | Economic integration | Political integration | Crises and setbacks |
|---|---|---|---|---|---|
| 1987 | | 14 April: Turkey applies for membership of the EC | 13 May: The Bank of Spain signs an agreement to join the European Monetary System (EMS). The Bank of Portugal follows suit on 10 November | | |
| | | | July: The SEA enters into force | | |
| 1988 | 27–28 June: Jaques Delors reappointed President of the Commission | | July: The EC and the communist East European trading block Comecon recognise each other, for the first time | | |
| 1989 | 9 November: The Fall of the Berlin Wall | 17 July: Austria applies to join the EC | | | |
| | Autumn: Democratic transformations throughout Central and Eastern Europe | | 18 December: An agreement on trade and economic cooperation is signed between the EC and the Soviet Union | | |
| 1990 | The end of communism in Europe | | | 28 April: At a Special European Council in Dublin, the Community agrees on a common approach to the German unification and on the relations with Central and Eastern Europe | |
| | EBRD | | | 29 May: The European Bank for Reconstruction and Development (EBRD) is established, to provide financial support to Central and Eastern Europe | |

Appendix: Chronology of European Integration         219

| | Treaties and key events | Member states | Economic integration | Political integration | Crises and setbacks |
|---|---|---|---|---|---|
| **1990** | August: Iraq invades Kuwait | 3 and 16 July: Cyprus and Malta apply to join the EC | 19 June: The Benelux countries, France and Germany sign the Schengen Agreement. Italy follows suit on 27 November | 15–18 June: Third direct elections to the European Parliament are held | |
| | German unification | 3 October: the *Länder* of Eastern Germany (former GDR) becomes members of the EC as part of unified Germany | 15 December: The new African Caribbean Pacific (ACP) – European Economic Community Convention is signed, for the fourth time, in Lomé, Togo | 19–21 November: 34 Heads of State or Government of the Conference on Security and Cooperation in Europe (CSCE) sign a Charter for a New Europe | |
| **1991** | June: Outbreak of war in the former Yugoslavia | 1 July: Sweden applies to join the EC | 14 April: The European Bank for Reconstruction and Development is inaugurated in London | | January: France break ranks with the EC position on the Iraq–Kuwait conflict and acts independently |
| | 22 August: Failed coup in the Soviet Union  25 December: Gorbachev resigns. The end of the Soviet Union | 16 December: Europe Agreements are signed with Poland, Hungary and Czechoslovakia | 1 September: The fourth Lomé Convention enters into force | | |
| | The Maastricht Treaty is presented | | | 9–10 December: At a European Council in Maastricht, a draft Treaty on the European Union is completed | |
| **1992** | The CFSP | 18 March: Finland applies to join the EC | 2 May: An agreement on the European Economic Area is signed in Porto | 7 February: The Treaty of the European Union is signed in Maastricht by the Foreign and Finance Ministers of the member states. The Treaty includes the reference to a Common Foreign and Security Policy (CFSP) | |

|  | Treaties and key events | Member states | Economic integration | Political integration | Crises and setbacks |
|---|---|---|---|---|---|
| 1992 | Treaty of the EU | 20 May: Switzerland applies to join the EC | | 18 June: In a referendum, the Irish people vote in favour of ratification of the Treaty on the European Union. On 2 and 31 July, Luxembourg and Greece ratify the Treaty on the European Union | 2 June: In a referendum, the Treaty of the European Union is rejected by Danish voters. At a European Council in Lisbon (26–27 June), the need for respecting the timetable for the ratification of the EU Treaty is underlined. 11–12 December: Denmark is offered special arrangements to enable her to hold a second referendum on the ratification of the Treaty |
|  |  | 25 November: Norway applies to join the EC | | 20 September: In a referendum, the French people vote in favour of ratification of the Treaty on the European Union. Italy (26 October), Belgium (4 November), Spain (25 November), Portugal (11 December), the Netherlands (15 December) and Germany (18 December) ratify the Treaty on the European Union | |
|  | Switzerland rejects the Community | | | | 6 December: In a referendum, the Swiss people vote against the ratification of the Agreement establishing the European Economic Area. The Swiss government withdraws its application for EC membership |

Appendix: Chronology of European Integration 221

|  | Treaties and key events | Member states | Economic integration | Political integration | Crises and setbacks |
|---|---|---|---|---|---|
| 1993 | January: Czechoslovakia splits into two separate states, the Czech Republic and Slovakia | Europe Agreements are signed with Romania (1 February) and Bulgaria (8 March) | 1 January: The Single European Market enters into force | May 18: In a second referendum in Denmark, the Treaty on the European Union is accepted (with special provisions for Denmark) | |
| | | October: Association agreement is signed with Slovakia and the Czech Republic | | 2 August: The UK ratifies the Treaty on the European Union | |
| | TEU: The Birth of the EU | | | 1 November: All ratification procedures are completed and the Treaty on the European Union enters into force. The EU now officially has a Common Foreign and Security Policy (CFSP) | |
| 1994 | | Hungary (31 February) and Poland (5 April) apply to join the EU | 1 January: The Agreement establishing the European Economic Area enters into force | | |
| | | Accession referenda in Austria (12 June), Finland (16 October) and Sweden (13 November). All in favour of joining the EU | | 19 April: The Council decides on joint action under the Common Foreign and Security Policy, in support of the Middle East peace process | |
| | 15 July: Jacques Santer is chosen to succeed Jacques Dolores as President of the European Commission | 14 June: A Partnership and Cooperation Agreement is signed between the EU and Ukraine | 18 July: Free-trade agreements are signed with Estonia, Latvia and Lithuania | 9–12 June: Direct elections to the European Parliament are held for the fourth time | |

|  | Treaties and key events | Member states | Economic integration | Political integration | Crises and setbacks |
|---|---|---|---|---|---|
| 1994 | Norway says no | | | | 27–28 November: In a referendum, 52.2 per cent of Norwegians rejects accession to the EU |
| 1995 | The EFTA enlargement | 1 January: Austria, Finland and Sweden become members of the EU | | February: The European Union web page is launched | |
| | Schengen Agreement enters into force | Belgium, France, Germany, Luxembourg, the Netherlands, Portugal, Spain and Austria | | 26 March: The Schengen Agreement comes into force. Austria signs the agreement on 28 April | |
| | Post-communist applicants | Romania (22 June), Slovakia (27 June), Latvia (13 October), Estonia (24 November), Lithuania (8 December) and Bulgaria (14 December) apply to join the EU | 20–21 March: The Stability Pact for Central and Eastern Europe is signed in Paris. 3–10 May: The Commission adopts a White Paper on preparing the associated countries of Central and Eastern Europe for integration into the EU | | |
| | | | 9 April: In a referendum, Liechtenstein ratifies its accession in the European Economic Area. The country participates in EEA from 1 May 1995 | | |
| | | 12 June: European Association Agreements are signed with Estonia, Latvia and Lithuania | | | |

Appendix: Chronology of European Integration 223

|  | Treaties and key events | Member states | Economic integration | Political integration | Crises and setbacks |
|---|---|---|---|---|---|
| 1995 | 14 December: The Dayton Peace Agreement for Former Yugoslavia is signed in Paris |  |  | 26 July: The Europol Convention for police cooperation is signed by the member states |  |
| 1996 |  | 1 January: Customs Union between EU and Turkey enters into force |  | 29 March: Opening of the Intergovernmental Conference to revise the Maastricht Treaty, in Turin | 27 March: The Commission adopts a decision on urgent measures to be taken for protection against BSE. A worldwide export ban on British meat products |
|  |  | The Czech Republic (17 January) and Slovenia (10 June) apply to join the EU. A cooperation agreement is signed with Uzbekistan (21 June) | 19 December: Sweden, Finland and Denmark sign the Schengen agreement |  |  |
| 1997 | Treaty of Amsterdam is drafted |  |  | 16–17 June: A new Treaty is drafted at a European Council meeting in Amsterdam. The national Ministers of Foreign Affairs sign the Treaty of Amsterdam on 2 October. The Western European Union (WEU) adopts a declaration (22 July) to be annexed to the final Act of the Treaty, on its role and its relations with the EU and NATO. The Amsterdam Treaty creates the post High Representative of the CFSP |  |

|  | Treaties and key events | Member states | Economic integration | Political integration | Crises and setbacks |
|---|---|---|---|---|---|
| 1998 |  | 1 January: A cooperation agreement with FYROM enters into force. | 25 March: The Commission adopts the convergence report and recommends that 11 member states adopt the euro on 1 January 1999 | 30 March: The accession process for the 10 Central and Eastern applicant countries and Cyprus is launched |  |
|  |  | 1 February: Europe Agreements with Estonia, Latvia and Lithuania enter into force | 3 May: The Council decides that 11 member states satisfy the conditions for adopting the single currency on 1 January 1999 | March: UK and France agree on European defence cooperation and greater autonomy for the EU to act without NATO (St Malo Declaration) |  |
|  | 30 April: Peace agreement on Northern Ireland | Partnership and Cooperation agreement with Ukraine (1 March) and Moldova (1 July) enter into force | 1 June: Establishment of the European Central Bank (ECB) in Frankfurt |  |  |
| 1999 | The euro | Austria, Belgium, Finland, France, Germany, Ireland, Italy, Luxembourg, the Netherlands, Portugal, and Spain | 1 January: The euro is officially launched | March: Czech Republic and Poland join NATO |  |
|  | The Santer affair | 1 February: A Europe Agreement with Slovenia enters into force |  |  | *The Santer affair* January: Increasingly concerned about fraud in the EU, the European Parliament put pressure on Jacques Santer, President of the European Commission. The whole Commission is close to being sacked |

## Appendix: Chronology of European Integration

| | Treaties and key events | Member states | Economic integration | Political integration | Crises and setbacks |
|---|---|---|---|---|---|
| **1999** | The Amsterdam Treaty | 1 May: The Amsterdam Treaty enters into force | | 10–13 June: European Parliament elections | 15 March: Official reports of fraud and mismanagement leads to the collective resignation of the Commission |
| | Prodi replaces Santer<br><br>CFSP and ESDP | 10–11 December: At a European Council in Helsinki, Turkey is recognised as a candidate country | | 3–4 June: At a European Council meeting in Cologne, the strengthening of the Common Foreign and Security Policy (CFSP) is discussed. The Union's determination to establish a common European security and defence policy is confirmed at a EU–US summit in Bonn, on 21 June, and again on 10–11 December at the European Council in Helsinki. Plans are made for the introduction of an EU Rapid Reaction Force (December 2003) | (24 March: Former Italian Prime Minster Romani Prodi is appointed new President of the Commission. Prodi is approved by the Parliament on 5 May) |
| **2000** | | | 2–3 February: The EU and the ACP countries agree on a plan of action that is to follow the fourth Lomé Convention that comes to an end in February 2000. On 23 June, the Cotonou Convention is signed, replacing the old Lomé Convention | 19–20 June: At a European Concil meeting in Santa Maria da Feira, Greece's entry into the euro is approved; a common strategy for the Mediterranean region is adopted; and an action plan for the northern dimension in external and cross-border policies of the EU is endorsed | |

| | Treaties and key events | Member states | Economic integration | Political integration | Crises and setbacks |
|---|---|---|---|---|---|
| 2000 | | | | | 22 September: The European Central Bank, taking joint action with the US Federal Reserve and the Bank of Japan, intervene to support the euro |
| | Denmark rejects the euro | | | | 28 September: In a referendum, the Danes reject joining the single European currency |
| | | | | 7–9 December: At a European Council meeting in Nice, the EU Treaty is amended in order to expand the Union | |
| 2001 | Treaty of Nice | | 2 January: Greece becomes the 12th member of the euro zone | 26 February: Following the December meeting in Nice, a new Treaty amending the Treaty on European Union and the Treaties establishing the European Communities is signed | 7 June: A referendum is held in Ireland, where a majority vote against the Treaty of Nice |
| | Anti-globalisation manifestations | | | The Treaty of Nice strengthens the European Security and Defence Policy (ESDP). The WEU is in effect incorporated into the EU | Intense anti-globalisation demonstrations accompany the European Council meeting in Nice, France (7–9 December 2000), the EU–US summit in Gothenburg, Sweden (14 June) and the G7/G8 Summit in Genoa, Italy |
| | 11 September: Terrorist attack on New York and Washington | | | 21 September: A special European Council is held in Brussels, to assess the international situation in wake of 9/11 | |

# Appendix: Chronology of European Integration

|      | Treaties and key events | Member states | Economic integration | Political integration | Crises and setbacks |
|------|----|----|----|----|----|
| 2001 |   |   |   | 19 October: Total solidarity with the US is reaffirmed |   |
|      |   | 29 October: A cooperation agreement between the EU and Croatia is signed |   |   |   |
|      | Laeken Declaration |   | 14 December: Euro coins available to citizens in the euro zone | 14–15 December: A European Council is held in Laeken. A Declaration on the future of the European Union: more transparent, more efficient and more democratic; and a commitment to strengthen the EU's role in the world |   |
| 2002 | The euro into circulation | Austria, Belgium, Finland, France, Germany, Greece, Ireland, Italy, Luxembourg, the Netherlands, Portugal and Spain | 1 January: Euro coins and notes enter into circulation. 28 February: The euro becomes the sole currency within the 12 euro zone countries | 28 February: The European Convention begins its work on a Constitution for Europe |   |
|      | 23 July: The Treaty establishing the European Coal and Steel Community (ECSC) expires after 50 years in force | In a second referendum, the Irish voters accept the Treaty of Nice |   | 26 September: The first European Day of Languages. 12 December: NATO formally invites seven post-communist countries to join the organisation |   |
| 2003 | War on Iraq | 8 March: A referendum is held in Malta. A majority in favour of joining the EU | 14 March: EU and NATO sign a Security Pact in Athens, Greece | 1 February: The Treaty of Nice enters into force | *The Iraqi Crisis* Spring: EU leaders fail to agree on a common position towards the US and President Bush's plans to invade Iraq |

|  | Treaties and key events | Member states | Economic integration | Political integration | Crises and setbacks |
|---|---|---|---|---|---|
| 2003 | No common position on Iraq | Accession referenda in Poland (7–8 June), the Czech Republic (13–14 June), and Latvia (20 September). A majority of voters is in favour of accession to the EU, in all three countries | | 20–21 June: At a European Coucil in Thessaloniki, a draft Treaty establishing a Constitution for Europe is presented. The Balkan countries are given a conditional invitation to join the EU | *Iraqi Crisis* (cont.) France, Germany, Belgium and Luxembourg hold their own summit meetings on the ESDP, which makes the UK and other member states furious |
|  | Sweden rejects the euro | | | 25 June: A EU–US Summit in Washington. The EU and the US decide to cooperate in the fight against terrorism | 14 September: Sweden holds a referendum, where a majority rejects the euro |
|  | | | | | 4 October: The draft Treaty establishing a Constitution for Europe is challenged by several member states |
| 2004 | The eastward enlargement<br><br>11 March: Terrorist attack in Madrid | 1 May: The Accession Treaty enters into force. Estonia, Latvia, Lithuania, Hungary, the Czech Republic, Poland, Slovakia, Slovenia, Malta and Cyprus become members of the EU | | The eastward enlargement<br><br>Rationale: ensure democratic consolidation in post-communist Europe and to 'unite Europe' | |
|  | | 17–18 June: Croatia is given the status as candidate country for membership of the EU. Membership negotiations set to start on 17 March, 2005 | | 29 June: Javier Solana is appointed as Secretary-General of the Council and High Representative of the CFSP | |

## Appendix: Chronology of European Integration

|  | Treaties and key events | Member states | Economic integration | Political integration | Crises and setbacks |
|---|---|---|---|---|---|
| 2004 | Barosso criticised for his Commission | 14 September: First meeting of the Stabilisation and Association Council between the EU and the Former Yugoslav Republic of Macedonia | | 29 October: a preliminary version of the Treaty establishing a Constitution for Europe is ratified by all member states in EU 25 | 26 October: The President-to-be Barroso is criticised for his line-up for the new European Commission. The proposal is withdrawn before it is submitted before the Parliament |
| | | 11 October: The EU and Tajikistan sign a Partnership and Cooperation agreement | | | (18 November: The European Parliament approves the new Barosso Commission. The result is 449 votes in favour, to 149 votes against with 82 abstentions) |
| 2005 | Croatia is put on hold | | | 20 February: First referendum on the European Constitution is held in Spain. The Spaniards vote in favour | 16 March: Negotiations with Croatia are put on hold by the EU and made contingent upon Croatia's cooperation with the international War Crimes Tribunal in the Hague |
| | | | 13 April: The European Parliament gives it approval for the entry of Romania and Bulgaria into the EU (2007) | | |
| | Constitution debacle | | | | *The Constitution crises* |
| | | | | | 29 May: French voters reject the Draft Constitution in a referendum |
| | | | | | 1 June: Dutch voters reject the Draft Constitution in a referendum |

|      | Treaties and key events | Member states | Economic integration | Political integration | Crises and setbacks |
|------|---|---|---|---|---|
| 2005 | | 3 October: Accession talks with Croatia re-open: Croatia expects to join the EU as a full member in 2009. The Council decides to open accession talks with Turkey as well | | | *The Constitution crisis (cont.)* June: Further referenda are put on hold |
| 2006 | | | | | Earlier deadline for ratification of the Constitution (November 2006) extended |
| 2007 | Projected enlargement | Bulgaria and Romania | | | |

*Sources*: George and Bache (2001); Bomberg and Stubb (2003); Bale (2005); and the official homepage of the EU (www.eu.int).

# REFERENCES

Bale, Tim (2005), *European Politics: A Comparative Introduction*, Basingstoke, Palgrave Macmillan.
Bomberg, Elizabeth and Alexander Stubb, eds (2003), *The European Union: How Does it Work?*, Oxford, Oxford University Press.
George, Stephen and Ian Bache (2001), *Politics in the European Union*, Oxford, Oxford University Press.
Official homepage of the European Union (www.eu.int).

# Index

11 September (9/11) 39, 123–25, 207, 226

Afghanistan 123, 215
Africa 50, 134
African Caribbean Pacific (ACP) 212, 219, 225
agrarian 92, 140
aid 113, 134
Albania 10, 86–88, 90, 98, 100, 107–108, 113
alienation 164, 181
Alps 21
Anglicans 41
Anti-American 136
Asia 50
Association Treaty 208
Austria 10–11, 16–17, 22–23, 36–39, 41, 43, 45–46, 48, 50–51, 64–65, 67–68, 70, 72, 74, 78, 80–84, 86, 88, 100, 102, 104–105, 108, 115–16, 118–19, 123, 129, 143–46, 149–52, 160, 167, 169–71, 177, 182, 184, 192, 207, 211, 218, 221–22, 224, 227
Austro-Hungarian Empire 3
authoritarian 11, 97
autonomy 9, 18, 25, 45, 224
Aznar, José Maria 113

Balkan 4, 12, 91, 113, 130, 146, 228
Baltic 3, 12, 47, 65, 68, 82–83, 90–91, 105, 119, 126, 131, 133, 146, 158
Bank of Amsterdam 20
Bank of Barcelona 20
Bank of Delft 20
Bank of England 20
Bank of France 20
Bank of Genoa 20
Bank of Hamburg 20
Bank of Middelburg 20
Bank of Nuremberg 20
Bank of Rotterdam 20
Bank of Scotland 20
Bank of St. George 20
Bank of Sweden 20
Bank of Venice 20
Barings Bank 20
Barosso Commission 229
Bauman, Zygmunt 3, 7, 164, 193
Beck, Ulrich 180, 192–93
Belarus 10, 86–90, 94, 98, 100, 102, 107–108, 128
Belgium 10, 18, 21, 23, 25, 36–8, 41, 43, 46, 48, 51, 64–65, 68, 72, 74, 77, 80–84, 86–88, 90–91, 102, 107–108, 115, 118, 123, 127, 129, 136, 144–45, 149–50, 152–53, 158, 160, 167, 169–70, 177, 182, 184, 192, 203–206, 217, 220, 222, 224, 227–28
Benelux 23, 47, 74, 114, 116, 118, 143, 183, 204, 219
Berlin Wall 218
Bismarck, Otto von 16
Blair, Tony 18, 113, 122, 195, 200, 202
Bohemia 151
borders 3, 9, 30, 34, 59, 85, 112, 127, 128, 186
Bosnia 10, 96
Brandenburg 161
British Empire 12
Brussels 1, 9, 19, 24, 70, 83, 103, 105, 118, 131, 135, 139, 141, 153, 158, 161–62, 200–202, 204–205, 213–14, 216, 226
Brussels Treaty 204–205
BSE 223
Bulgaria 3, 10, 25, 36, 41–42, 44, 46, 48, 51, 56, 64–66, 68, 80–84, 86–88, 90, 96, 98, 100, 107–108, 114–15, 118–19, 131, 143–46, 151–52, 155, 158–60, 184, 221–22, 229–30
*Bundesländer* 161
*Bundestag* 153, 161
bureaucrats 142, 166, 200–201
Bush, George W. 113, 122–23, 136, 227
business 112, 165, 172

231

Candidate Countries Eurobarometer 6, 63–65, 69, 71, 78–79, 105, 109, 111, 115, 118–20, 122, 130–31, 134–35, 143, 161, 172, 174–75, 184
capitalism 122, 180
Carolingian Empire 13
Catalonia 18, 21
Catholic 10–11, 13, 16, 40–44, 46, 53, 144–45, 170
Catholic Church 41–42, 44
Catholicism 4, 42
Central and Eastern Eurobarometer (CEEB) 63, 109, 134
Central and Eastern Europe 3, 12, 23, 74–75, 82, 92, 106, 122, 127–28, 136, 139, 143, 145–47, 218, 222
Central European Opinion Research Group 56
Centre Party (*Keskerakond*) 151
Charlemagne 7, 13
Charles V 13
China 25, 111, 123–24
Chirac, Jaques 3, 113, 149, 200
Christian League 150
Churchill, Winston 203
citizenship 6, 14, 16, 24, 27–39, 53, 56, 134
city-belt 10–11, 17, 21–22, 101, 145–46, 199
Civic Democratic Party 151
civil society 56, 146, 181, 184, 189–90, 193
Clearing House 20
clergy 9, 12
clientelism 146
Colbert, Jean Baptiste 15
Cold War 3, 9, 63, 77, 83, 85, 112, 118, 122–23, 126, 128, 147, 203
collective 33, 50, 53–55, 78, 175, 187–88, 191, 225
Colombia 50
Comecon 218
Committee for European Economic Co-operation 203
Common Agricultural Policy 206–207
Common Customs Tariff 209
Common Foreign and Security Policy (CFSP) 112, 114, 117, 119–21, 134–37, 219, 221, 223, 225, 228
Commonwealth 15
communism 11, 31, 34, 37, 40, 52, 54, 118, 126–27, 185, 218
Communist Party of Finland 150
communitarian 31, 33, 187
Community Free Trade Agreement 211
companies 2, 172–74, 178
Compromise of Verdun 11, 13
conceptual map 9–14, 140, 142, 144
Conference on Security and Cooperation in Europe 212, 219

Conservative Party 150
consolidation 17, 198–99, 215, 217, 228
constitution 18, 33, 42, 50, 55, 74–75, 91, 103
Constitution for Europe 227
constitutional 1, 2, 7, 17, 33, 49, 53, 74–75, 102, 146, 163, 201
Costa Rica 50
Costa/ENEL ruling 208
Cotonou Convention 225
Council of Europe 34, 36, 38, 50, 57, 204, 206
Council of Ministers 4, 79, 103, 142
courtoisie 13
*Crédit Agricole* 20
Croatia 10, 25, 30, 36, 38, 41, 44, 48, 51, 66, 84, 86–88, 90, 97, 100, 107–108, 128, 151–52, 160, 227–30
currency 'snake' 210
customs union 14, 203–204, 209
Cyprus 3, 10, 12, 23, 36, 38, 43, 46, 48, 51, 56, 64–66, 72, 80–84, 115–16, 118, 127, 130–31, 144–45, 151–52, 158, 160, 167, 169, 211, 219, 224, 228
Czech Republic 3, 40, 43, 46, 51, 56, 64–65, 72, 77, 80–84, 86, 88, 90–91, 102, 105–108, 114–18, 127, 131, 143–46, 149, 151, 153, 158, 160, 167, 169, 221, 223–24, 228
Czechoslovakia 151, 219, 221

Danish People's Party 149–50
Davignon Report 209
Dayton Agreement 112, 223
de Gaulle, Charles 75, 142, 208–209
death penalty 28, 34, 50–53, 56
Defrenne ruling 213
deliberative democracy 192
Delors, Jacques 217–18
Democratic Unionist Party 150
Denmark 10–12, 16, 22–23, 36–43, 46, 48, 51, 56, 64–65, 72, 74, 80–84, 86–88, 90–91, 98, 102–104, 107–108, 113–16, 118–19, 123, 125–26, 129, 139, 143–46, 149–53, 155, 160, 167, 169–71, 176–77, 182, 184, 195, 204, 207–209, 211, 215, 220–21, 223, 226
disillusionment 166, 171
dissatisfaction 60, 74, 90, 103
diversity 158–59, 161, 185–86, 188
division 4, 13, 46, 60, 84, 128, 136, 162, 179
Draft Constitution 2, 33, 54, 59, 66, 113, 195–97, 200–201, 229

Easton, David 4, 8, 59–62, 77, 105, 133, 135

## Index

eastward enlargement  68, 77, 119, 126, 139, 200, 228
*ecclesia*  9, 11
Eco, Umeberto  184, 186
ECSC High Authority  205–207
Ecu  214
Ecuador  50
education  31, 42, 44, 49, 53–54, 56, 179
EFTA enlargement  222
Eire  10–11, 144
Elbe  17
electoral  6, 37, 47–48, 148–49, 152–53, 155, 159, 167
elite (-s)  1, 2, 4, 10, 18, 33, 52, 103, 111–12, 122, 130, 132, 139–40, 154, 197, 200
England  10, 18, 20, 44, 144–45
enlargement (-s)  2, 3, 11, 23, 62, 66–68, 72, 74, 77–81, 83, 86, 112, 128–32, 136, 139, 142, 145, 149, 153, 162, 173, 197–99, 201, 209, 211, 215, 217, 230
Enlightenment  29
entrepreneurs  17, 154
environment  102, 125–26, 132, 187
environmental  113, 122, 174
equality  49, 187
Estonia  3, 10, 35–38, 40–41, 43, 46, 48, 51, 57, 64–65, 68, 72, 80–84, 86, 88, 90, 98, 100, 102, 107–108, 114–16, 118–19, 130–31, 134, 143–47, 151–52, 158, 160, 167, 169, 179, 221–22, 224, 228
Estonian Rural People's Party (*Rahvaliit*)  151
estrangement  164, 173
ethnic cleansing  112
ethnicity  56
euro zone  226–27
Eurobarometer  6, 49, 63–65, 67, 69–73, 75–76, 78–80, 82, 84–85, 88–89, 92, 104, 109, 111, 114–15, 117–22, 124–27, 129–30, 134–35, 143, 156–57, 159, 162, 168–69, 172, 174–75, 177–78, 184, 186
Eurofriendly  119, 143, 146–47, 154
*Europaverdrossenheit*  190–91
European Association Agreement  222
European Atomic Energy Community (Euroatom)  206
European Bank for Reconstruction and Development (EBRD)  218–19
European Central Bank (ECB)  19, 224, 226
European citizenship  24, 33, 59
European Coal and Steel Community (ECSC)  204–207, 211–12, 227
European Commission  2, 4–6, 11, 59, 62–63, 66, 68, 75–78, 85, 105, 128, 134–35, 142, 155, 161–62, 195–96, 201, 221, 224, 229

European Constitution  103, 168, 229
European Convention  56, 214, 227
European Convention for the Protection of Human Rights and Fundamental Freedoms  56, 214
European Council  59, 103, 212–20, 223, 225–27
European Court of Justice  59, 142, 208, 213
European Day of Languages  227
European Defence Community  204–205
European Defence Community Treaty  205
European Economic Area (EEA)  219–22
European Economic Community (EEC)  10–11, 106, 206–208, 215, 219
European Economic Space (EES)  139
European External Action Service  114
European Free Trade Association (EFTA)  74, 78, 80, 82, 85, 87, 99, 102, 207, 222
European identity  3, 6, 65, 168, 189, 211
European Monetary System (EMS)  214, 218
European Monetary Union (EMU)  209–10, 213
European Monitoring Centre on Racism and Xenophobia  156–57, 162
European Parliament  4, 47–49, 59, 62–63, 76–79, 103, 142–43, 166–69, 197, 206, 212, 214, 216, 219, 221, 224–25, 229
European Parliamentary Assembly  206
European Parliamentary elections  59
European Political Community (EPC)  205
European Political Cooperation  118, 209
European Recovery Programme  203
European Regional Development Fund (ERDF)  212, 214
European Security and Defence Policy (ESDP)  113, 117, 119–21, 134, 137, 226, 228
European Social Survey  156, 162, 169–70, 182
European Union of Federalists  203
European Union web page  222
European Values Study  56
Europeanisation  6, 29, 50, 52–53, 134, 147
Europol Convention  223
Eurosceptic  12, 98, 126, 133, 140, 143, 146, 148–49, 151–54, 163
Euroscepticism  129, 139, 140–53, 158–62, 166, 197–99
Eurostat  36, 38
Evangelicals  41
Exchange Rate Mechanism (ERM)  214
exclusion  3, 5, 27–29, 31–34, 47, 52, 54–55, 84, 154
exclusiveness  27, 34, 50, 159, 197–99
extreme right  149, 161

federalists 2, 32
female suffrage 47
Fifth Republic 75
Finland 10–11, 23, 25, 35–36, 38, 41–43, 46, 48, 51, 64–65, 70, 72, 80–84, 86, 88, 96, 100, 102, 104–105, 108, 114–16, 118–19, 123–24, 126, 129, 143–46, 150, 152, 159–60, 167, 169–71, 176–77, 182, 184–85, 211–12, 219, 221–24, 227
First World War 3, 12, 14, 21, 23, 46
Flash Eurobarometer 123–25, 135, 175, 192
Flemish Bloc 149–50
Florence European University Institute 212
Fortuyn, Pim 150
Fouchet plans 207
Fourth Republic 75
fragmentation 56
France 10, 14, 16–17, 20–21, 23, 26, 30–31, 36–38, 40–43, 46–49, 51–52, 64–66, 74–75, 80–84, 86–88, 90–91, 96–97, 101, 103–104, 107–108, 114–16, 118, 122–23, 125, 127, 129, 134, 143–45, 149–55, 158, 160, 167, 169–70, 177–79, 182, 184, 192, 195–96, 200, 204–206, 208, 217, 219, 222, 224, 226–28
Franco, General Francisco 56, 202, 216
Franco-German Agreement 216
Frankfurt Parliament 16
Free Trade Agreement 211
French Revolution 13, 18, 22
functionalists 2

German Democratic Republic (GDR) 51, 161, 219
Georgia 86–88, 90–91, 98, 100, 107–108
German unification 218–19
Germany 10, 16–18, 20, 23, 30–31, 33, 35–36, 38–41, 43, 46, 48, 51, 64–66, 72, 74–75, 78, 80–84, 86–88, 90–91, 96, 101, 104, 107–108, 114–16, 118, 123–25, 129, 134, 136, 144–46, 149–53, 158–60, 162, 167, 169–71, 177, 182, 184–85, 200–201, 204–206, 217, 219–20, 222, 224, 227–28
Giddens, Antony 193
globalisation 2, 6, 124–25, 135, 163–66, 171, 173–79, 185, 188–92, 198–199, 226
glocalisation 164
God 42, 56
Gorbachev, Michail 219
Great Britain 11, 64, 80–84, 89–90, 104, 107–108, 116, 134
Greece 10–11, 23, 25, 36, 38, 41, 43, 46, 48, 51, 64–65, 68, 72, 77–78, 80–84, 86, 88, 90–91, 100, 107–108, 113, 115–16, 118, 123–25, 127, 129, 144–45, 150, 152–53, 158–60, 167, 169–71, 175, 177, 182, 184–85, 192, 207, 212–13, 215, 220, 225–27

Green parties 140, 150
Greenland 11, 23, 215–17
Greens 150

Habermas, Jürgen 135
Habsburg 13, 16, 146
Haider, Jörg 149
Hamburg Girobank 20
hedonism 164, 180–81
hedonistic 6
Hegel, Friedrich 189
Helsinki Final Act 52
High Representative 113, 223, 228
Hitler, Adolf 7, 14
Hohenzollern 16
Holocaust 135, 147, 162
Holy Roman Empire 13, 16, 18, 142, 161
Holy Roman Empire of the German Nation 16, 18
Holy Scripture of the Koran 10
homogeneity 33, 35, 37, 40, 42
human rights 29, 34, 50, 52, 87, 111, 114, 120–21, 128, 134, 192
Hungarian Justice and Life Party 151
Hungary 3, 10, 12, 22–23, 36, 38, 41, 43, 46–48, 51, 56, 64–65, 72, 77, 80–84, 86, 88, 90–91, 96, 102, 105, 107–108, 115, 118, 131, 144–46, 149, 151–52, 160, 167, 169–70, 182, 206, 219, 221, 228

Iceland 10–12, 23, 96, 204, 211
identity 2, 33, 54, 64–65, 80, 111, 147, 168, 173, 185, 187
Imia islands 113
immigration 28, 37, 39, 56, 103, 141, 155, 158–59, 196
inclusiveness 27, 34, 39, 50, 55, 159, 199
Independent Smallholders' Party 151
India 123–24
indifference 6, 32, 165, 190
individualism 6, 32, 49, 56–57, 163–65, 180–85, 187–88, 190–92
Inglehart, Ronald 180, 192–93
intergovernmentalists 32
International Metric Commission 22
International Metric Convention 22
International Postal Union 5, 21, 25
Iran 123, 132
Iraq 6, 113, 119–20, 122–24, 127, 133, 135, 171, 219, 227–28
Ireland 18, 23, 35–36, 38, 41, 43, 46–48, 51, 64–65, 68, 72, 77, 80–84, 86–88, 90–91, 96, 98, 100, 103–104, 107–108, 115–16, 118–19, 123, 125, 129, 145, 150–52, 160, 167, 169–70, 177, 182, 184–85, 193, 207–209, 211, 224, 226–27
Iron Chancellor 16
iron curtain 4

Islam 146
Israel 123, 132
Italy 10, 17, 20–21, 23, 36–37, 40–41, 43, 46–48, 51, 64–65, 68, 74, 80–84, 86–88, 90–91, 94, 102, 107–108, 113–16, 118–19, 123–24, 129, 132, 143–45, 150–52, 158–60, 167, 169–70, 177, 182, 184, 193, 204–206, 219–220, 224, 226–27

Jewish 41
*jus sanguinis* 30, 35
*jus soli* 30, 35–36

Kazakhstan 86–88, 90, 94, 97, 98, 102, 107, 108
Kazoo 10
Kemal, Atatürk 46
Kissinger, Henry 24
Korean War 204
Kosovo 113
Kuwait 219
Kwasniewski, Alexander 130

*Länder* 134, 219
Latin America 50
Latin Monetary Union 21
Latvia 3, 10, 35–38, 40–41, 43, 46, 48, 50–51, 64–65, 68, 72, 77, 80–84, 86, 88, 90, 100, 105, 107–108, 115–16, 118–19, 131, 134, 143–47, 151–52, 158–60, 167, 169, 179, 221–22, 224, 228
Law and Justice Party (PiS) 151
*le Front National* 37
le Pen 149–50
League of Polish Families 151, 154
Left Party 150
legitimacy 5, 21, 50, 76, 103, 133, 163, 167, 177, 188, 190
Lenin, Vladimir I. 25
Libya 123–24
Liechtenstein 23, 222
Lipset, Seymor Martin 4, 8–9, 26, 87, 92, 106
Lithuania 3, 10, 36, 41, 44, 46, 48, 51, 56, 64–65, 68, 72, 74, 77, 80–86, 88, 90, 98, 100, 104–105, 107–108, 115, 118, 127, 131, 144, 145–47, 151–52, 158, 160, 168–69, 221–22, 224, 228
Lomé Convention 212–13, 215–17, 219, 225
Lomé II 215
Lutherans 41
*Lutte Ouvrière* 150
Luxembourg 17–18, 36, 38, 41, 44, 46, 48, 51, 64–66, 68, 77, 80–84, 86–88, 90–91, 100–101, 107–108, 112, 115, 118–19, 123, 129, 134, 150–52, 158, 160, 203–206, 208–209, 215, 217, 220, 222, 224, 227–28
Luxembourg compromise 208

Macedonia 86–88, 90, 98, 100, 107–108, 118, 158, 229
Malta 3, 10, 12, 23, 36, 38, 41, 44, 46, 48, 51, 56, 64–65, 72, 80–84, 114–16, 118, 130–31, 143–47, 149, 151–52, 159–60, 167, 169, 210, 219, 227–28
market economy 66, 128
Marshall Plan 203
medieval Europe 9
Mediterranean 4, 12, 23, 35, 215, 217, 225
Mégret, Bruno 149–50
Merger Treaty 208
Metric Convention 22
metric system 5, 22
Middle East 124, 211
Middle East peace process 221
Moldova 96, 224
Monnet, Jean 32, 57, 205, 214
Montenegro 87, 98, 102
multiculturalism 140, 158–60
Muslim 10, 12, 40, 41, 44–45, 103

Napoleon, Bonaparte 13
National Christian Alliance (ZCHN) 151
National Front 149–50
national identity 30, 147, 168
National Republican Movement 150
nationalism 6, 25, 30, 32, 139–41, 147, 158, 197–99
nation-building 10–13, 15, 24, 47, 141, 147
nationhood 33, 54, 83
Nazi Germany 14
neo-liberal 164
Netherlands 10, 17–18, 20, 22–23, 36, 38–39, 41, 43–46, 48, 51, 56, 64–65, 74, 80–84, 86–88, 90–91, 97–98, 102–104, 107–108, 113, 115, 118, 123, 125, 129, 144–45, 150, 152, 160, 167, 169–71, 175, 177, 182, 184, 195–96, 203–206, 217, 220, 222, 224, 227
Nixon, Richard 74
Nord-Deutscher Zollverein 17
North Atlantic Treaty Organization (NATO) 9, 113, 118–20, 122, 126, 132, 136–37, 204–205, 215, 223–24, 227
North German Customs Union 17
North Korea 123, 132
Northern Ireland 64, 80–84, 86, 88, 90, 100, 107–108, 116, 134, 145, 158, 160, 224
Northern League 150

Norway 10–12, 23, 25, 57, 71, 82–84, 86, 88, 90, 98, 100, 102, 104–108, 116, 134, 143–44, 160, 170, 182, 204, 207–209, 212, 220, 222
Norwegian Social Science Data Services 134

occupation 16, 18, 146
Organisation for Economic Co-operation and Development (OECD) 38, 207
Organisation for European Economic Co-operation (OEEC) 204, 207
Orthodox 10–11, 41–44, 130, 144
Organisation for Security and Cooperation in Europe (OSCE) 34, 57

Pakistan 123
Paksas, Rolandas 74
pan-Europeanism 141
parliamentary 25, 46, 59, 124, 149, 152–53, 159, 161, 167–68, 195–96, 200
participation 28, 46–49, 53, 55, 59, 168–69, 171–72, 190
passport union 212
Peace of Westphalia 9, 12, 18
periphery 4, 9, 11, 21, 65, 68, 72, 92
Persson, Göran 140, 155
Philip II 13
Plevnen Plan 204
pluralism 66
Poland 3, 10, 36–38, 41, 42, 44, 46, 48–49, 51, 56, 64–65, 72, 80–84, 86, 88, 90, 96–98, 100, 102, 107–108, 115, 118, 131, 143–46, 151–53, 155, 158, 160, 167, 169–70, 182, 219, 221, 224, 228
police 39, 171–72, 223
Polish Peasant Party 151
political parties 44, 148, 159, 166, 171
*Politikverdrossenheit* 163–64, 166, 173, 188, 190
Poos, Jacques 112
Portugal 10–11, 18, 23, 36, 38, 41, 44, 46, 48, 50–51, 64–65, 68, 77–78, 80–84, 86, 88, 90–91, 97, 102, 107–108, 115–16, 118, 123, 129, 144–45, 150, 152–53, 159–60, 167, 169–70, 177, 179, 182, 184–85, 204, 207, 211, 213–14, 217–18, 220, 222, 224, 227
post-communist 56, 115, 130, 134, 146, 168, 175, 181, 227–28
post-materialist (-ism) 164, 180, 187, 192
Prodi, Romani 63, 128, 225
Progress Party 149–50
Protestant (-ism) 4, 9–13, 16, 41, 44, 46–47, 144–45, 170
Prussia 16, 17, 18, 146
Public Bank of Barcelona 20

public opinion 5, 52, 111, 114, 122, 127, 132, 135, 154, 160
Putnam, Robert D. 180, 193
Radio Free Europe/Radio Liberty 126, 128, 131, 134, 136, 140, 162
Rapid Reaction Force 225

referendum (referenda) 2, 54, 71, 91, 102–104, 143, 154–55, 168, 195–96, 206, 210, 212, 215, 220–22, 226–29
reflexive politics 192
Regional Policy Committee 212
regionalism 141
religion (-ious) 4, 6, 9, 12, 28, 31–33, 40–45, 52–56, 144–45, 172
religious freedom 28, 33, 43, 45
representation 4, 7, 46–47, 49, 141, 153, 159, 161
repression 31
resistance 12, 25, 31, 54, 56, 118, 140, 155, 158
Revolutionary Communist League 150
revolutions 16, 168
Rhine 17, 18
Richelieu, Cardinal 15
right-wing 11, 37, 39, 140, 149, 153
*Riksdag* 155
Rokkan, Stein 4, 8–10, 12, 14, 25–26, 87, 92, 106, 140, 142
Roma 16
Romania 3, 10, 25, 36, 39, 41, 44, 46, 48, 51, 64–66, 68, 78, 80–84, 86–88, 90, 98, 100, 107–108, 114–15, 118–19, 127, 131, 143–46, 151–52, 158, 160, 184, 221–22, 229, 230
Royal Exchange 20
rule of law 66, 84, 87, 128, 146
Russia 10, 12, 20–23, 25, 32, 56, 86–88, 90–91, 94, 98, 102, 107–108, 111, 119, 123, 128, 134, 136–37, 146
Russian Revolution 10
Russian State Bank 20

*Saarland* 206
Santer, Jacques 221, 224–25
Santer affair 224
Saudi Arabia 123–24
Saxony 161
Scandinavia 22, 53, 129, 146
Scandinavian Monetary Union 21
Schengen Agreement 217, 219, 222
Schröder, Gerhard 113, 124, 140, 200
*Schwyz* 15
Scotland 10, 18, 21, 44
seaward empire 10, 12, 144–45
Second World War 2, 3, 9, 18, 46, 51, 83, 122, 147, 201

Self Defence (*Samoobrona*) 151, 154
Serbia 10, 87, 98, 102
Silesia 17
Simmenthal ruling 213
Single European Act (SEA) 217
single voice 132, 209
Slovakia 3, 10, 36–39, 41, 44, 48, 51, 64–65, 72, 77, 80–84, 86, 88, 90–91, 96, 98, 100, 105, 107–108, 115, 118–19, 130–31, 144–46, 151–52, 158, 160, 167, 169, 221–22, 228
Slovenia 3, 10, 36, 38, 41, 44, 48, 51, 64–65, 68, 72, 77–78, 80–84, 86–88, 90, 96, 100, 105, 107–108, 115, 118, 131, 144–46, 151–52, 159–60, 167, 169, 170, 182, 223–24, 228
Slovenian National Party 151
social trust 182
Socialism 153
Socialist People's Party 150
Solana, Javier 63, 113, 228
Solemn Declaration on the European Union 216
Somalia 123–24
Soviet Union 3, 11, 14, 23, 64, 83, 85, 126–27, 204, 206, 215, 218–19
Spain 10–11, 17–18, 20, 22–23, 36, 38, 40–42, 44, 46, 48, 51, 64–65, 68, 72, 78, 80–84, 86, 88, 90–91, 97, 107–108, 115–16, 118, 123–25, 129, 144–45, 149–53, 159–60, 167, 169–70, 176–77, 182, 184, 213, 215, 217–18, 220, 222, 224, 227, 229
Spanish Armada 13
Special Eurobarometer 172, 187, 192
St Malo Declaration 224
state-building 10–12, 14, 16, 24
statehood 4, 9, 13, 16, 18, 54, 59
Stockholm Convention 207
Stoics 29, 30
Strasbourg 139, 143
sub-politics 192
Sweden 10–12, 21, 23, 25, 35–36, 38, 41, 44, 46–48, 51, 64–65, 70, 72, 74, 78, 80–88, 96, 100, 102, 104–105, 108, 113–16, 118–19, 123–25, 129, 133, 139, 143–46, 150, 152–53, 155, 158, 160–61, 167, 169–71, 176–79, 182, 184–85, 195, 202, 207, 211, 219, 221–23, 226, 228
Switzerland 10, 12, 14–15, 17–18, 21, 23, 25, 96, 144, 162, 170–71, 182–83, 207, 211, 220
Syria 123–24

Tajikistan 229
technocrat (-s) 2, 32, 142, 146
Tell, Wilhelm 16

territorial 15, 17–19, 30
terrorism 124–27, 133, 228
Thatcher, Margaret 215
The euro 224, 227
trade unions 124
transatlantic 112, 118, 122, 126, 132
transformation 147, 168, 175, 181, 185
transition 75, 102, 128, 179, 197
Treaty establishing a Constitution for Europe 1, 228–29
Treaty of Accession 215
Treaty of Amsterdam 112, 219–21, 223, 225–26
Treaty of Maastricht (EU Treaty) 24, 102, 113, 143, 219, 223
Treaty of Nice 112, 226–27
Treaty of Paris 204
Treaty of Rome 14, 65, 77, 80, 82, 195, 206, 217
Treaty on Economic, Social and Cultural Collaboration and Collective Self-Defence 118
True Finns 150
Truman doctrine 203
Tsarist Russia 25
Turkey 10, 12, 23, 25, 36–38, 40–44, 46–48, 51–52, 64–66, 68, 77, 80–81, 84, 96, 113–16, 118, 127, 130–31, 143, 155, 160, 207–208, 211, 218, 223, 225, 230
Turks 31
turnout 24, 59, 104, 143, 166, 168

Ukraine 10, 86–88, 90–91, 94, 97–98, 100, 107–108, 128, 221, 224
Ulster 10, 144
unemployment 91, 103, 121, 186, 214
unified Germany 134, 219
United Dutch Provinces 18
United Kingdom (UK) 7–8, 17, 23, 25, 36, 41, 44–46, 48, 51, 57, 65–66, 68, 72, 74, 77–78, 80, 85–88, 96, 101, 104–106, 114–16, 118–19, 123–26, 129, 134–35, 139, 143, 146, 150–52, 158, 160–61, 167, 169–70, 177–78, 182, 184–85, 193, 195–96, 200, 204, 207–209, 211–12, 216–17, 221, 224, 228
United Nations Security Council 9, 120–21, 132
United States (US) 6–8, 14, 18, 24–25, 36, 50, 52, 57, 74, 104–106, 111–13, 119–27, 132–33, 135–36, 161, 178, 197–99, 203–204, 225–28
United States of Europe 7, 104, 197, 198–99, 203
Unity List 150
universal suffrage 29, 46, 212–214

universalism 29, 141
*Unterwalden* 15
*Ur* 15
Uruguay 50
Uzbekistan 223

Venezuela 50
Venice Declaration 215
*Vergangenheitsbewältigung* 31
Victorian era 18
Vilnius 135, 137
*Vlaams Belang* 37
*Vlaams Blok* 37
von Bismarck, Otto 16

Wales 10, 18, 25
war against terrorism 6
War Crimes Tribunal 25, 229
war on Iraq 113, 124
Washington 25, 125, 226, 228
Washington Treaty 204
Waterloo 13

*Wehrmacht* 14
Werner Plan 210
West Roman Empire 13
Western Europe 2, 12, 34, 37, 51–53, 56–57, 72, 83, 89, 91, 116, 118, 122, 129, 136, 139, 144–46, 149, 155, 170, 179, 205, 223
Western European Union (WEU) 118, 205, 223, 226
Westphalian system 9, 13, 21
World Bank 178, 191
World Values Survey 48

xenophobia 32, 141, 149, 160
xenophobic 158, 161, 199

Yaoundé Convention 208–210
Yugoslavia 30, 46, 83, 86, 88, 90–91, 98, 100, 102, 107–108, 112, 118, 122, 136, 219, 223

*Zeitgeist* 34, 188